'Essential reading and an urgent and chastening warning to our leaders and voters. This important book chronicles how illiberal, intolerant, authoritarian activism, often linked to a menu of ideologies such as decolonialism and antiIsraelism, is a threat to liberal democracy itself' **Simon Sebag Montefiore**

'Nobody reading this book can be left in any doubt: the fight against the latest evil upsurge in antisemitism must be won to ensure Western civilisation has a future. It's that fundamental' **Andrew Neil**

'A compelling and timely call to fight for our Western values' **Nigel Farage**

'A timely diagnosis that captures the flawed mindset that is undermining the confidence of the West and weakening our resolve in dealing with today's threats' **Kemi Badenoch**

'This is much more than a book about the travails of Israel or the suddenly fashionable prejudices against Jews. It is a book about Western civilisation, the highest and freest form of social organisation since we discovered farming. It is a book about the self-recrimination that infects that civilisation, and that often manifests itself as antisemitism. And it is a book about how to recover our confidence. All recounted in a civil, Scrutonian and occasionally elegiac tone by a man who has lived the story he is telling' **Daniel Hannan**

'This book is a searing indictment that must be heeded before it is too late. It is well written, deeply documented and reflects a brave and sane voice in a debate all too often shorn of either. As a Gentile, I felt hot with shame reading it, asking myself: when will the West finally wake up?' **Andrew Roberts**

'Jake Wallis Simons is a brave and brilliant writer who can be trusted to bring rare moral clarity to the most contested issues of our times' **Michael Gove**

'A critical and lucid book that should be required reading as our societies navigate today's dangerous waters of extremism. As the world's oldest hatred mutates into anti-Zionism and accelerates around the world, and there is a betrayal of reason and universal values in the West, Jake Wallis Simons unravels what went wrong, and offers answers about how moral inversions may be remedied and a collective moral compass found again. An essential book for our troubling times' **Bernard-Henri Lévy**

'With the West cut adrift from its foundational values, it falls to the Jews, a "seismic people", to feel the tremors of the coming earthquake. In this thrillingly good and timely book, Jake Wallis Simons provides an acute analysis of what ails us and issues an urgent rallying cry to the "sensible, complacent majority" to rediscover what it was our forefathers died for and to fight for it once again with all our might and love. In short: Be more Israel! I felt a whole lot better after reading this book' **Allison Pearson**

'A must-read for scholars, activists and concerned citizens alike. Jake Wallis Simons makes crystal clear that the resurgence of antisemitism we are currently witnessing is here not only to annihilate the Jews. Simultaneously, it is here to destroy the West. If met with more complacency, it may very well succeed' **Ayaan Hirsi Ali**

Never Again?

How the West betrayed the Jews and itself

JAKE WALLIS SIMONS

CONSTABLE

First published in Great Britain in 2025 by Constable

1 3 5 7 9 10 8 6 4 2

Copyright © Jake Wallis Simons, 2025

The moral right of the author has been asserted.

All rights reserved.

No part of this publication may be reproduced, stored in a retrieval system, or transmitted, in any form, or by any means, without the prior permission in writing of the publisher, nor be otherwise circulated in any form of binding or cover other than that in which it is published and without a similar condition including this condition being imposed on the subsequent purchaser.

A CIP catalogue record for this book
is available from the British Library.

ISBN: 978-0-34900-043-5 (hardback)
ISBN: 978-0-34900-044-2 (trade paperback)

Typeset in Electra LT Std by SX Composing DTP, Rayleigh, Essex

Printed and bound in Great Britain by Clays Ltd, Elcograf S.p.A.

Papers used by Constable are from well-managed forests
and other responsible sources.

Constable
An imprint of
Little, Brown Book Group
Carmelite House
50 Victoria Embankment
London EC4Y 0DZ

The authorised representative
in the EEA is
Hachette Ireland
8 Castlecourt Centre, Dublin 15,
D15 XTP3, Ireland
(email: info@hbgi.ie)

An Hachette UK Company
www.hachette.co.uk

www.littlebrown.co.uk

For Mutti and Gramps

'I know of nothing like it in all the history books. Millions of educated, well-mannered people are being driven towards the edge of a cliff. What do they do? One cries, one smokes a cigarette, one sings, but no one can be found to jump to his feet, grab the reins and change the wagon's direction.'

Ze'ev Jabotinsky, 1938

Contents

Introduction

SIR, I WOULDN'T START FROM HERE!

Never say never

As she was dragged backwards across the hall, her blazer rucked up about her head and her trousers torn, the slight, bookish woman was speechless with shock. Around her, the Holocaust memorial ceremony was proceeding as if nothing unusual had occurred: on the stage, the Irish president was continuing his address and most of the audience did not even turn their heads. A few people pleaded, 'Leave her alone, it's a ceremony,' and 'How dare you treat her like that?' They were ignored. Eventually, as she was bundled towards the door, the woman, a granddaughter of Holocaust survivors, found her voice. 'This is my ceremony!' she shouted. 'No! No! No!'

This was thirty-seven-year-old Lior Tibet, an Israeli academic at University College Dublin who teaches about the Holocaust as part of a course on modern European history. Together with several other Jews, including a pregnant woman, she had stood up and silently turned her back when the president, Michael Higgins, shamefully started talking about the war in Gaza at the Holocaust Memorial Day ceremony in Dublin. Higgins, who has a history of Israelophobic rhetoric,[1] had been begged by two elderly survivors not to politicise the ceremony by shoehorning the Palestinians into his speech. The event was intended to mourn the genocide of the Jews; this was no platform for bigoted rants about Israel's conflicts. When the president ignored their pleas, Tibet and her friends felt compelled to act. The reprisal was immediate. It is difficult to understand how the security officers were not crippled with irony as they prevented Jews from standing up for themselves – literally – at an event dedicated to the promise of 'Never Again'.

As this was the year that marked the eightieth anniversary of the liberation of Auschwitz, that Holocaust Memorial Day was expected to be especially poignant. But in this post-October 7 world, it quickly became poignant in a very different way. Across the board, Jews found that their pockets were being picked of their own grief. A presenter on *Good Morning Britain*, one of the country's leading breakfast television programmes, spoke of the deaths of six million 'people', editing out both their identities and the reason for their extermination at a stroke. Deputy Prime Minister Angela Rayner followed suit, posting a picture of herself on social media lighting a candle for 'all those who were murdered'. This vanishing-Jew approach was adopted by everyone from the Labour MP Sarah Champion to the then Canadian prime minister Justin Trudeau, from the councils of Bury and Cambridge City to the Humanists, who tweeted their sorrow for 'all the victims of genocide'. At the Lowestoft Council wreath-laying, Jews were not invited to participate. The message was clear. Eighty years on from the most appalling racist crime in modern European history, the victims were being told: 'It's not about you.'

This was just the latest ripple in the tsunami of antisemitism which had been unleashed when six thousand jihadis and civilians launched their pogroms in southern Israel at the close of 2023. In Britain, the oldest hatred soared by 150 per cent directly after the massacres,[2] before hitting a record high in the first half of 2024, with 121 incidents of assault, a 246 per cent rise in vandalism and an astonishing 465 per cent spike in antisemitism at universities.[3] A similar story played out across the Western world, with such depravities as the antisemitic rape of a twelve-year-old girl in a Paris suburb,[4] mob violence against Israelis in Amsterdam,[5] and the firebombing of synagogues from Melbourne[6] to Warsaw[7] regularly appearing in the news. For the first time since the war, Jews across Europe were forced to hide their identities;[8] in Berlin, the police even gave them explicit advice to do so.[9]

On the other side of the Atlantic, things were no better. Antisemitism more than tripled across the United States in a wave of vandalism, campus occupations and physical assault;[10] in November 2023 it claimed the life of Paul Kessler, a sixty-nine-year-old Jewish Californian who was struck on the head with a megaphone at a rally.[11] In May 2025, two young Israeli diplomats were shot dead in Washington, DC, apparently in the name of 'Palestine'. The following month, a rally for the Israeli hostages in Boulder, Colorado was firebombed, claiming the life of an elderly woman. The main drivers of this violence have been Islamist extremists and, in a phenomenon this book will explore, their progressive allies.

Looking back, many Jews still struggle to comprehend how the mob can have been roused to the side of the jihadis rather than the families they butchered. They also look at how the majority stood silently by – as exemplified in the apathy of that audience in Dublin – and feel a deep betrayal. The isolation is reinforced by trends like the double standards of policing, by which nationalist protests are routed with horses and batons while Gaza rallies are treated with kid gloves. Bloodcurdling Israelophobic chants go unpunished at music festivals. Again and again, antisemitism is excused, downplayed, denied and defended, whereas hypervigilance is shown in cases of bigotry towards other groups. Meanwhile, the silent majority, if indeed it remains a majority, is too demoralised to find its voice.

Now more than ever, Israel needs friends. But who is stepping forward to be counted? Whatever the state of politics in Jerusalem, this is a civilisational struggle between the free world and the forces of jihad, yet most of our energy is devoted to condemning and subverting our democratic ally. If we had reacted to October 7 by putting pressure on the terrorists rather than the people they attacked, the war would have been won much quicker, with far less human cost. How can we question which side we are on?

All this did not emerge out of nowhere. This book will argue that antisemitism cannot be addressed in isolation from the deeper social trends that produce it. When seen in this light, the betrayal of the Jews is symptomatic of how in recent years, the democracies have incrementally betrayed our own values, bankrupting our inheritance and opening the door to an age of radicalism. Twilight has fallen on the great liberal experiment that came about in response to the Cold War and Second

World War. Perhaps this was only to be expected: over the decades, elitist rule has become a vehicle for complacency and cultural suicide, stamped with the hallmark of Israelophobia. By depriving us of pride in our identity and tolerating no dissent, the leadership classes of the West disabled society's immune system towards the viruses of progressive fanaticism, Islamist extremism and nationalist chauvinism that now run rampant around us, pumped up by the digital revolution. As the old certainties collapse around our ears, those who are awake to these dangers face a fundamental question: what next?

Amid the long civilisational landslide that began on 9/11, the bombastic reprise of Trump in January 2025 came to represent an upheaval in the Pax Americana and the return of Great Man power politics, while enabling the mainstreaming of brazen antisemitism, conspiracy theories and Putinism amongst segments of his Maga followers. Meanwhile, hordes of organised Islamists embedded in the democracies are emboldened and progressive cultists are dismantling what remains of our sense of self.

Without ending the decline, the Jews will shrink from the West while the open civilisation that has given the world so much will become dominated by outside powers and ideologies. A remedy may be mapped out, but achieving such renewal requires resolute leadership and is the task of at least a generation. Who will 'grab the reins and change the wagon's direction,' as the Jewish visionary Ze'ev Jabotinsky cried despairingly amid the apathy on the eve of the Second World War? For those in the eye of the storm, complacency is the most disturbing symptom of all. As they worry about the futures of their children, the Jews face questions that should trouble all of us. What do the disturbing events of recent years tell us about our societies? Where do we go from here?

Wrestling with the angel

The Irish writer Conor Cruise O'Brien famously described antisemitism as a 'light sleeper'. The bitter irony is that while the demon has awoken with a vengeance around the world, causing many to reach for those perennial tickets to Tel Aviv, Israeli society is in political turmoil and an unprecedented level of violence has been unleashed upon the Jewish state. In 2024, as bewildered reservists closed their businesses, kissed their children and marched for war, more than eighteen thousand attacks, from assaults with stones to stabbings, shootings and bombings, were carried out against Israelis on the home front. These claimed almost 150 lives and wounded some 1,300,[12] in a country with a population about the same as London. A flight to Tel Aviv will still get you out of the frying pan of Paris, Berlin or Amsterdam, but it may take you no further than the fire.

I have lost count of the times that despairing Jews have asked me at panel discussions how we can possibly make things better, both at home and overseas. Yet this is not only a Jewish problem. Take any group that threatens the wellbeing of society, whether from the far left, far right or the sphere of Islamism, and you will find that their most vicious hatred is reserved for the Jews. It is becoming ever clearer that the current wave of antisemitism is a symptom of a sickness that has been spreading through the West, as well as the Middle East, for decades. Everybody fears that the breaking point is approaching but nobody knows where it lies. Even fewer know what to do about it.

In many countries across the West, our leadership class has long done its best to make us forget who we are. An obsession with open borders has seen millions of new arrivals over a very short period, mostly from failing countries with no democratic tradition, producing parallel communities blighted by criminality and welfare dependency. European armed forces are on their knees, levels of debt and taxation are at record levels, and our economies groan under the weight of regulation and empty climate targets. The population is ageing while the birthrate plummets. The disruption of social media and artificial intelligence threatens the foundations of psychological wellbeing. As we squander the momentum of previous generations, the old seeds of antisemitism sprout. People are lost. We are facing the greatest test of Western resilience since the Second World War, and we have spent decades running down the very resources required to weather it.

There's an old Irish joke in which a tourist asks a local man for directions to Dublin. 'Sir,' the man replies, 'if I were you, I wouldn't start from here!' Restoring our societies is indeed a daunting task, but we have no choice but to begin where we are standing. We need a strong set of values and clear goals, and must not rest until we tame the antidemocratic forces that are tearing us apart. Bold political leadership will be vital, but it will be as nothing without the unsilencing of the silent majority. Our restoration will depend upon that patchwork of families, communities, churches, clubs, regiments and voluntary groups that together form the repository of our culture and hold the instinctive understanding of who we are and how we do things. These are the decent citizens famously described by the eighteenth-century philosopher Edmund

Burke as the 'little platoons' of society. Above all, we need these good people to find their voices and remind the elites that they cannot ignore the electorate forever.

My podcast *The Brink*, which I present with the former Parachute Regiment officer and geopolitical analyst Andrew Fox, and which is available to download now, offers the full interviews from which I have cited extracts in this book (released one by one over the period following publication). In one episode, the American Jewish journalist Bari Weiss, editor of the *Free Press*, painted a poignant picture of today's United States. 'Jews feel homeless,' she told me. 'They feel like the centre has collapsed. People still feel that the vast majority of ordinary Americans are profoundly good people, who reject the woke right and woke left, the identity politics that says either that white men are the best, or white men are the worst. The problem is that the centre has increasingly less power and purchase in the culture and politics. The most extreme versions of the argument are the ones that have most cachet and go most viral online.' Jews are now looking over their shoulders, she said, for both jihadists and white supremacists who have spilled their blood in recent years.

'Is there a version of centrism that feels alive and authentic and sexy to people?' she asked. 'Not centrism in the political sense, but in the sense of a sane view in which the rule of law matters, due process matters, and everyone is equal in the eyes of God and under the law. The normal values that liberals and conservatives used to take for granted. It's crazy but at the moment, it doesn't seem like it. It's crazy that we are having to make the argument again and again for our most foundational, basic principles.'

Many are plagued by such despair. Given the last three millennia of history, however, the truth is that the Jewish people are not the ones in danger of extinction. Since October 7, the world has thrown the kitchen sink at Jerusalem as it desperately tried to eliminate the savage threat to its people. The result? Humiliation for those who made the mistake of betting against the Jews. Israel may be suffering unprecedented enmity abroad, but it has not been this mighty since 1967. As Jabotinsky put it: 'We are not to sit for anybody's examination, and nobody is old enough to call on us to answer. We came before them and will leave after them. We are what we are, we are good for ourselves, we will not change, nor do we want to.'[13] Where else can such certainty be found in the West? Whereas the Jews continue to thrive, other great and ancient civilisations, from the Babylonians to the Romans, have become dust.

In the moving conclusion to his 2010 book *Future Tense*, the late chief rabbi Lord Jonathan Sacks reflected on his people's resilience. 'Yes, the Jewish fight is a losing battle,' he wrote:

> It always was. Moses lost. Joshua lost. Jeremiah lost. We have striven for ideals just beyond our reach, hoped for a gracious society just beyond the possible, believed in a messianic age just over the furthest horizon, wrestled with the angel and emerged limping. And in the meanwhile those who won have disappeared, and we are still here, still young, still full of vigour, still fighting the losing battle, never accepting defeat, refusing to resign ourselves to cynicism, or to give up hope of peace with those who, today as in the past, seek our destruction. That kind of losing battle is worth fighting.[14]

This passage was shared with me recently by a London rabbi called Daniel Epstein, as we talked in the echoing lobby of his synagogue, which was founded in 1761. He followed it with his own observation. 'The Jewish people have never wanted victory, only survival,' he said. 'We have survived for three thousand years, and we will survive for another three thousand years. The future of the West is more of a worry.'

The three tribes

The Third Reich, to which the vow of Never Again was an answer, emerged out of a firmament of radicalism. Amid the humiliation and economic ruin of the Great War and the subsequent hyper-inflation in Germany, the value of the dollar surged from four marks before the war to more than four trillion in 1923. Then came the Great Depression, developing with the help of the 'Smoot-Hawley' tariffs imposed by the United States in 1930, which ignited trade wars and destroyed international business confidence. Between 1929 and 1932, global trade volumes fell by more than 60 per cent. This economic and political turbulence contributed towards the collapse of the German centre, as fascists and communists vied for supremacy and the affections of a downtrodden people. The historical contexts may be sufficiently divergent to make drawing too many lessons from that period unwise, but it would be equally unwise to ignore the many resonances. Once again, the West has lost confidence in the views quietly held by the majority. Once again, amid economic strain and geopolitical uncertainty, society has become increasingly captured by antidemocratic radicalism. Once again, antisemitism is on the rise.

Broadly speaking, the new radicalism – a term I began using in 2024 – is championed by three tribes: progressives, Islamist extremists and nationalist chauvinists. They share many common denominators, but the most fundamental is that all are built upon the very tolerance that they reject. As the writer Douglas Murray told me when I interviewed him on *The Brink*: 'People have treated themselves to completely absurd ideologies, which are all reliant on a set of presuppositions which are not supported by the ideology they've fallen into. Things like human rights, things like tolerance, things like freedom.'

Although these radicalisms exert growing influence throughout the West, their appeal to the majority of people remains very limited. By doing ourselves down so determinedly in recent decades, however, we have made society vulnerable to these ideological forces, allowing them to infiltrate, mutate and replicate without meeting serious opposition. This is a phenomenon I think of as the 'funhouse mirror effect', in which hubristic overextension by the elites conjures distorted political movements that proceed to take it to task.

These range from newly emerged parties that react powerfully against the status quo but rest upon no established political philosophy to diluted versions of fascist groups that were founded decades before. To make matters worse, with the roots of radical Islamism, progressivism and chauvinism now so deeply embedded in our societies, populations are so demoralised and confused that they can barely remember what their older values were, let alone stand up for them.

In Britain, which has never had much of a taste for fascists, the dominant strains of radicalism remain the Islamist extremists and progressives. Europe and the United States are more closely stalked by a danger from the right; five out of the seven terror attacks in America in 2023 were linked to people with such sympathies.[15] Either way, another common denominator of this unholy trinity is that they all have a problem with the Jews, around whom the various tribes have been circling more tightly since October 7.

Most Jewish people share an intense anxiety as they struggle to read the runes of history. According to Christopher Hitchens, the twentieth-century German diarist Viktor Klemperer once described the Jews as a 'seismic people',[16] attuned by generations of persecution to the early tremors of a coming quake. What are they sensing now? In the democracies of the West, the security that has been enjoyed for generations is dissolving amid hushed conversations about whether children should be told to cover the emblems of their Jewish schools in the street, and if it would be best to remove mezuzot from the doorposts of Jewish houses, and whether any university is safe for Jewish students any more.

Jews of middle age and older spend much time battling antisemitic trolls online, or writing to politicians, or lodging complaints to broadcasters over their biased coverage of Israel's wars, or arguing with friends and acquaintances who have turned on their people and their state. Amid the two-tier policing, combined with the Israelophobia found everywhere from the media and the arts to the education system and the health service, they fear that this hollowed-out society can no longer be relied upon to keep them and their children safe.

In 1790, a year after the storming of the Bastille, the Irish philosopher Edmund Burke published a pamphlet called *Reflections on the Revolution in France*, warning his more excitable countrymen against expecting similar scenes in Britain. 'Because half-a-dozen grasshoppers under a fern make the field ring, while thousands of great cattle, reposed beneath the shadow of the British oak, chew the cud and are silent, pray do not imagine that those who make the noise are the only inhabitants of the field,' he wrote.

So much may be true now as it was then. But it only provides comfort if the thousands of great cattle retain the pluck to trample the grasshoppers when it counts. History demonstrates that great disasters can be brought upon the heads of a population at the hands of a radical minority, especially when the sensible majority is too complacent or confused to do anything about it.

What is the West?

On my father's side, my great-grandfather, Sir William Carr, was from an evangelical Christian family, one of nine children of a Lancaster cotton manufacturer. He won a place in the Indian Civil Service and in 1893, at the age of twenty-one, he was appointed Assistant Commissioner to Moulmein, Lower Burma, in charge of revenue, education, health, roads, jails, local taxation and government in an area about half the size of an English county.[17] Later, he became a judge. Sir William must have been of an independent cast of mind because in 1906, he defied convention to marry Ma Khin Hnyaw, an impoverished cheroot roller whom he had met at the local bazaar, and they went on to have eight half-Burmese children who were educated in Britain.

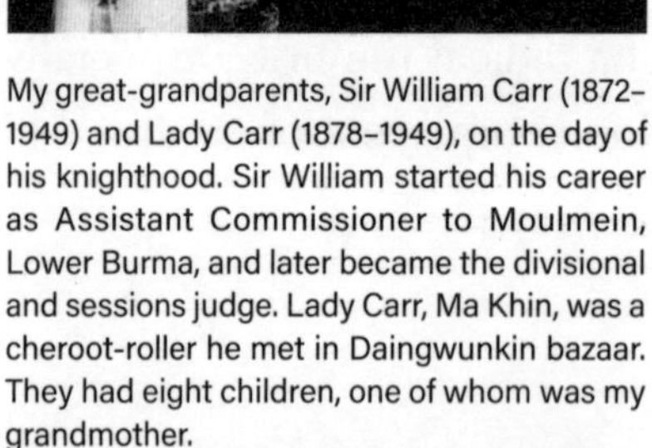

My great-grandparents, Sir William Carr (1872–1949) and Lady Carr (1878–1949), on the day of his knighthood. Sir William started his career as Assistant Commissioner to Moulmein, Lower Burma, and later became the divisional and sessions judge. Lady Carr, Ma Khin, was a cheroot-roller he met in Daingwunkin bazaar. They had eight children, one of whom was my grandmother.

ALL EYES ON TO-DAY'S RACE—P. 2

Wireless on Page 14

Daily Mirror

THE DAILY PICTURE NEWSPAPER WITH THE LARGEST NET SALE

FREE £500 PICTURE CONTEST P. 19

One Penny

£3,000 Cross-Word on Page 16

HINKLER—THE SOUTH ATLANTIC LINDBERGH

OPENING OF BURMA CONFERENCE

NATIVE GIRL'S SPEECH

The front page of the *Daily Mirror*, November 28, 1931, was devoted to the 'native girl's speech' at the House of Lords, remarking that 'she replied to the Prince's speech in English.' My great-aunt Gertrude Daw Saw Yin (1906–1996) is on the right of the main picture. (*Daily Mirror*)

My great-aunt Gertrude Daw Saw Yin (1906–1996) and Louis Mountbatten, 1st Earl Mountbatten of Burma (1900–1979), at the Inter-Asian relations conference in New Delhi in 1946.

My great-aunt Gertrude Daw Saw Yin (1906–1996), right, and her friend May Oung, left, on a visit to London to attend the Round Table Conference on Burma in 1931. Note the gawping man in the background.

My great-great-great grandfather, Benjamin Simons (1817–1891), whose forefathers had arrived in Britain from Spain and Portugal in the 1700s. After starting life as a barrow trader selling fruit in Covent Garden, he walked to Glasgow in search of better prospects and founded the largest fruit importers and brokers in Britain.

My great-great grandfather Bailie Michael Simons (1842-1925), son of Benjamin. He was a philanthropist, patron of the arts and the first Scottish Jew to hold public office.

My ancestor John Wallis, the seventeenth-century mathematician and clergyman known for introducing the infinity symbol into mathematics. *(Pictorial Press/Alamy Stock Photo)*

My Jewish grandfather, Gramps, who took part in the D-Day landings while serving in the RAF, and my grandmother Mutti, pictured on Remembrance Sunday, 2011. This book is dedicated to them.

There is a possibly apocryphal story of Sir William's butler booking a suite at the Savoy for the summer holidays, only for his master to be told upon arrival that the rooms were not available, once the concierge had clocked that Lady Carr was an Oriental and their several children were half-castes. They were forced to spend the entire summer in a rented flat on Prince of Wales Drive on the edge of Battersea Park. There is also a photograph – definitely not apocryphal – on the front of the *Daily Mirror* from November 28, 1931, showing one of their daughters, my great-aunt Gertrude, standing in traditional Burmese dress beside her friend May Oung, the only female delegate to the Burma Round Table Conference, held to discuss the partition of Burma from India. In the background a man is gawping as if they are aliens. Yet my grandmother, Dorothy Carr, the sixth of those eight half-Burmese children, became a botanist and married my grandfather, Jack Wallis, a descendant of the clergyman and mathematician John Wallis; my father was a chorister at Eton. Although racism in their lives was always unpleasant and often a social stumbling block, ultimately it did not stand in their way.

Similarly, my great-grandfather on my mother's side was Ernest Simons, a scion of one of the world's largest fruit importers, whose father Michael had funded and built Garnethill synagogue in Glasgow with his own father Benjamin, a Jewish immigrant who had established the family firm. A patron of the arts, Michael was behind the great Glasgow Exhibitions of 1890 and 1901 and founded both the Theatre Royal and the King's Theatre in the city. He also established the first Jewish Freemasons' Lodge (Montefiore number 753) and was recognised as the pre-eminent Scottish Jewish leader of his day. Again, although Britain was hardly free of antisemitism, this did not hold the Simons family back. My mother received a good education and met my father in Winchester. She later turned to orthodox Judaism.

Despite the strange interplay of Jewish, Burmese, Scottish and English heritages, patriotism runs strongly through my family. Both of my grandfathers served in the Royal Air Force during the War and love of country was passed down the generations. Yet although I am not a citizen of Israel and have never lived there, like most Jews I feel a bond to the place in my blood. As I explore in these pages, this has only been strengthened by the totemic significance the Jewish state has come to assume in our own politics; for a number of reasons, a person's feelings towards Israel have become a shorthand indicator of moral substance. Partly because of this, perhaps, it has never conflicted with my Britishness.

Nonetheless, I have been left with an enduring sense of being both an insider and an outsider, Jewish and Gentile, somebody with an instinctive understanding of religious communities – whether Jewish, Christian or Buddhist – but not a regular member of any, both the product of immigrant stock and an inheritor of a paternal bloodline that stretches deep into our Anglo-Saxon past by way of one of our country's most prominent mathematicians. This has been enhanced by my life as a writer and reporter, which has taken me all over the world, from Europe to Africa, Latin America to the Middle East, as an observer of some quite remarkable events. It is this range of influences that informs my perspective on the Jews, their relationship to the wider world and the condition of society at large.

My insider-outsider selfhood is hardly unusual these days. In fact, it seems more common than one of true belonging and is something to which most readers perhaps will relate. Am I a Westerner? Certainly. But pinpointing this becomes more complicated. I'm not a Christian. Some of my blood comes from Asia and – originally at least – the Middle East. Much of my childhood was spent in a Jewish bubble with its own particular identity, lexicon, social structure, faith, food and traditions. But English is my mother tongue, I share that loyalty to Britain of the generations that preceded me, and my sensibility, values and tastes are surely the legacy of that broad and multifarious culture to which we refer loosely as the West.

The psychoanalyst Erik Erikson, the twentieth century's leading scholar of selfhood, who popularised the terms 'identity' and 'identity crisis', observed that our cultural identity may be 'as indispensable as it is unclear', as it was 'manifold, hard to define and evades many ordinary methods of measurement'. Perhaps, therefore, we cannot define the West without citing every word of our literature, every note of our music, every chapter of our history, every scientist and engineer and renegade that made our civilisation flourish, every person who has died for our freedom and every thinker who gave us the system of governance under which we continue to thrive, to the extent that we do, today.

As Douglas Murray has pointed out, 'cultures and countries are like people: they have certain characteristics that are recognisable, but they contain multitudes, and they are in the ultimate stage at once knowable and unknowable'.[18] It is certain, however, that our civilisation is not defined by its geography or bloodlines so much as its history, social customs, outlook, traditions, values, art, humour, sensibility and taste. It is those things that bind us, those things that are ours, those things that we naturally love.

In broad terms, our layered heritage includes Greek and Roman strata but is more richly rooted in the Judaeo-Christian tradition, together with ideas that emerged during the Renaissance, Reformation and Enlightenment. The American political scientist Samuel Huntington, who famously coined the notion of a 'clash of civilisations', may have added an appetite for empire-building overseas (rather than territorial expansion) and 'superiority in applying organised violence' to that list, which, he pointed out, has been less easily forgotten by those who suffered it. The late English philosopher Sir Roger Scruton, meanwhile, emphasised that our singular flourishing has stemmed from the Jewish and Christian desire to comprehend and express the sacred through a span of achievements such as our musical traditions, the architecture of the Renaissance and the enshrinement of the rights of the individual. Leo Strauss, the American Jewish émigré who had fled Nazi Germany, worried that individualism and secularism had gone too far; faith was a fundamental companion to reason that would guard the West against totalitarianism, he argued. As we shall see, his wisdom rings loudly today.

This rich and conflicted cultural inheritance, which may contain deep shadows but holds far more light, has produced such wonders as representative democracy, the separation of church and state, the elevation of reason and the rejection of ethnic tribalism, few of which can be found in any comparable way in other parts of the world. In the Middle East, for example, before the influence of Western ideas of patriotism and citizenship, human loyalty was ethnic while political loyalty was owed to dynastic overlords. Under Ottoman rule, Jews were expected to give allegiance to the sultan but were excluded from the full mantle of citizenship, usually prohibited from such rights as bearing arms, which was seen as the duty of Muslims alone. By contrast, the West's unique style of governance and political and legal systems, which rest on such principles as the secular rule of law, religious choice, free association, personal rights and the democratic nation-state, have in their best and most realised expressions – though obviously not always – allowed Jews to live as equals. From this sensibility has flowed the great intellectual, cultural and spiritual achievements of figures from Mahler to Elgar, from Chaucer to Dickens, from Disraeli to Brunel, from Julian of Norwich to Moses Mendelssohn, as well as the ordinary lives of people like you and me.

The Wykehamist fallacy

For all its complexity, our identity is not a nebulous concept or a purely private concern. It informs the way in which we relate to the world, from our manners to our foreign policy. In a particularly fine passage in his final book, Huntington wrote:

> If American identity is defined by a set of universal principles of liberty and democracy, then presumably the promotion of those principles in other countries should be the primary goal of American foreign policy. If, however, the United States is 'exceptional', the rationale for promoting human rights and democracy elsewhere disappears.

> If the United States is primarily a collection of cultural and ethnic entities, its national interest is in the promotion of the goals of those entities and we should have a 'multicultural foreign policy'. If the United States is primarily defined by its European cultural heritage as a Western country, then it should direct its attention to strengthening its ties with Western Europe.
>
> If immigration is making the United States a more Hispanic nation, we should orient ourselves primarily toward Latin America. If neither European nor Hispanic culture is central to American identity, then presumably America should pursue a foreign policy divorced from cultural ties to other countries. Other definitions of national identity generate different national interests and policy priorities. Conflicts over what we should do abroad are rooted in conflicts over who we are at home.[19]

It is perhaps the way in which our leaders tried to base Western identity on supposedly universal values in recent decades that led to our disastrous military interventions overseas. The British philosopher Isaiah Berlin pointed out that different moral principles, such as freedom and justice, may sometimes come into conflict without either one being invalid. He resisted the notion of 'moral monism', or a belief in a single, universal ethical truth, which only leads to oppression and eventually totalitarianism. Recent history, not least the Iraq War, has shown he was right to do so.

In contrast, however, democratic leaders after the Cold War embraced what Robin Renwick, the Labour peer and former Foreign Office mandarin, referred to as the 'Wykehamist fallacy', which affected young diplomats of a certain breeding. This, he said, was the tendency to assume that even the most bloodthirsty despot had an inner civilised chap as one might find at Winchester College. Treat him decently and that fair-minded fellow would float to the surface.

If the Western identity is built upon such beliefs, and if democratic values are a universal human good, then all one needs to do is remove Saddam Hussein or Colonel Gaddafi and their people will naturally embrace liberalism. In truth, however, there are other ways of structuring a society, particularly in tribal cultures, that might not be democratic but still hold their own forms of morality. The freedoms we enjoy in the West are a gift from the previous generations that laboured so hard to develop and protect them. They are ours. Place such things in the hands of corrupt men of tyrannical tendencies and what one soon discovers, as Lord Renwick used to point out, is that 'actually, they're a bunch of thugs'.

This is why – though so few people seem to hold it these days – our true moral position can only be to back both Israel and Ukraine with great resolve. Despite their many darknesses, and the blood, chaos and innocent suffering that stalks all warfare, these two countries are defending our shared inheritance against a bunch of thugs that wish to do away with it, and us into the bargain.

Israeli and Ukrainian armed forces have shared a bond since the latest catastrophes fell upon both their heads. In March 2022, a month after the Russian invasion, a viral video showed a Ukrainian soldier with the nom de guerre of 'Zion' proudly taking a biography of the Israeli wartime leader Golda Meir, who was born in Kyiv, out of his backpack. 'This is my favourite book,' he said. 'I will take it with me even if it will be my last battle.'[20] Indeed, the quote often attributed to Meir – 'if the Arabs put down their weapons today, there would be no more violence. If the Jews put down their weapons today, there would be no more Israel' – would apply equally well to the war with Russia.

'It's so clear that in the two cases, there is an aggressor and a victim,' said the French philosopher and adventurer Bernard-Henri Lévy when I interviewed him on *The Brink*. 'The aggressor is Putin for Ukraine, and Hamas, Hezbollah and Iran for Israel. Israel and Ukraine are equally victims of an aggression.' Lévy has spent much time on the Ukrainian front lines and shared two observations with me. 'Number one: the Ukrainian army very often sees the Israel Defence Forces as a model army, as a sister army,' he said. 'There are a lot of common points between the two. Second: I met many veterans of the Israel Defence Forces battling, struggling, fighting in the ranks of the Ukrainian army. In one of my films, there is an important segment when I film a band of five men, three ethnic Ukrainians and two Israeli veterans. They formed a real combat unit. They shared with me their absolutely heartbreaking experience of combat, of mutual sacrifice. So for me, it is clear that Israel and Ukraine are on the same side of the barricade.'

At the same time, it must be acknowledged that the West is hardly a monolithic cultural or political entity. This has always been the case, with different countries ploughing different furrows under different conditions; in particular, the United States stands out among the otherwise imperialist histories of Britain, Canada, Australia and New Zealand. From 1945 until the re-election of Donald Trump, however, those furrows ran more or less in parallel, as there was a consensus of alliance based on shared values, forged by the courage of Woodrow Wilson and Franklin Roosevelt. America's forty-seventh president, however, has made a historic departure from this principle, often eschewing old alliances in favour of pragmatic dealmaking with the strongest powers and personalities. As a result, Canada, Europe and Australasia have found themselves cast adrift and scrambling to cope with the new order; the revised configuration of global power will take time to settle. Moreover, although the different nations of the West generally contend with similar challenges stemming generally from complacency and radicalism, the specific constellation of dangers facing individual countries may vary.

Now more than ever, we must value the gifts of our long civilisation. The West is not located purely in place or in policy, but in the hearts of the many millions who have emerged as the holders of our collective endowment through the generations. They have been, to use that much-abused term, diverse. Our societal genius can be found in what the political scientists Gabriel Almond and Sidney Verba called our 'civic culture' of tolerance, freedom and consent that has developed since the Enlightenment, turning away from gatekeeping rites that guarded against the pollution of other races, religions and tribes. As Sir Roger Scruton observed: 'Our obligations to others, to the country and to the state have been revised in a direction that has opened the way to the admission of people from outside the community – provided that they, too, can live according to the liberal ideal of citizenship.' This lies at the heart of the miracle.

So the West does not depend on race, though in some contexts it could be said to play a part; neither does it depend on religion, though again that is hardly irrelevant; and it does not rest on dry questions of birth. At bottom, the West is a spiritual affair. It depends upon the individual embodiment of certain foundational values and sensibilities and our love for them. This allows us to share that feeling of belonging, that combination of home, kinship, values and culture in our hearts which we naturally seek to hold and defend. The West is broad enough to embrace the stranger yet consists of a distinct people, culture and way of life. It is at once elusive and abundantly obvious. If it can be shared by someone like me – with a Burmese great-grandmother sired by a Hokkien trader who sold cheroots from a stall in Daingwunkin bazaar (not Rudyard Kipling's 'whackin' white' ones but the brown stumpy variety),[21] as well as Jewish antecedents who fled from eastern Europe to peddle fruit from a hand barrow while trudging from London to Glasgow on foot – it can be shared by someone like you. It is under assault as never before. Let's not lose it.

Chapter One

CENTRIST FUNDAMENTALISM

Strangers on the earth

October 7 marked the end of a golden age in which antisemitism was relatively taboo – at least in polite society – yet the volcano had been boiling for decades before the eruption. This process was embedded in a greater cultural shift that occurred gradually after 1945 and then suddenly upon the collapse of the Soviet Union. The postwar period, described by the historian Simon Sebag Montefiore as the 'Great Liberal Reformation', produced great wealth and human flourishing, as well as advances in freedoms including the acceptance of homosexuality, contraception and abortion. The 'seventy-year peace', he observed, comprised two movements: 'forty-five years of Cold War, then twenty-five of American unipotency'.[1] Yet particularly in the latter phase, the familiar shape of society in the form of family, traditions and beliefs, which had balanced and channelled human instincts for centuries, was jettisoned.

In Britain, Tony Blair's landslide victory in 1997 entrenched social democracy as the template for decades of governance, whether under Labour or the Conservatives. Our liberties came to be viewed as universal, not the hard-earned legacy of our forebears; lawyers, judges and other experts were granted power over politicians and the voters they represented; people from all cultures were seen as interchangeable, so mass immigration could be used as a tool of economics.

As in European countries, we were sold a selective or falsified version of history that suggested we were a 'nation of immigrants', or that our country was built by foreign newcomers rather than emerging as an endeavour to which they were attracted. In truth, of course, migrants did not deliver to us democracy, or universal suffrage, or individual rights, or the Industrial Revolution. Those things were ours. Yet in May 2025, research by the Policy Exchange think tank found British schools widely teaching from the 'decolonisation' textbook *Brilliant Black British History*, which asserted that black people had built Stonehenge and that 'Britain was a black country for more than seven thousand years before white people came'. Its research showed that important elements of national history had been erased from state syllabuses, with fewer than one in five schools teaching the Battle of Agincourt and just 11 per cent teaching the battles of Trafalgar and Waterloo. The following month, it emerged that children were being taught that Vikings were 'diverse' and some were Muslim, seemingly on the strength of a few Islamic goods being found in the graves of some Vikings, who had traded with the Muslim world.[2]

Speaking on *The Brink*, the historian Sir Niall Ferguson told me: 'In the 1990s, when the Cold War had been won and all the arguments seemed to be over – when Francis Fukuyama said that history had ended – that was when projects that had produced globalisation suddenly were let loose. And those projects were quite radical in terms of trade, capital flows and flows of migrants.' Over time, those at the top of society turned their backs on patriotism and tradition, loyalty to peoplehood and homeland, a belief in borders to distinguish a nation from outsiders, and the peculiar religious and cultural sensibilities of their countries. Beginning around the turn of the millennium, these expressions of the old identity found themselves mocked and downtrodden, with our history, language, faith, values and customs slowly suffocated in the grip of secularisation, the sexual revolution, moral relativism and mass immigration. The elevation of other cultures was accompanied by heavy social penalties for dissenters, with pride in our way of life condemned as bigoted and any hesitation about the ways of others seen as racist.

In April 2024, a group of former British ministers, national security advisers, permanent secretaries, ambassadors and senior officials produced a policy paper entitled, *The World in 2040: Renewing the UK's approach to International Affairs*. 'The UK has often sought to project an image of "greatness" to the world that today seems anachronistic,' they said. 'Former colonies are making increasingly vocal demands around the need for reparations from colonialism and compensation for the loss and damage arising from historical industrial emissions . . . We cannot simply brush aside concerns around the UK's historical legacy and questions of nationhood.' They did not feel the need to justify that last statement.

The former mandarins even went on to recommend a 'new brand' for the Foreign Office, in order to 'signal a forward-looking ambition for the twenty-first century'. The magnificent buildings at King Charles Street, built by George

Gilbert Scott in 1868 as 'a kind of national palace or drawing room for the nation',[3] should be muted, they argued. 'A new Department for International Affairs (or Global Affairs UK) would signal a potentially quite different role. The physical surroundings on King Charles Street also hint at the Foreign Office's identity: somewhat elitist and rooted in the past. Modernising premises – perhaps with fewer colonial era pictures on the walls – might help create a more open working culture and send a clear signal about Britain's future?' To most ordinary people, these people were undermining their country, not strengthening it.

The writer David Goodhart once recalled a conversation with Gus O'Donnell, then Britain's most senior civil servant, over dinner at Oxford. Goodhart mentioned that he was writing a book on immigration. 'When I was at the Treasury, I argued for the most open door possible,' the cabinet secretary replied. 'I think it's my job to maximise global welfare, not national welfare.' The director-general of the BBC at the time, Mark Thompson, who happened to be sitting nearby, concurred that 'global welfare was paramount'.

This is not a fringe view in certain circles. When he was prime minister of Canada, Justin Trudeau, for instance, once told the *New York Times* magazine that Canada could be the 'first postnational state', claiming that 'there is no core identity, no mainstream in Canada'.

Such opinions, which have been normal among the elites for decades, are not shared by at least 90 per cent of the population. 'Is it healthy for democracy when such powerful people hold views that are evidently at odds with the core political intuitions of the majority of the public?' Goodhart wondered.[4] It was no surprise that by May 2025, foreigners were claiming £1 billion a month in benefits in Britain,[5] a fact that enraged a burdened and beleaguered country. Yet this top 10 per cent of society polices its position by way of condescention towards everybody else. It is this attitude that I have come to call 'centrist fundamentalism'.

In a world still trying to outrun the psychological shadow of the Second World War, the values that anchored society since the dawn of history have come to be seen by the elites as a reservoir of chauvinism from which the toxic stream of the Third Reich flowed. Democracies across the West have applied different versions of the same worldview, creating a global leadership class and technocratic retinues who governed according to a shared ideology, regardless of their political shade and oblivious to the deeper sensibilities of those to whom they were supposed to answer. Ordinary people, meanwhile, are obliged to silence their beliefs for fear of pillory or cancellation.

If the ideology could be personified, it would perhaps be in the figure of 'Davos man', the corporate executive found haunting the moneyed World Economic Forum event in the Alps, where the scent of cigars and illicit perfume is never far away, and where private jets touch down just in time for their occupants to attend hand-wringing sessions on climate change – often including a good telling-off by Greta Thunberg – and hungover men in tailored suits pay tens of thousands of francs to show their faces at lectures on social inequality. Huntington, who coined the 'Davos man' moniker, provided a description that well captured the high priests of centrist fundamentalism. 'These transnationalists have little need for national loyalty, view national boundaries as obstacles that thankfully are vanishing, and see national governments as residues from the past whose only useful function is to facilitate the elite's global operations,'[6] he wrote. It goes without saying that both Gus O'Donnell[7] and Mark Thompson[8] are Davos attendees.

As conservatism has long understood, it is far better to allow human instincts to be healthily expressed in an organic social system of checks and balances than to attempt to stamp them out, or to dilute them into nothingness by universalising every value and mark of identity. 'Now, there is no such thing as "man" in this world,' wrote the French philosopher Joseph de Maistre in his 1796 pamphlet *Considérations sur la France*. 'In my life I have seen Frenchmen, Italians, Russians, and so on. I even know, thanks to Montesquieu, that one can be Persian. But as for "man", I declare I've never encountered him.' For normal voters, these sentiments of national belonging remain as vivid as they were in the eighteenth century. By necessity, however, they are driven underground. As the debates surrounding Brexit, immigration and the elections of Trump showed, anybody who persists in surfacing such older sensibilities is now branded a racist and a fascist.

This malady has long affected every corner of the West. For decades, the only acceptable consensus among the elites has held that liberal values are universal; no culture has superior qualities, least of all our own, and exotic evils like Islamist radicalism are basically fine; open borders and free trade guard against war and instability; policymaking should take place on universal moral and humanitarian grounds rather than in the national interest; and Western norms represent a gold standard that every part of the world respects and is destined to emulate.

It is this bastard child of various political, cultural and economic movements that is implied by 'centrist fundamentalism', in which 'centrist' implies a habit of self-fashioning as a grownup moderate, while 'fundamentalism' suggests the dogmatic mockery of dissenters and the weaponisation of taboo.

The damage of such a worldview is everywhere around us today. As the political philosopher Leo Strauss argued as early as 1965: 'The recognition of universal principles . . . tends to alienate [men] from their place on the earth. It tends to make them strangers, and even strangers on the earth.'[9] His words were nothing if not prophetic. Six decades later, in May 2025, the British prime minister, Sir Keir Starmer, confessed that after decades of mass immigration, the country he led was becoming an 'island of strangers'. Although he later apologised, polling showed that the nation agreed with him.[10]

What would Hitler do?

The historian Jonathan Clark has coined the term 'far-Centre'[11] to characterise those who 'depict themselves as balanced moderates, as experienced technocrats, as the only sensible adults in the room'. As the self-styled grownups, he argued, they take for granted that their enlightened position must be imposed upon an unwilling and unenlightened population. The core far-Centrist belief lies in 'universal human rights', which justifies 'deference to an idea of higher law, enforced by the UK's Supreme Court, the European Court of Human Rights and such bodies' and makes government answerable to lawyers. 'They talk about democracy, but are unwilling to listen to its results,' he wrote, thinking perhaps of Brexit.

'They believe in "humanity", made real by diversity and mass immigration', and were willing to use their power to mould society according to this ideal.

In Clark's view, this 'far-Centre' dogma was characterised by an absence of a belief system from which it could draw principled positions. Instead of conservatism or socialism, its only guiding light was secular pragmatism. 'In the absence of these grand ideologies, politics has become a matter of focus groups, public opinion surveys and news management,' he wrote. 'Parliamentary politics, instead, becomes a matter of mutual and empty denigration, taking the place of argument about great systems of ideas.' He identified this trend – in which 'the most intolerant people of all' became 'those who insist most loudly on their moderation' – as emerging in the nineties. Its most vocal advocates, of course, became known as 'centrist dads'.

But I think there *is* a grand ideology to this doctrine, albeit one that is rarely articulated, even by the believers to themselves. It is one that became so ubiquitous among the educated classes from the latter twentieth century onwards that it now feels invisible to those who imbibed it with their mothers' milk. It is enforced by a psychological system of stubborn but thinly examined positions, set against the conjured bigotry of the plebeians and their class-traitor allies, fuelled by instinct and reinforced by scoffing at opponents. But in its remoteness from the values and sensibilities of ordinary people, and its drive to silence their views, this 'centrism' – which is really an elite species of leftism – is nothing if not fundamentalist. In the United States, it was mass frustration with the failures of centrist fundamentalism, and the disdain of the human fondness for faith, flag and family that it entailed, which led to the explosive overreaction of Trumpism.

Philosophically, the new dogma had its origins in the idea of the 'open society', or '*société ouverte*', coined in 1932 by the French philosopher Henri Bergson.[12] This was a system of moral universalism inspired by Classical Greece and intended to replace the 'closed society', which he saw as running on baser, tribal instincts. The open society was later proposed by figures like the philosopher Karl Popper as the best way to confine totalitarianism to the past and fulfil the ambition of Never Again. In *The Open Society and Its Enemies*, published in 1945, Popper argued that a system of universal humanism was the only way forward. 'The fascist appeal to "human nature" is to our passions,' he wrote, but 'the wise man belongs to all countries, for the home of a great soul is the whole world'. Popper derided the traditional history taught in schools as simply the promotion of 'political power', which he saw as 'an offence against every decent conception of mankind'.[13] This way of thinking gradually emerged as the orthodoxy of Western elites who embarked on a project of building world dynamics according to its principles, over the heads of everyday voters.

Over time, this brewed a great popular resentment towards politics. With all mainstream parties dominated by centrist fundamentalism, differing only in flavour and emphasis, the electorate repeatedly voted for change yet received only more of the same. In Britain, Tory leader David Cameron promised in the 2010 election campaign that his party would limit immigration to the 'tens of thousands', as welcoming two hundred thousand a year – as was then the case under Labour – was 'too much'. He was duly elected; but by the end of fourteen years of Tory rule, net migration had hit a record high of more than nine hundred thousand.

This was a matter of design, not just incompetence. Policies such as the graduate visa route, the salary threshold for work visas and the rules for dependants had all been drawn up to encourage a huge influx of newcomers, as successive administrations relied upon cheap foreign labour to bolster the economy while record numbers of Britons languished on benefits. In this and many other areas, the Conservatives showed themselves not only to be untrustworthy but also unconservative. In truth, they had left the principles of Edmund Burke behind long ago and had become simply a variety of centrist fundamentalist, like Labour and the Liberal Democrats.

Over time, voters clearly saw that their governments were more concerned with open borders, self-indulgent climate change dogma, international commitments, the quangocracy, unelected judges, incontinent tax and spend, compulsive borrowing, red tape, social engineering and petty nannying than fulfilling the wishes of the electorate. Ordinary people could only stand by and watch while their countries changed in a way that nobody had wanted and that had no democratic legitimacy. People started to feel that they were being treated with contempt, a sense that was only reinforced when they were attacked by their rulers with a soaring tax burden, patronising rhetoric and open disdain. In 2016, when Hillary Clinton memorably demeaned millions of Trump supporters as a 'basket of deplorables', it contributed greatly towards her drubbing at the ballot box.

In a sense, this can be seen as a cultural backlash to Hitlerism that went wrong. Speaking on *The Brink*, the historian Tom Holland, co-presenter of the podcast *The Rest Is History*, told me:

> We've already had an experience in the West of what happens when people jettison the Christian idea that the strong owe a duty of care to the weak, that there is 'neither Jew nor Greek', as Paul wrote in his letter to the Galatians, that all are one. We've already seen what happens when great European countries reject that as their core ideology.
>
> I think the shock of the experience of Nazism was so profound that it kind of inoculated us against the possible consequences of the collapse of Christian teaching to valorise the weak, and the disadvantaged, and the foreign, as a way of being 'not Hitler'. So whereas a hundred years ago, even if people were not believers in Christian teachings, the gut instinct in the West morally would be to say 'What would Jesus do?' and then do it, I would say that since the Second World War, the instinct has been to say 'What would Hitler do?' and do the opposite.

Down with us!

Centrist fundamentalism also contained a reaction to the way in which totalitarian demagogues had cranked up popular support for their quixotic visions or personal ambitions. Trump may have brought subtle shades of this phenomenon back into vogue, but for decades Western leaders placed their faith in creating governments to govern our governments. This instinct played a role in the birth of supranational institutions like the United Nations and the European Union, as well as arbiters of global legal standards such as the International Court of Justice and the International Criminal Court, economic authorities like the World Trade Organisation, the World Bank and the International Monetary Fund and the entire edifice of the rules-based international order.

All of these institutions fulfilled different purposes and each has its own merits. The World Trade Organisation, for instance, countered economic nationalism and offered a means to settle disputes. But it was all part of a slow drive towards universalism that carried deep disadvantages as well as profits, not least of which was the ideological climate within these gleaming buildings in Brussels, Geneva, Washington, New York and the Hague. As time went on, many of these organisations, from the United Nations to the International Criminal Court, became dominated by centrist fundamentalism and then, ironically enough, hijacked as Trojan horses for Israelophobia.

The way this hijacking took place was partly explored in my book of that name (*Israelophobia* was published on 7 September 2023, exactly a month before world history took a darker turn). As I described in that volume, the phenomenon of international institutions so readily hosting the parasite of antisemitism is nothing new and has much to do with the influence of the Soviets. As an illustration, a single vignette from a United Nations seminar on 'religious tolerance', in Geneva in December 1984, will suffice. As the late historian Bernard Lewis noted, during his speech, the Saudi delegate, Dr Maruf al-Dawalibi, attributed to the Talmud the supposed dictum that 'if a Jew does not drink every year the blood of a non-Jewish man, then he will be damned for eternity'. Drily, Lewis added: 'Most of Dr Dawalibi's contribution to religious tolerance and freedom consisted of a detailed account of the Damascus blood libel case of 1840, assuming the complete guilt of the accused and the accuracy of all the charges brought against them.'[14]

If this episode appeared to embody both medieval Christian and Nazi antisemitism, well, that is because it did. As we shall see, Muslim antisemitism is well rooted in both. Indeed, Dr Dawalibi had spent the Second World War in German-occupied Europe and was described by SS Obergruppenführer Erwin Ettel, the Arab liaison, as 'our man of confidence' in a secret missive to the German embassy in Paris in 1943. But these are matters to which we shall return in a later chapter. The point to emphasise here is that Dr Dawalibi was allowed to make his remarks unchallenged at a United Nations seminar on religious tolerance, where he found himself most welcome.

This outrage was a natural result of the new moral relativism of the elites, who had denied themselves the right to name evil and condemn it. As Leo Strauss warned back in 1953: 'Liberal relativism has its roots in the natural right tradition of tolerance or in the notion that everyone has a natural right to rhetorical pursuit of happiness as he understands happiness; but in itself it is a seminary of intolerance.'[15]

Over the decades, belief in the centrist fundamentalist worldview, both domestically and on the world stage, became default for most of the educated middle classes. It became what evolutionary biologist Richard Dawkins called a 'meme';[16] not a trending online joke but a viral idea that is able to replicate itself, pursue its own interests and mutate over time, just as natural selection drives the development of biological genes. As it emerged as the established ideology of the elites, they naturally took a disparaging attitude towards those who clung to the older values of tradition and love of country, feeling like they were policing the boundaries of an enlightened society by doing so, even as the evidence mounted that their luxury beliefs were failing ordinary people and navigating the world into increasingly treacherous waters. The quagmire created by this meme is one in which the West is sunk to the armpits.

'The "down with us" mentality is devoted to rooting out old and unsustainable loyalties,' Sir Roger Scruton argued, 'and when the old loyalties die, so does the old form of membership. Enlightenment, which seems to lead of its own accord to a culture of repudiation, thereby destroys enlightenment, by undermining the certainties on which citizenship is founded. This is what we have witnessed in the intellectual life of the West.'[17] What Sir Roger did not point out, but could have, is that when it comes to 'us', there is no people to do down more aggressively than the Jews.

Around the world, populations have reacted against years of such dogma by turning to the funhouse mirror. Donald Trump, nothing if not a product of such resentment and frustration, swept all before him in the United States, while at the last British election, mainstream parties attracted the least support since the 1920s, possibly midwifing a new, pentapolar political system. Amid the birthing pangs, Labour managed a landslide victory on just a third of the vote, fewer than even Jeremy Corbyn had won; but such a unique weather event is unlikely to arise again.

The growing dominance of Reform UK in Britain, Rassemblement National in France, Alternative für

Deutschland in Germany, and many other anti-establishment outfits across the West, is testament to the years of myopic centrist fundamentalism that left voters in a sulphurous temper. Amid this crisis of politics in the West, a University of Gothenburg study in March 2025 found that autocracies now outnumbered democracies around the globe.[18] Looking back over recent decades, the volumes of energy and ingenuity applied at the top of society to the project of dismantling the great cathedral of our civilisation, and the synagogue within it, is remarkable. As the great novelist Saul Bellow noted, 'a great deal of intelligence can be invested in ignorance when the need for illusion is deep'.[19]

Blancmange

Centrist fundamentalism may have little appeal to the majority, but its suffocating effects are now woven into the fabric of everyday life. Take, for instance, the dilution of our national religion that has formed part of the project. Even though Muslims account for just 6 or 7 per cent of the population, Ramadan has become a national event in Britain. Writing in the *Spectator*, the Irish journalist Melanie McDonagh noted the supermarkets displaying posters asking, 'Are you Ramadan ready?', to advertise foods with which to break the fast, while a Belgravia hair salon opened late to offer 'a little luxurious self-care after Iftar'. Central London was adorned with conspicuous 'Happy Ramadan' lights for the third year in a row, she wrote, accompanied by special Ramadan offers at restaurants. Numerous councils offered guidance to schools on presenting the Muslim festival in a positive way.[20]

This presents no problem in itself, especially as some of the businesses and institutions had an Islamic clientele. But in a country in which 46 per cent of the population is still Christian, the enthusiasm with which Ramadan was embraced provided a powerful contrast with our neglect of the calendar of our national religion. Most younger people are no longer familiar with the customs of Lent, Ash Wednesday, Whitsun and Good Friday, while our discomfort with using the gentle 'Merry Christmas' greeting has led to it being erased in favour of the harsh and agnostic 'Happy holidays'. As a result, we often see a prouder public display of Muslim traditions than those of the majority. Of course, there are no Ramadan posters that erase the festival in favour of 'Happy holidays'. During that month, as the writer Douglas Murray drily remarked, 'a tourist travelling through central London should be under the impression that they were in Islamabad, just with better lighting'.[21] All of this has had a drip-drip effect on our national selfhood.

This is not an argument in favour of evangelism. Rather, it is to point out that in actively advancing secularism as a replacement for Christianity – though not for Islam – and wilfully washing out our traditions, we have rather lost the baby with the bathwater. This can be seen as the effect of the centrist fundamentalist ideology. As spring 2025 approached, for instance, Norwood Primary School in Hampshire scrapped its Easter celebration and service out of 'respect for diversity'. In a letter to parents dripping with fundamentalism, Stephanie Mander, the headmistress, explained: 'By not holding specific religious celebrations, we aim to create a more inclusive atmosphere that honours and respects the beliefs of all our children and their families.' She added: 'We understand that this change may be disappointing for some, especially those who have cherished these traditions over the years,' – did she mean Christians? – 'however, we believe that this decision aligns with our values of inclusivity and respect for diversity.'

The religion of secular centrist fundamentalism, of course, would still be observed; the school planned to celebrate 'Refugee Week' in June, she confirmed.[22] Once again, it is simply impossible to imagine any other culture, from Shinto Japan to Hindu India and the proud Muslim civilisations of the Middle East, systematically erasing their national traditions in this way.

Yet Norwood Primary School was no outlier. On Palm Sunday 2025, Downing Street's official X account wished its followers a 'Happy Nepali New Year', a 'joyous Tamil and Sinhala New Year', a 'Happy Bengali New Year' and 'Happy Vaisakhi' to Sikhs, but offered no mention of a certain Christian celebration. Little wonder that a 2017 poll found that almost half of Britons failed to associate Christ with Easter.[23]

Most people roll their eyes and mutter darkly under their breath at this sort of thing. But such is their submergence in centrist fundamentalism that their opinions no longer produce the normal social checks and balances – like a sufficiently heavy texture of communal disapproval – that create a natural taboo in a healthy society. Instead, Norwood Primary School was later targeted by protests by the Disciples of Christ,[24] a radical Christian group linked to the fringe UK Independence Party, whose activists have protested outside a BBC staff celebration while holding wooden crosses aloft and chanting 'Communist scum'.[25] It could not be clearer: when the sensible majority are cowed, radicals of all stripes flow into the vacuum.

Not just the radicals. With our culture dissolving into a blancmange of platitudes served up on the iron spoon of intolerance, minority groups with a stronger sense of self have stepped into the breach, usually upon invitation. In 2025, St Albans City and District Council voted to abolish the traditional Christian prayer that had been recited before meetings for generations. This, according to Liberal Democrat councillor Sinéad Howland, was because it 'may inadvertently exclude or alienate individuals of different faiths' in a council committed to 'equality and inclusivity', even though almost half the local population were Christian.[26]

By contrast, such concerns were nowhere to be seen when Islamic prayers were recited in the council chambers everywhere from Redbridge to Romford, Bradford to Birmingham City, with non-Muslim councillors standing in respectful silence. Again, there is nothing wrong with such prayers. By the same token, however, there is nothing wrong with Christian prayers and this remains, after all, a Christian country.

At the heart of all this is the centrist fundamentalist belief that in order to be 'inclusive' we must be 'diverse', which is code for undoing what is ours; and most in need of undoing are the Jews, who are more ourselves than ourselves. This is what the demographer and political scientist Eric Kaufmann was gesturing towards in his 2004 book *The Rise and Fall of Anglo-America*, when he coined the term 'asymmetrical multiculturalism'. At home, this means erasing our patriotism, pride in our history and Christian heritage in order to cede the space to minorities. Overseas, it means softening our borders and making Parliament subservient to international institutions. Like socialism, this is an attempt to win heaven that only succeeds in finding a new way to hell.

My abiding memory of the Orthodox Jewish bubble in which I grew up is that although we wanted to be left alone to observe our faith, we preferred to live in a secure Christian country rather than one that no longer valued itself. Every Shabbat, almost all synagogues recited prayers for the royal family, the words of which were often displayed in pride of place on the wall. Until the seventies or eighties, people would sing the national anthem at the conclusion of bar mitzvahs. Partly, this was an anxious performance of loyalty born from centuries of persecution. Mostly, however, it was an expression of patriotism, deriving from the conviction that a people secure in their own identity would allow space for ours.

My Jewish grandfather, a D-Day veteran, was one of the most patriotic men I've ever met. To him, the notion of moving to a Christian country only to take offence at its Christianness, or to demand that it dilutes its customs to elevate yours, or to expect exceptional treatment, would have seemed the epitome of boorish ingratitude. This attitude was shared by most Jews. Keep your head down; work hard; do the right thing; be respectful. Push your shoulders back. Sing the anthem. These were our instincts.

Speak to any member of a minority who loves and respects this country and you will find the same sensibility. The truth is that to feel part of a nation, there needs to be something solid to which you may pledge allegiance. Weakening the dominant culture only fosters anxiety all round, particularly for people of faith. When a member of a minority sees the majority laying aside their own traditions, how can he have confidence in the protection of his own? A similar principle applies to foreign policy. The hand of friendship can only be extended from a country that has conviction in itself. Undermining our Britishness does not make foreign states feel secure in an alliance, any more than it makes minorities feel at home on our shores. It projects a sense that you are too weak to be relied upon, emboldens those who mean you harm, and advertises yourself as an easy target for exploitation.

The funhouse mirror effect

As society became more and more dogmatic, anything that could be conceived as belonging to an older system of values found itself in the crosshairs, no matter how benign. Under the principle of the funhouse mirror, this spirited up distorted versions of lost virtues to take their place. Take the simple act of being male, for instance, which, though obviously unavoidable for about half the population, has been seen as a rebuke to diversity.

According to the Civitas think tank, a quarter of parents now believe that boys are made to feel ashamed of themselves at school.[27] A report by the Higher Education Policy Institute found that they were subjected to 'lower educational aspirations, a shortage of role models of the same sex and bias among teachers'. In the foreword to the report, Mary Curnock Cook, former chief executive of Ucas, wrote: 'We want girls to have role models to motivate them to achieve, yet we seem to be intensely relaxed about so many boys growing up with few male teachers, often in single-parent households (where the single parent is usually a mum, not a dad) and in places where their doctor, the vet and the solicitor are also increasingly likely to be female. Is it any wonder they look to social media for their icons and heroes, and are drawn too often to highly toxic versions of masculinity?' So we find funhouse mirror effect at work: in stamping down healthy expressions of masculinity, centrist fundamentalism sets the conditions for the emergence of distortions like 'manosphere' influencer Andrew Tate, who incidentally has posted 'I can only pray for a death as heroic as [Hamas leader] Yahya Sinwar'.[28]

Other unfashionable characteristics, such as being white, Jewish or heterosexual, have also been mocked, denigrated and marginalised in favour of other more celebrated races and sexualities. Ironically, as more and more areas of society pursue the doctrine of 'diversity', they grow increasingly intolerant towards a greater number of people. The fact that this divisive and unbalanced *Weltanschauung* is both damaging to our national spirit and self-evidently absurd has done nothing to hamper its spread. In England, even flying the national flag has long been mocked by the middle classes as an expression of knuckle-dragging nationalism akin to Nazism. In 2014, when the Labour politician Emily Thornberry notoriously posted on social media a patronising picture of a working-class house displaying the George Cross,[29] she was simply displaying an attitude that was common in her social strata of centrist fundamentalists.

In the years that followed, the mood was typified by a viral video suggesting that being British was 'all about driving a German car to an Irish-themed pub to drink Belgian beer, then going home, buying an Indian takeaway to sit on a Swedish sofa in front of a Japanese television to watch American shows, and all the while being suspicious of anything foreign'.[30] It was as if our country alone was devoid of a distinctive culture, able to offer the world nothing other than xenophobia.

By 2025, even Shakespeare's Birthplace Trust was planning to 'decolonise' itself, by which it meant celebrating the poets of other cultures to relativise the Bard. Of course, as the Trust apparatchiks would have understood if they had better studied their Jacques Derrida, there can never be an escape from one's own subjective cultural scene. As the deconstructionist philosopher famously observed in *Of Grammatology*, '*il n'y a pas de hors-texte*', or 'there is nothing outside the text'. On that note, we may deconstruct the Trust: in demanding levels of abasement from Britain that they would never dream of expecting of any other culture, they were themselves showcasing the sort of 'West-centric worldview' that they pretended to deplore. After all, what African, Asian or Middle Eastern society would denigrate its own icons to elevate those of foreigners?

Britain's self-deprecating humour has reached the depths of self-abnegation. Everything that can boost national pride is up for grabs. We have even lost that quality for which we are most famous: our sense of irony. As Douglas Murray has put it, 'only a country that does not know anything about its history or its culture could put up with what Europeans are being asked to put up with today. Only a culture that has been told that it has nothing worth protecting would agree not to protect itself.'[31]

Like everyone else, but more so

The Jews have occupied a complicated position in this

emerging cultural firmament. On the one hand, as the victims of Hitler's genocide, they stood at the heart of Never Again. On the other, as the world's oldest religious, cultural and ethnic group, they represented many of those values of faith, peoplehood and belonging that centrist fundamentalism was designed to repress.

The long currents of history elevated this neurosis. In the Middle Ages, many Jews had lived as marginal nonconformists within the great new cities of Paris, Florence and Seville. 'Europeans belonged to a civilisation that had long been exceptional for its degree of cultural homogeneity,' the historian Tom Holland observed. 'For centuries, pretty much everyone – with the exception of the occasional community of Jews – had been Christian.'[32] In an age when God and the Bible were ubiquitous, the Jews, who had rejected Christ, embodied an existential insult by maintaining their traditions even after they had been vanquished, exiled from their land and set adrift in an ocean of Christendom.

Moreover, Christianity – which defined membership purely through faith, not ethnicity – held an identity complex of its own. On my podcast, *The Brink*, Holland told me: 'The dissolution of peoplehood was a fundamental part of Christianity's appeal. The Romans struggled to get a hold on it. They couldn't make sense of a people who said, well, we have no mother city, we have no fatherland, we have no fields or soil that is ours.' Later, when established Christian powers were confronted with the defiance of Jewish peoplehood in their midst, much blood and tears would flow.

Over time, as the norms of a religious society were augmented and supplanted by the secular über-tolerance of centrist fundamentalism, the Jews, who stubbornly continued to find value in their particular traditions, provoked new flavours of the old bitterness. As Holland explained on *The Brink*, in order to function within Western democracies, diaspora Jews had been 'obliged to accept' that they belong not so much to a people but to a religion, respecting 'Christ's injunction to render unto Caesar what is Caesar's and unto God what is God's', and enabling the emergence of a citizen who is, to borrow a Christian lens, both 100 per cent citizen and 100 per cent Jewish. Israel, which precariously holds a belief in peoplehood within the norms of a secular democracy, is 'a repudiation of the idea that Judaism is a religion', Holland argued, and 'clearly a reaction against the French revolutionary understanding of the secular, of *laïcité*'.

But this is no zero-sum game. In my view, as the growing global backlash to centrist fundamentalism is proving, peoplehood may be dialled down in pursuit of social harmony but never erased; with much effort it may be suppressed, but not for long. Such is human nature. The French writer Renaud Camus – who coined the idea of the 'great replacement' of European populations, which was later stolen as the starter culture for the noxious white supremacist conspiracy theory – expressed an envy of Jewish-style peoplehood in an age of centrist fundamentalist erasure. In his writing, he yearns for 'a simple, self-evident sense of belonging, one that doesn't force you to keep asking questions about it . . . I wish I could be French in the same way that Arabs are Arabs, Jews are Jews, Japanese are Japanese, Poles are Polish.'[33]

In an impoverished culture, such yearning could only breed resentment; such admiration only hostility; such repression only chauvinism. The underlying dynamic was hardly new. As the original 'chosen people', whose inheritance had been forfeited by the rejection of Jesus and bestowed instead upon his Gentile followers, the Jews had for centuries survived as a living provocation to Christianity. By the late twentieth century, however, the old dynamic had taken on new particulars. With the West tying itself in knots trying to respond to the racist outrages of the Holocaust and slavery, Jewish selfhood again became a challenge to a society that had embarked upon the impossible project of tamping down its own.

The late Rabbi Lionel Blue once remarked that the Jews are 'like everyone else, but more so'. For those unable to say 'Merry Christmas', seeing Jews thriving without apology could only feel awkward, especially as what remains of their own religious inheritance evolved from a Jewish kernel. While the West shamefully felt little solidarity as the Christian population of the Middle East shrank from 20 per cent a century ago to 4 per cent today – by 2019, four out of five persecuted religious believers were followers of Christ[34] – Jews worldwide wept whenever their people suffered and rallied to help them (the Jewish community gives exceptionally large sums to charity).[35] As had been the case throughout history, the Jews became the mirror in which society attacked both its own reflection and its own conscience. Before long, the rise of centrist fundamentalism presented the Jews with a familiar choice: join us or be attacked as representatives of everything we have blindly come to deplore.

As the West struggled with the hot potato of national selfhood, matters that had been previously viewed with natural clarity were called into question. It became impossible to imagine most democratic leaders telling the Arabs, as Winston Churchill did unequivocally on a visit to Jerusalem in 1921, that 'it is manifestly right that the Jews, who are scattered all over the world, should have a national centre and a national home where some of them may be reunited. And where else could that be but in this land of Palestine, with which for more than three thousand years they have been intimately and profoundly associated?'[36] Or to describe, as he did in 1908, a 'centre of true racial and political integrity' based on the 'historical traditional aspirations of the Jews' as a 'tremendous event in the history of the world'?[37]

Although displaced Syrians were welcomed into Europe with signs saying 'refugees welcome', displaced Jews with their ancient roots in the land of Israel were branded as perennial invaders, no matter how many generations were born there. During a ceasefire in the 2023 war in Gaza, the residents of that benighted territory were told by the West to remain with their children in the rubble to preserve fantasies of a two-state solution. No 'refugees welcome' for them. The racist Palestinian demands for *Judenrein* territory, meanwhile, both in Gaza and on the West Bank, were championed as naturally just. This thicket of contradictions and double standards revealed the confusion at the heart of centrist fundamentalism, whose emptied soul was blurring with identity politics in the funhouse mirror.

Part of the West's difficulties in relating to Israel lay in its own elongating distance from conflict. The collapse of the Soviet Union in 1991 provoked the belief among the democracies that war was over, or at least the kind that might sully our own doorsteps. This contributed towards what Simon

Sebag Montefiore has called the 'comfort democracies'. As the Kremlin found its way into the G8 – this was 'a very strong message of support for President Putin and his reforms in Russia', Prime Minister Blair observed in 2002[38] – and China was suicidally admitted into the World Trade Organisation, European countries eagerly diverted their defence budgets to pad out the provision of welfare, a handy election winner. In Britain, as huge sums were shovelled into the maw of the inefficient National Health Service, parents were handed free nursery places and the elderly, who tend to turn out to vote, were showered with television licences, winter fuel allowances and triple-locked pensions. Vast capital resources were diverted to costly vanity projects, like net zero targets, which further choked productivity while China and India fired up their coal furnaces. Complacent under the American security umbrella, European countries rapidly reduced their armed forces; by 2005, British troops found themselves being ordered to shout 'bang, bang' in training as they had run out of ammunition,[39] and by 2025, they were smaller in number than those of Romania and Bangladesh (separately, not put together).

Before long, the peace dividend had led to a culture of welfare dependency which took on a life of its own, helping to drive up national debt to almost 100 per cent of gross domestic product. That figure snowballed even more dramatically in many democracies, including France, Italy, Spain and Canada. The United States, which was footing the bill for Europe's defence, had a debt burden of around 124 per cent at the start of 2025.[40] Accelerated by the Covid years, Britain's national inactivity rate – the number of working-age people who are neither employed nor seeking work – came to stand at about

22 per cent,[41] with more than half a million never having had a job.[42] In some parts of the north, as many as 83 per cent of people were 'economically inactive',[43] and nationwide, one in ten children was growing up in a household in which none of the adults were employed.[44] Enjoying lifelong support from the taxpayer, they were better off than they would have been with a job paying £70,000 a year.[45] With a quarter of working-age people registered as 'disabled',[46] a staggering £65 billion was being splurged on incapacity and disability payments annually;[47] that figure alone amounted to £6 billion more than our entire defence spending in 2024, and is projected to rise by tens of billions in the coming years.[48]

The Continent took a similar trajectory. Angela Merkel once observed that although Europe was home to 7 per cent of the global population, it was responsible for half of the world's welfare expenditure.[49] This is not just a matter of economics: the status quo has been deeply harmful to the soul of the nation. Once again, this degeneration was reflected in hostility towards the Jews. With enemies crouched on its every frontier, Israel has never enjoyed the luxury of such lavish spiritual and material sloth. In the milky eyes of the West, however, the military activity of the Jewish state came to be seen as inherently savage and deplorable, as we could no longer relate to its tragic moral necessity.

Chapter Two

WAR AND PEACE

The eternal Sunday

When it comes to national service, recent polling has shown a sharp divide between the comfort democracies and the rest of the world. In the event of war, 41 per cent of Americans, 34 per cent of Canadians and 32 per cent of Europeans say they would take up arms to defend their people. More than a third of Britons under forty say they would refuse to serve their country.[1] By contrast, 77 per cent of those in west Asia, 76 per cent of Indians and 73 per cent of people in the Middle East would fight.[2] As the world enters a period of greater instability than it has seen for generations, this cultural gulf between ourselves and our potential enemies is obviously of grave concern for the security of the West. It also speaks of the broader malaise affecting our societies, reflecting not just the complacency and indolence that has been permitted to develop since the end of the Cold War but also the diminution of our sense of national pride, moral character and social bonds.

'Our sense of history, we lost that,' Bernard-Henri Lévy told me on *The Brink*. 'We are sleeping in a strange dream of what the twentieth-century philosopher Alexandre Kojève called an "eternal Sunday". We believe that it's Sunday every day. We are living in a week of seven Sundays. Kojève said that this was the definition of the end of history, and that this was the result of the animalisation of human society. When we become like farm animals, as in Orwell's novel, we lose our sense of history. We lose the very conception that our world, our values, our way of life can be destroyed, so we don't resist.'

This epochal languor has created two additional gulfs of understanding in the West. The first lies between the citizens of democracies and the generation of their grandparents, for whom the values of wartime fortitude, pride and national sacrifice were deeply instilled. The second divides us from Israel, a democratic outpost that has drifted from the West over time by virtue of constant enemy pressure, meaning that citizens are still called upon to endure hardships for their people and if necessary sacrifice their lives in defence of their homeland. Israel has never had an alternative to living in the real world. While the comfort democracies have enjoyed the luxury of relaxing their borders in line with their 'open society' ideals, if Israel did so, the ensuing carnage would make October 7 look like a cake walk. Similarly, while Westerners have had the luxury of being able to believe that deep down, Middle Eastern rulers were the same as us, who if shown enough love would embrace democracy – the 'Wykehamist fallacy' – Israel has been disabused of this illusion by repeated collisions with reality.

As I described in *Israelophobia*, corrupt Palestinian leaders have repeatedly turned down offers of statehood which would have delivered 100 per cent of their demands, from a Palestinian state with a capital in East Jerusalem to an internationally administered Old City. So much is a matter of historical record. Why? Because their goal was not peaceful coexistence with Israel but the eradication of the Jewish state as a matter of Muslim honour. Speaking to me on *The Brink*, the former Islamist turned intellectual Ed Husain described how the history of the Middle East in recent centuries has bequeathed such neuroses to many Muslims. 'They have a kind of post-traumatic stress disorder after their ancestors lost global power,' he said. 'The old Islamic empire subjugated hundreds of millions of people, from Asia to the borders of France. In the nineteenth century, all of this was lost amid the unstoppable might of the West.'

Once again, the Jews were viewed as the most potent expression of the enemy. During the centuries they had spent under Islamic rule, they had been seen as weaklings, living as 'dhimmi', or second-class citizens. In Muslim eyes, the idea that they could now carve out and defend part of the Middle East, even just the 0.2 per cent of the region to which they have an ancestral claim, compounded the humiliation of history. As the late historian of the Middle East Bernard Lewis observed, for centuries, Jews living in Arab lands had been expected to keep their place, and the rare outbreaks of Muslim violence against them had almost always resulted from a belief that they had resisted doing so. He drily concluded: 'They have conspicuously failed to do so in recent years.'[3]

This has informed the development of a Palestinian Arab identity based upon the rejection of the Jewish state as a point of Muslim pride, rather than a desire for state-building on behalf of its own people. Yet as the dove of peace choked in blood and tears, the blinkered comfort democracies could only scold Israel for the plight of the Palestinians. Opening their eyes to reality and defending freedom and democracy was clearly too unfashionable.

Ironically, by preserving what the West has jettisoned, Israel has been remarkably successful. Without wishing to downplay its problems, by retaining a fidelity towards the old values of tradition, shared identity and devotion to a greater good, its social bonds are enduring, with close-knit, multi-generational families and a keen sense of national duty. Universal military service lies at the heart of this solidarity, contributing towards a high-trust society with exceptionally low crime rates.

As countries get richer, citizens typically have fewer children, leading to an ageing population that falls below the replacement level of fertility. Israel has certainly been getting richer. The Jewish state's GDP per capita surpassed that of Britain – its former colonial ruler – in 2020; two years later, *The Economist* ranked it fourth best performing economy in the OECD, while Britain came in twentieth.[4]

In spite of the raging war, in March 2025, Google's parent company, Alphabet, bought the Israeli cybersecurity startup Wiz for a record-breaking $32 billion.[5] But this remarkable economic success has been accompanied by a sustained baby boom, from religious Jerusalem to secular Tel Aviv, creating a nation that is affluent, young and growing. At 2.9 children per woman, Israel's birthrate is easily the highest in the OECD, where the average is just 1.5.[6] Moreover, in the final months of 2024, newborn numbers jumped by 10 per cent, making Israel probably the only country in history to have increased its birthrate during a war rather than afterwards.[7]

The strength of the Israeli family is apparent from the briefest visit to the country. Both government and company policies are child-centric, grandparents are typically very involved in bringing up younger generations, strangers naturally look out for children in public and the traditional Friday night dinner provides a generous social glue. This is reflected on a national level, as the spirit of patriotic self-sacrifice runs deep. In an interview with podcaster Dan Senor, the Israeli civil servant and veteran peace negotiator Tal Becker described how one morning, in the days after the soldier Gilad Shalit had been kidnapped by Hamas, his young son came into his room. 'Dad, I've made a big decision,' he said. 'I've decided to swap myself for Gilad Shalit. Gilad is a soldier and we need him. I'm already seven, I'll be fine.'[8]

This attitude came to the fore after October 7, when men and women in their late teens and twenties – the 'TikTok generation' – rose as one to face down evil with exceptional fortitude. While reporting from Israel in September 2024, I met ordinary soldiers the same age as British university students who had spent months entering the claustrophobic tunnels under Gaza to do battle with Hamas in the dark. These were narrow catacombs with arched ceilings built to a standard height of five and a half feet, meaning that troops could not even stand up straight underground. One cannot imagine the horrors these youngsters encountered. Here were men produced on the Israeli conveyor belt of heroes. Here were people who truly understood the lessons of Never Again.

One phrase I have heard many times from Israeli servicemen is 'this is our shift'. This spirit, which resembles that of 'the Few' who won the Battle of Britain in 1940, is now alien to many in the West. Yet it continues to radiate throughout Israeli society. In May 2025, ninety-six-year-old Magda Baratz, who had survived the notorious Auschwitz death march in 1945, attended a Holocaust memorial ceremony at Bergen-Belsen concentration camp in northern Germany. While she was being honoured at the event, 2,400 miles away in Gaza, her great-grandson, Asaf Cafri, a plump, twenty-six-year-old reservist with a ginger beard and an easy smile, was shot dead by a jihadi sniper when serving in Beit Hanoun. Two weeks later, a heartbroken Mrs Baratz also passed away.

This tragic vignette embodies how in a very real way, citizens of the Jewish state are brought up within the bond of duty between 'the dead, the living and those who are to be born'. The country's former defence minister, Yoav Gallant, summed the ethos up in a separate conversation with Senor. 'A lot of things are more important than your life: your people, your nation, your country, your family and your unit,' he said. 'In those dramatic days [after October 7], you saw the unity, the willingness to sacrifice of Israeli society. People walk empty-handed into the fire . . . You wake up in the morning, you drink coffee, or you go to play sport at six o'clock, and by six thirty, you hear the news. By seven thirty, these people, reservists and civilians, are on the battlefield fighting for their lives and others' lives.'[9]

The results of such a culture – one that we used to recognise – speak for themselves. Whereas the West struggles with an ageing demographic and low birth rates, Israel's average age is more than a decade lower than in Europe. Whereas levels of addiction and mental illness are soaring across the West, Israel's levels of alcoholism, drug abuse, suicide and loneliness are negligible; the ultra-Orthodox, among the poorest in society, suffer from almost zero crime, substance addiction, broken families or unhappiness, which accompanies poverty in every other country on earth.[10] In Israel, men spend three years in the armed forces, often seeing combat, and women serve for eighteen months. In Britain, however, just 10 per cent of those aged between eighteen and twenty-four would risk their lives for their country,[11] or even support a year of mandatory national service,[12] amid plummeting levels of patriotism. Ironically, however, devotion to your people forms the bedrock of a happy life.

Before October 7, the United Nations world rankings placed Israel as the fourth happiest country in the world. After the atrocities, the trauma, bereavements and multi-front conflict had caused the country to slip just one place to fifth, behind only Finland, Denmark, Iceland and Sweden. Following a further year of war, Israel had descended to eighth; by comparison, Australia was eleventh, Canada eighteenth, Britain twenty-third and the United States twenty-fourth. France, meanwhile, was thirty-third, Spain thirty-eighth and Italy languished at forty. Interestingly, all these Western countries had joined Israel in sliding down the rankings in 2025 (aside from poor old Italy, which managed to climb one place).[13]

The Blitz of 1940–41 has become a symbol for a rosy past in which working-class Londoners 'pulled together' in the face of adversity.[14] Our affection for it hints at our hidden craving to feel a sense of belonging within a national family. Study after study has shown that regardless of race, class or sexuality, the more people feel a meaningful part of a nation, the less alienation, disenfranchisement, discrimination and resentment there will be. Deaths of despair from drug abuse or suicide will reduce, as will poverty, depression and family breakdown. Productivity, optimism and wellbeing will increase.

Different countries have different historical and demographic challenges, but from South Korea, where researchers found that 'national pride is positively associated with happiness',[15] to the United Kingdom, where the Office of National Statistics concluded that 'perceptions of unity within Britain are associated with higher average life satisfaction, happiness and feelings that things done in life are worthwhile',[16] strong social bonds are essential to the health of the body politic. Yet a recent study found that just 15 per cent of British people between the ages of eighteen and twenty-four felt that the country was united.[17]

Research into 'common ground and division' by the More in Common think tank, responding to the worldwide social divisions that followed the death of George Floyd, concluded that we faced a choice. 'One path leads to the deepening polarisation that is being experienced in other countries, where "us-versus-them" dynamics shape national debates, causing distrust and even hate between people on either side of the divide,' it said. 'The other path leads to a more cohesive society where we build on common ground and focus on the issues that we agree are more important than anything else.'[18]

If we wish to undo the deep betrayal to which we have been subjected and heal our fractured communities, the remarkable social cohesion of Israel – a country that so many blindly deplore, and that is undergoing such physical and spiritual turbulence – should be a source of inspiration. This national spirit used to be familiar across the West. In recent decades, however, with the fading of our own memories of wartime, we have been engaged on a project of self-sabotage. We now find ourselves more complacent, miserable, atomised and confused than ever before, surrounded by funhouse mirror replacements of things we formerly cherished, in countries that are ageing fast, having fewer babies and losing themselves amid soaring levels of immigration. On top of all this, we are facing an ideological assault on multiple fronts which, either explicitly or subliminally, aims to undermine the very foundations of our way of life. We must wake up.

Hath not a Yehud eyes?

The tragedy of the war in Gaza and the depressing response of the international community to Israel's struggle of self-defence is exhaustively addressed in other books, such as Douglas Murray's excellent *On Democracies and Death Cults*. But at this point, for the sake of grounding my discussion about Israel, it is worth briefly interrogating the popular view that the Gaza campaign went too far, and from where this perception derives. In truth, although the conflict is appalling – all wars are appalling, even the most just – in terms of the relative numbers of innocents who have lost their lives, Israel has been very cautious by global standards.

There have certainly been examples of rule-breaking and criminality, as there are whenever any democracy deploys its armed forces in such numbers. By and large, however, great care was taken to protect civilians, with up to a hundred thousand telephone calls and tens of millions of messages and voicemails instructing people to evacuate by designated routes to safe areas. Giant speakers were dropped by parachute that began broadcasting warnings once they touched the ground. Military maps were handed out and tracking technology was used to keep people safe. 'Ironically, the careful approach

Israel has taken may have actually led to more destruction,' wrote John Spencer, a world authority on urban warfare at the United States Military Academy at West Point. 'Since the Israel Defence Forces giving warnings and conducting evacuations helped Hamas survive, it ultimately prolonged the war and, with it, its devastation.'[19]

Much research has shown that Hamas manipulates the tally of casualties by exaggerating the numbers of women and children; counting natural deaths, such as cancer patients found on hospital lists and those who had died before the conflict began; including Palestinians murdered by Hamas or killed by misfiring homemade rockets; and, most significantly of all, failing to distinguish between dead combatants and civilians. Even if the total is taken at face value, however, placing it alongside Israel's count of terrorists killed means that between one and two civilians lost their lives for every combatant. Every death is surely an unspeakable tragedy. But according to the United Nations, an average of nine civilians perish for every combatant in wars around the world, meaning that Israeli operations have been unusually restrained, especially given that Hamas intentionally embedded its fortifications among the innocent.[20] This view, however, is rarely projected by the media.

It is surprising how rarely the most obvious questions are asked. Did Britain, the United States and our Iraqi and Kurdish allies evacuate civilians from Mosul before we sent in the bombers to hit Islamic State in 2016–17? Did we deliver waves of aid into the hands of the enemy? Did we agonise about our targeting, with legal experts sitting alongside military decision makers at several levels, as the Israelis did? Did anybody even question the number of civilians we killed? 'The battle for west

Mosul has caused a civilian catastrophe,' opened an Amnesty International report in 2017, as Western-backed Iraqi and Kurdish forces battled the soldiers of jihad. 'Civilians have been ruthlessly exploited by the armed group calling itself the Islamic State, which has systematically moved them into zones of conflict, used them as human shields and prevented them from escaping to safety. They have also been subjected to relentless and unlawful attacks by Iraqi government forces and members of the US-led coalition. Residents of west Mosul count themselves lucky if they escape with their lives.'

At the time, the RAF and US Air Force provided air support while local troops undertook the fighting on the ground. But some American special forces were embedded as spotters with the Iraqi army, responsible for calling in air strikes on enemy targets. A veteran from this campaign described to me how he would be stationed just behind the front-lines, waiting for information about Islamic State positions. From time to time, Iraqi soldiers would inform him that a jihadi sniper was firing from this building or that. Without hesitation, he would call in an airstrike. Within minutes, a two-thousand-pound bomb would fall. No more sniper. No more building, either, and no more civilians inside. In his estimation, about sixty non-combatants had at times been killed for every terrorist.

'Islamic State tactics and violations created particular challenges for pro-government forces in terms of civilian protection in west Mosul,' the Amnesty report observed. 'Iraqi government and US-led coalition forces failed to adequately adapt their tactics to these challenges – as required by international humanitarian law – with disastrous consequences for civilians.' It went on to accuse coalition forces of 'a series of unlawful attacks' using 'explosive weapons with wide area effects' that had 'crude targeting abilities'. As a result, 'these weapons wreaked havoc in densely populated west Mosul, where large groups of civilians were trapped in homes or makeshift shelters,' it said. By some estimates, by the end of the battle, up to forty thousand civilians had been killed.

At the time, the key findings were handed both to the Iraqi defence minister, Irfan al-Hayali, and to the American secretary of defence, James Mattis, in an attempt to stop the massacre of the innocent. Yet this was in the aftermath of the Bataclan attack in Paris, the Brussels bombings, the Nice truck massacre and the Berlin Christmas market ramming, all of which had been perpetrated by Islamic State (and all of which I witnessed first hand as a reporter). Our blood was up. Nobody demanded a 'ceasefire'. The campaign continued until the battle was won.

This Israelophobic myopia has a blood cost. Understanding the pull of Palestinian suffering upon the hearts of the world, Hamas stokes the misery of its own people as propaganda. Over almost twenty years, it spent billions building up to 450 miles of tunnels at various depths[21] – the London Underground is 200 miles shorter – beneath a territory spanning just 25 square miles. Yet when war broke out, not a single civilian was allowed to take refuge there from the bombardment, in case the stream of gory footage dried up. Was this the first regime in history to have behaved in this way? Even the worst leaders in the world made some attempts to protect their people in shelters or metro stations. Hamas, on the other hand, has constructed not a single civilian defence while embedding its forces in schools and hospitals. The tiny number of civilians killed when Israel fought Iran shows how the Jewish state operates when it is not up against a cult of human sacrifice.

'Radical evil has emerged in connection with a system in which all men have become equally superfluous,' observed Hannah Arendt in her 1961 masterwork *The Origins of Totalitarianism*.[22] She could have been talking about Hamas, the especial evil of which views both fighters and civilians alike, whether young or old, as entirely expendable. With the fetishisation of death – any death – at the core of their ideology, the Hamas strategy holds its own depraved logic. Yet it depends upon the complicity of journalists. If it wasn't for the attitude of the media, many more Palestinian civilians may be alive today.

In April 2024, the Israeli authorities released a video of an interrogation of an Islamic Jihad spokesman called Tarek Abu Shaluf. 'The international media differs from the Arab ones,' he said. 'They focus on humanitarian issues. We don't speak to them in the language of violence, destruction and revenge. They come and say, "only talk to me about the humanitarian side", meaning, for instance, you'd say, "it's our right to live", or "we want the situation to return to normal and our children to live like other children in the world".' This partial reporting is bad enough. On some occasions, he added, reporters have even agreed to publish misinformation so they do not lose access to Islamic Jihad officials.[23] One would like to think such behaviour is rare. But it is an extreme instance of an overall trend. When interviewing Palestinians, the BBC, for instance, regularly mistranslates the Arabic word 'Yehud' as 'Israeli' rather than 'Jew', covering up the base antisemitism that is sadly so widespread in Gaza.[24]

According to a report produced by Andrew Fox in December 2024, only 5 per cent of the media organisations surveyed cited casualty figures issued by the Israeli authorities. By contrast, 98 per cent used those provided by Hamas.[25] Quite apart from the contrast between the fraudulent nature of the jihadi data and Israel's democratic standards of accountability, the refusal to include both sides of the story speaks volumes. The sorry truth is that many Western media outlets have unflinchingly disseminated Hamas propaganda to tens of millions of viewers. Moreover, the Islamist overlords in Gaza suppress footage of wounded and dead jihadis, intentionally creating the illusion that Israel is targeting the innocent. Does nobody wonder why we see so many injured civilians on our televisions but never any wounded Hamas terrorists? It is unusual even to see a gun being brandished during reports from the Strip. All in all, this comprises one of the most scandalous betrayals of journalistic ethics in history.

The dark triad

This onslaught of disinformation has been profoundly effective in turning public opinion against Israel. In the aftermath of October 7, Britons were almost twice as likely to hold Hamas more responsible for the war than the Israeli government. A year later, however, 60 per cent considered Israel to have gone too far, with only 12 per cent thinking it was 'about right'.[26] Such has been the power of the Hamas propaganda, amplified by the media, that anybody who tells the truth about this war today risks being laughed out of the room. This affects government policy, isolating the Jewish state and pressuring it to remove its boot from the throat of Hamas, a group which would murder us all if it could.

The way in which Hamas has managed to manipulate the West can be understood in psychological terms. In April 2025, the cognitive scientists Scott Barry Kaufman and Craig Neumann published research which found that 'citizens in democratic countries have more benevolent traits, fewer malevolent traits, and greater well-being'.[27] Based on a study of 200,000 people from seventy-five countries, they found that people living under autocracies were more likely to exhibit the 'dark triad' of negative personality traits: narcissism, Machiavellianism and psychopathy. In democracies, by contrast, more people displayed the 'light triad' of humanism, faith in humanity and 'Kantianism', or treating people with dignity in their own right rather than viewing them as a means to an end.

This may help explain the dynamic. When a light triad Westerner, who enjoys a privileged life of *le dimanche éternel* within a comfort democracy, encounters a dark triad Hamas terrorist, who has grown up in one of the world's worst autocracies and risen to become one of its enforcers, the stage is surely set for manipulation. The underlying presence of centrist fundamentalism and Israelophobia only makes it that much easier.

The neuropsychologist Dr Orli Peter has described this phenomenon in terms of two different types of empathy. 'Cognitive empathy is the ability to accurately understand and model the thoughts, feelings and values of others,' she writes. 'It's like hacking into someone else's algorithm for how they think and feel, enabling you to predict their reactions to your actions.' This is a primarily cerebral, calculating quality. Emotional empathy, on the other hand, is about warmth, described as 'the ability to feel what you believe the other person is experiencing'[28] and be moved by their suffering. Hamas, with its preponderance of dark triad traits, holds a malign cognitive empathy, giving it a gimlet-eyed insight into how the Western mind works. People in the democracies, however, where light triad traits are more common, have little cognitive empathy. This keeps them ignorant of the way jihadis think and inclined to view them as basically fine.

On the other side of the equation, dark triad jihadis have little 'emotional empathy', leaving them unmoved by human misery. In the West, by contrast, we have a glut of the stuff. Show a soft-hearted Westerner a picture of Palestinian suffering and they're anybody's, even when it has obviously been generated by artificial intelligence. From a neuropsychological point of view, as Andrew Fox has argued, exposure to images of suffering activates our amygdala, which sits in the brain's limbic system and is responsible for emotional reactions. This in turn shuts down critical thinking by suppressing the logical prefrontal cortex, submerging us too deeply in the amygdala stress process to analyse the situation properly. This is true at the highest levels. Time and again, we find world leaders citing 'the pictures coming out of Gaza' when taking steps against Israel, often backed up by bogus casualty figures. Since when were television pictures a sound basis for policy? And why do people still dignify those figures? All of this makes it easy for the jihadis to play with our passions to achieve their goals.

Tender turtles

It is surprising how many Jewish people have become bogged down in the swamp of Israelophobia. While the majority have despaired at the spotlight of condemnation cast upon them since October 7, others have opted instead to downplay the alarm or even join the ranks of the critics. Many Jewish people have long feared that the tolerance that has characterised the West is in terminal decline. But just as there are untold numbers of ordinary Gentiles who throughout history have reacted to signs of totalitarianism with a shrug, a glass of wine and the equivalent of Netflix, an influential minority of secular Jews in cosy corners have allowed themselves to forget their peoplehood entirely and fall asleep with their eyes open.

In terms of the scale and nature of the oppression, it is hardly appropriate to compare Germany of the thirties to the brewing dangers of today; but a tendency towards complacency can be seen in both cases. In some ways, it is understandable. By the time Hitler was elected, a remarkable 44 per cent of Jews were marrying outside the faith and many held positions of distinction in German society.

'Jews mistook such prominence as an index of their successful integration,' observed the writer Amos Elon in his magisterial *The Pity of It All*. 'The few who suspected otherwise must have repressed their concerns.'[29] After Hitler's inaugural speech, a young Jewish copy editor on a Berlin tabloid proofread the transcript 'without the slightest feeling [or] concern that it might affect me'.[30] Even after the Nazi victory, when the brownshirts staged an infamous torchlight procession through Berlin, wealthy Jews left for the usual ski resorts and the writer Arnold Zweig and his wife holidayed at a thermal spa. 'An exaggerated faith in *Kultur* blocked awareness of the danger and produced a highly selective sense of reality,' Elon wrote.[31] Today, with many liberal Jews with comfortable lives and good standing embracing centrist fundamentalism, it is fashionable in those circles to emphasise the remaining tolerance of the West rather than its growing decline. The concerns of the majority are dismissed as bigoted or reactionary, in true centrist fundamentalist fashion.

These are the Jews lampooned in Howard Jacobson's novels. In *Kalooki Nights*, the narrator, Max Glickman, recalls how as a child he once began to chant, 'Jew Jew, Jew Jew, Jew Jew', while on his mother's lap on the train. Max's father, a secular, progressive type, pretends that his son was simply imitating the 'whoo whoo' of the whistle. When Max corrects him, his father turns icy, 'as though I'd informed him I wanted to be a rabbi when I grew up'. This was the centrist fundamentalist instinct writ large.

A similar disavowal is evident when privileged Jews take a dim view of their own homeland, even repeating the cant common to their class that the special form of malice facing Israel is somehow disconnected from the special form of malice that happens to be facing the Jews. These people tend to focus on the faults of the Jewish state, such as its small number of chauvinist politicians, and train their guns on the right wing of their own community while overlooking those who would have them and their children driven out or dead, both in the Middle East and at home, regardless of their support for the two-state solution. It is hard not to call to mind the words of Martin

Luther King at the height of the Cold War. 'We cannot sit complacently by the wayside while our Jewish brothers . . . face the possible extinction of their cultural and spiritual life,' he said. 'Those that sit at rest while others take pains are tender turtles and buy their quiet with disgrace.'[32]

Speaking of disgrace, a handful of Jews even join the Gaza rallies, fêted on account of their useful Jewishness and invited into the vanguard as mascots. Over the years, this craven idiocy – too distorted even for the funhouse – has become an unwelcome feature of Jewish life. During the violence along the Gaza border in 2018, for instance, a group of progressive Jews gathered in Parliament Square to recite kaddish, the Hebrew prayer of mourning, for the sixty-two dead, fifty of whom happened to be Hamas terrorists.[33] Further back, in 1972, four Jews and an Arab were arrested in Israel for spying for Syria on behalf of the KGB; the inquiry revealed that all were leftists and most were members of the 'Israeli Communist Party'.[34]

Such complacency, appeasement and treachery have been an ignominious part of Jewish history for many centuries. One of the earliest examples in the West came in 1144 with the first recorded blood libel, when the murder of a boy called William in Norwich was falsely blamed on the ritual practices of local Jews. This lie was invented by a man called Theobald of Cambridge, himself a Jew who had later converted to Christianity. 'I was, at that time at Cambridge, a Jew among Jews, and the commission of the crime was no secret to me,' he claimed after his conversion.[35] It seems that Theobald had adopted the antisemitic narratives to which he had been subjected and appointed himself their most insidious proponent. In the centuries that followed, the suicidal Jewish innovation was enthusiastically taken up by Gentiles across the globe, claiming countless lives. It remains widespread today, not least in the Israelophobic 'baby killer' smears which are so shamefully amplified by the modern bearers of the mantle of Theobald of Cambridge.

It is not just the radicals. Whenever they have adopted centrist fundamentalism, the tender turtles of the Jewish world have ended up betraying themselves. In truth, when Angela Rayner, Sarah Champion, Justin Trudeau, the Humanists and the others erased the Jews from Holocaust Memorial Day in 2025, the ground for doing so had been laid by the Jewish elites. The Holocaust Memorial Day Trust, the body responsible for the annual commemorations that was founded by the Blair government in 2001, is run by Jewish officials. From the beginning, it agreed to act as a portmanteau for all genocides. Officially, the day of remembrance in 2025 marked not just eighty years since the liberation of Auschwitz but also the three decades since the genocide in Bosnia, an entirely unrelated tragedy, as well as other acts of depravity around the world.

Indeed, the shameful scenes in Dublin were even presaged by the behaviour of the Trust itself: in its invitation to the annual ceremony in London, its leaders felt obliged to state that they were 'horrified' by the 'devastating violence against Palestinian civilians in Gaza', implicitly endorsing the blood libel.[36] They were later forced to apologise. As we have seen, this tendency to beckon one's own undoing is not a Jewish phenomenon but part of centrist fundamentalism, which works ruination through whomever it touches.

The great primæval contract

It goes without saying that the suffering of innocent Palestinians – for which Hamas is, of course, principally to blame – is deeply upsetting, but bringing it into Holocaust Memorial Day holds disturbing implications. Firstly, it gives tacit credence to the vindictive claim that Israel is conducting a 'genocide', rather than simply waging a just war against a savage enemy in Gaza. Secondly, it chimes with the false equivalence drawn between Israel and the Nazis, a smear relished by antisemites since its invention by Cold War propagandists (as I explored in *Israelophobia*). Thirdly, it grotesquely minimises the Holocaust. Lastly, it opens the door for those with malicious intent to hijack the Holocaust to blacken Israel's reputation, a principal feature of the strategy for its dismantlement. With the Trust opening these gates wide, was it any wonder that people like President Higgins – who was branded an 'antisemitic liar' by Jerusalem's foreign minister after he falsely claimed that Israel wished to occupy Egypt – strolled so blithely through them?

Although October 7 accelerated this assault on Jewishness, things had been going in this direction for decades. Every year, when candle lightings are held to remember the victims of the Holocaust, there is not one but five, the others marking the genocides in Bosnia, Cambodia, Rwanda and Darfur. Seeing Rwandan officials bowing their heads for the victims of 1994 in front of a Holocaust Memorial Day banner seems rather reductive for the Rwandans, but it is even worse for those who until recently had been granted natural ownership of the horrors that took their families. The universalisation of antisemitism – Jeremy Corbyn was only ever able to stand against 'all forms of racism', not the particular hatred of Jews[37] – always removes the necessary defences against this specific bigotry, allowing it to creep quietly on. When it comes to the Holocaust, by stealing Jewish suffering and sharing it out across the world, the genocide is laid open to the winds of forgetting.

It is hard to ignore the stench that hangs around this debate. Depriving Jewish mourners of the straightforward right to grieve unravels the weft of their selfhood, replacing it with a fixed template of universal ideals that may add up on paper but have never been rooted in any human heart. It subverts the bond between 'the dead, the living and those who are to be born', which Edmund Burke identified as the 'great primæval contract of eternal society, linking the lower with the higher natures, connecting the visible and invisible world, according to a fixed compact sanctioned by the inviolable oath which holds all physical and all moral natures, each in their appointed place'.[38] It fosters the sly advancement of the spiritual destruction of the Jews, under the guise of mourning those who were physically destroyed. Once again, irony abounds.

If there is any lesson at all from the Nazi period, it is that when it meets no resistance, antisemitism progresses by increments. All too often, centrist fundamentalism removes that resistance. As Holocaust Memorial Day stepped annually along its benighted path, such was the taboo and groupthink that nobody was able to stand firm with the obvious objection: why must the Jews, and the Jews alone, be called upon to relinquish ownership of their personal loss? Surely this is like being told that in order to gain society's approval, you must expand your grandfather's funeral to include dead men in distant countries. One bereavement may not be worse than another, but to deny the private nature of grief is to deny what it means to be human. It seems self-evident that the appropriation of the Holocaust as a synonym for all genocides relativised the Jewish tragedy and set the conditions for the erasure of Jewish selfhood that arrived in 2025.

The degradation of Holocaust Memorial Day represented something worse than a straightforward victory for hostile forces, as in battle; it represented a process in which Jewish elites became themselves complicit by conforming to an alien and hostile ideology, as did the Hellenised Jews in the story of the Maccabees. Jews are no monolith. Although they may share certain common denominators, their dispositions and outlooks are refracted through a complex set of religious, cultural, economic and political lenses, as is the case in the population at large. With the modern left providing a welcoming home for Israelophobia, both brazen and covert, many Jews with progressive tastes have absorbed the code for their own demise.

In 2023, the Board of Deputies, the main leadership organisation of Anglo Jewry which has for many years been dominated by liberal elites, attacked the Conservative government for seeking to limit the flow of undocumented migrants crossing into Britain on small boats.[39] Some resigned from the organisation in protest, accusing it of 'political grandstanding'.[40] The president at the time visited Dunkirk to be pictured handing out food to the migrants; a year later, she stepped down from that politically neutral role and immediately joined the Labour Party.[41] Without question, the way Britain opened its doors to so many immigrants from Muslim countries over the last thirty years, at a rate that did not allow for assimilation, has been one of the main drivers of antisemitism on our shores. By espousing centrist fundamentalism, Britain's Jewish leadership had become an agitator against the interests of its own community.

This is, however, a question on which good people may disagree. To consider the counter argument: Daniel Finkelstein, a columnist for *The Times*, recalled that his father, a Holocaust survivor, 'regarded the prevention of other genocides as part of Holocaust commemoration'. Indeed, he continued, 'he had always asserted that the reason the Nazis had to be stopped was not just because of what they were doing to the Jews, but because of the result of this for everyone'. In addition, he pointed to the 'acres of media coverage' that Holocaust Memorial Day has produced as evidence of its value.[42]

In my view, however, for all the media coverage, a universalist morality unburdened by peoplehood is no morality at all. Relativising the Holocaust always ends up erasing the Jews. The national attention that Lord Finkelstein values for its educational benefit would not, I think, be hampered at all by limiting Holocaust Memorial Day to the Holocaust. Moreover, it is perfectly possible to underline the sombre imperative to guard against other genocides without resorting to some Frankenstein's monster of memorial. Singularity offers greater depth, making for a more powerful moral message with respect to other unique peoples threatened by mass murder. As Joseph de Maistre put it, 'as for "man", I declare I've never encountered him'. Create a general 'genocide day' if you must. Holocaust remembrance must remain a Jewish affair. The alternative is to conspire in the dilution of your grief until you can no longer taste it.

Chapter Three

DADS AND MUMS

The new authoritarianism

In 2024, on her way to becoming Conservative leader, Kemi Badenoch – the daughter of Nigerians – wrote in a column that 'not all cultures are equally valid' when it comes to immigration. 'We cannot be naïve and assume immigrants will automatically abandon ancestral ethnic hostilities at the border,' she argued. 'I am struck, for example, by the number of recent immigrants to the UK who hate Israel. That sentiment has no place here.' She concluded: 'Those we chose to welcome, we expect to share our values and contribute to our society.'[1] One might be forgiven for thinking that this was an eloquently expressed statement of the obvious. To most of the population, it probably was. Predictably, however, the centrist fundamentalists and leftists did their best to silence such forbidden opinions.

Zarah Sultana, for instance, the progressive MP, branded Badenoch 'one of the most nasty and divisive figures in British politics'. This hysterical climate of supercharged taboo in the service of national self-harm went far beyond the vision that had inspired the drive for an open society in the first place.

In *The Open Society and Its Enemies*, Popper had warned: 'If we are not prepared to defend a tolerant society against the onslaught of the intolerant, then the tolerant will be destroyed, and tolerance with them.' As the West grew plump on the peace dividend, however, elite centrism became increasingly fundamentalist until it mutated into a caricature of itself.

This did not happen automatically. Over the years, the ideology was normalised and enforced by a rapidly expanding managerial bureaucratic state that fed itself on swollen taxes, sweeping even conservative politicians along with its agenda. Inherent within the ideology is an intolerance towards those who do not share it. Because it had its hands on the levers of power, centrist fundamentalism eventually moved beyond mockery and cancellation and started to enlist the muscle of state enforcement. Particularly in Britain, newly authoritarian tendencies developed, with the West's belief in the importance of free expression trampled in a drive to force people to 'be kind'. Before long, the demand for a suicidal level of tolerance was being enforced with an almost totalitarian spirit of intolerance.

The process accelerated during the Covid years, when reasonable questions about government pandemic policy were treated as taboo and our civil liberties took an unprecedented battering. Within a few years, custody data revealed that British detectives were arresting thirty members of the public every day for making offensive posts on social media that may cause 'annoyance', 'inconvenience' or 'anxiety',[2] including – bizarrely – a grandmother in Stockport who had criticised a Labour councillor on Facebook.[3]

In November 2024, Julie Bindel, one of Britain's most prominent feminist writers, received a visit from the police investigating a 'hate crime' after a 'transgender man' from the Netherlands reported one of her social media posts. Figures released by the Department of Education revealed that in 2022–23, a toddler, aged either three or four, was one of ninety-four pupils suspended from school – or nursery, in this case – for 'abuse against sexual orientation and gender identity'.[4] Quite how a child barely out of nappies could possibly be transphobic remained unexplained.

In April 2025, Hertfordshire police sent six officers to detain a middle-aged couple and held them in a cell for eight hours after their child's primary school complained about 'disparaging' remarks made in a WhatsApp group.[5] An academic who believed in biological sex, an eminently reasonable position shared by the vast majority of the population which was later confirmed by the Supreme Court, was hounded out of the university where she worked.[6] A retired special constable was held in a cell overnight after daring to criticise the Palestine marches on Facebook; six officers arrested him at home and searched his property for right-wing material, criticising his 'Brexity' bookshelves.[7] (The fact that the Home Office responded by pointing out that 'this incident occurred under the previous government' is a measure of the way mainstream parties have universally embraced centrist fundamentalism, despite their superficial political shade.)

The list could go on and on. Ordinary people caught up in this new authoritarianism reacted with disbelief. How could the fundamental freedoms of our society have become so debased? How could those trusted to keep us safe turn their authority against us? Here was a betrayal of the first order. In poignant remarks, a woman in her forties, who had been summoned for interview under caution by Cambridgeshire police after calling a man a 'pikey', told the press: 'We are a military family, and this just rocks us to the core that we are living in a world, in this country, where this is allowed to go unchecked.'[8]

As if this wasn't enough, a new category of 'non-crime hate incidents' allowed British police to impose ideological conformity even without the pretext of a crime. In the five years leading up to 2023, as many as 120,000 such transgressions were recorded. These included a man who was interviewed by Humberside police after liking a limerick on social media that was seen as offensive to transgender people; a Bedfordshire resident who had taunted a neighbour by whistling the theme tune from the *Bob the Builder* cartoon; and a West Yorkshire schoolboy who had mistakenly dropped a Quran.

This style of enforcement was no accident. It radiated from an approach towards policing that put ideology first. In March 2025, for instance, the Police Race Action Plan told officers to give ethnic minorities special treatment in order to 'put an end to racial disparities', stating that arrest rates must be equalised between groups. Meanwhile, the Sentencing Council put forward two-tier rules that would give more lenient sentences to members of 'an ethnic minority, cultural minority, and/or faith minority community', as well as transgender people, young people and women, provoking a showdown with ministers. Not only free expression but equality under the law was being trampled by the new authoritarianism.

Inevitably, this dismantlement of our own national selfhood paved the way for the advance of the three tribes. How were people who had been stifled by cultural universalism under threat of arrest supposed to condemn Islamist radicals and demand their prosecution? How were those who were no longer permitted to respect their history supposed to challenge those progressive radicals who insisted that we had always been the most racist country on earth? And with Britain's expressions of patriotism limited to the veneration of the National Health Service, 'diversity' and Paddington Bear, is it any wonder that ordinary people turned their gaze to the nationalist chauvinists, the only ones still showing pride in their country? With ordinary people pressured into docility, often at the hands of the police, our doors were inadvertently opened to the most dangerous people and ideologies.

The late Christopher Hitchens once remarked that 'the barbarians never take a city until someone holds the gates open to them'.[9] In the midst of our addiction to disrespecting our own culture while venerating those of others, countries across the West began holding the gates wide to the barbarians, allowing them to enter amid reckless waves of immigration for which nobody had voted and about which nobody was allowed to complain.

All three Islamic State terrorists who killed eight people and injured almost fifty in the London Bridge attack of 2017 – which I vividly recall, having seen it as a reporter – were immigrants, with one, Rachid Redouane, an asylum seeker whose claim had been rejected eight years earlier. Most of those responsible for other Islamist atrocities, from the 7/7 London bombings to the 2021 murder of Conservative MP David Amess, were sons of immigrants, many of whom had entered the country in the nineties. The same was true of the terror attacks in Europe in the late 2010s, most of which I covered as a correspondent on the ground, and several of which targeted Jews, not least the 2015 siege of the kosher supermarket in Paris where four people were murdered.

It wasn't just headline-grabbing acts of terror. From the Blair years onwards, our soft borders and growing cultural relativism degraded social trust and allowed insular societies to sprout. The problem was not immigration in principle but the sacrifice of common sense on the altar of ideology. Cities across Britain and Europe began to change at a rapid cadence. In 2015, during the manhunt that followed the Bataclan attacks in Paris, I reported from Saint-Denis, now home to more than 130 nationalities, after the police raided a flat used as a headquarters by the terrorists. One of them, a second-generation immigrant from Morocco, had blown himself up in protest and his severed head had landed on a parked car across the road. Five years later, in Gothenburg, Sweden, which has an immigrant population of 34 per cent, I found myself covering the rise of the migrant mafia clans, who had carried out more than 250 bombings and three hundred shootings that year. The mob had even had the audacity to set up roadblocks in the north-east of the city.

A further five years later, the depraved scandal of the Pakistani child rape rings came fully to light in Britain after an intervention by Elon Musk. In many countries, however, the borders remain very lax, with politicians unable to resist importing foreign workers as an apparently quick and easy solution for economic woes. According to the latest projection, by 2032, 14 per cent of the population of Britain will have arrived in the previous decade alone, while a quarter of the workforce is unemployed and more than three million languish on sickness and disability benefits.[10] Yet even today, it remains difficult to express concerns about all this without fear of being smeared as racist.

You can't say that!

It could not be clearer: the more people distrust their own instincts and suspect themselves of being congenitally racist, the more society's immune system fails. A terrible example came in 2017 when Salman Abedi, a twenty-two-year-old Mancunian of Libyan descent, murdered twenty-two children and adults in a suicide attack at an Ariana Grande concert. His father had been part of a jihadi group that fell out with Colonel Gaddafi in the nineties, after which he was for some reason awarded British citizenship and settled in Manchester. Clearly, the jihadism flowed down through the generations. Salman's younger brother, Hashem, was imprisoned for assisting in the attack and his older brother, Ismail, refused to cooperate with the inquiry before fleeing justice.

Did immigration officials fear that denying entry to such people would have been 'Islamophobic'? Did this anxiety dull their instincts when they allowed him to return to Britain after a year with militants in Libya? We will never know. But a public enquiry later found that a security guard at the Manchester Arena, Kyle Lawler, failed to raise the alarm when he saw Abedi walking in with his heavy backpack because he worried that his 'bad feeling' was an expression of 'Islamophobia' in his unconscious. 'I did not want people to think I am stereotyping him because of his race,' Lawler said. If the intolerance of the tolerant had not robbed him of his judgment, the atrocity may have been limited or even prevented.[11]

My memories of that attack are vivid. I was among the journalists who arrived first on the scene, as I happened to be covering a different story down the road at the time. I will never forget the bloodied and desperate parents searching for their children through the streets and, in the days that followed, the bereaved families behind shuttered windows. Many Jews in Britain and around the world looked on with a special shudder. They need only cast their eyes to France to find the repeated murder of their people at the hands of Muslim radicals, including Sarah Halimi, a sixty-five-year-old retired teacher, who in 2017 was hurled out of a window to her death by a man yelling, 'Allahu Akbar'. In 2022, the same fate awaited an eighty-nine-year-old Jewish gentleman called René Hadjaj, who was defenestrated from the seventeenth floor by a neighbour in Lyon.

There have been many other examples, and – probably out of the same dulling ideology that had been drummed into the head of Kyle Lawler – the antisemitic motive is always either downplayed or covered up by the authorities. Security is tight around synagogues, schools and community centres. But when those who are charged to keep people safe fail in this duty because they have been bullied out of their senses by centrist zealots, it underlines the vulnerability of the community that is doomed to be the first target of Islamist radicals.

The child rape gang scandal in Britain, described as 'the biggest child protection scandal in UK history' by the criminal justice expert Angie Heal, was similarly enabled by a fear of being branded 'Islamophobic', combined with a disdain for poor, white girls. Rapists, paedophiles, sadists and murderers, mostly of Pakistani heritage, were protected by social workers and police as they abused many thousands of children over several decades. The 2014 Jay Inquiry into child sexual abuse found that in at least two cases, distraught fathers tracked down their daughters and tried to rescue them from their abusers, only to be arrested themselves. In Rotherham, officers told a father that his fifteen-year-old daughter might 'learn her lesson' from being raped. The town 'would erupt' if the routine abuse of white children by men of Pakistani heritage became public knowledge, they said. In other instances, police arrested child victims for being 'drunk and disorderly' rather than the men who were abusing them and plying them with alcohol and drugs.

The link to elite centrist radicalism was far from fanciful. In 2019, a definition of 'Islamophobia' was adopted by the Labour Party. In the sixty-nine-page document presenting it,[12] the term 'grooming gangs' – which by then had been a problem for decades, and had already been exposed in a series of high-profile investigations by *The Times* – was presented only in inverted commas, with concern about them branded a 'subtle form of anti-Muslim racism'. The top two 'tropes used to justify Islamophobia', the document informed us, were 'paedophilia' and 'rape'. At one point, the report even asserted that 'dangerous brown men' were no more than a figment of the 'Islamophobic' imagination. 'Age-old stereotypes and tropes about Islam, such as sexual profligacy,' the document insisted, had a 'modern-day iteration in the "Asian grooming gangs".'

No allowances were made for language to describe those Muslim men who may genuinely be dangerous. Instead, in the style of true centrist fundamentalism, we were warned that breaking the silence would be 'Islamophobic'. One Muslim, we were told, was 'fearful of being injured by a taxi driver in the wake of a child rape case involving Asian men'. In his testimony, the man said, 'Taxi driver drove his car dangerously and carelessly, frightening me.' This was used as evidence of the dangers of drawing attention to the abuse of children. The message was clear. Keep your mouth shut. In their foreword, the Labour politician Wes Streeting and former Conservative Anna Soubry wrote: 'We hope our working definition will be adopted by Government, statutory agencies, civil society organisations.' Thus the suffocation of critical thought migrated from centrist fundamentalists in Parliament to officials in the real world, with depraved and tragic results. (Streeting later admitted that 'well meaning, but ultimately fundamentally misguided and warped views of political correctness' had enabled the crimes, but took no responsibility himself.)[13]

Deep concerns already surrounded the efforts to create a new crime of 'Islamophobia'. There have been several awful murders of Muslims over the years, including those of Mohammed Saleem in 2013, Muhsin Ahmed in 2015 and Makram Ali in 2017. Clearly, prejudice can have deadly consequences and must be dealt with decisively. But murder, of course, is already illegal. Moreover, the 2010 Equality Act and the 2006 Racial and Religious Hatred Act already protect minorities, while allowing 'discussion, criticism or expressions of antipathy' towards their beliefs. A broader crime of 'Islamophobia' would run the danger of stifling scepticism about the religion as a kind of blasphemy. Indeed, many moderates opposed the document that was adopted by Labour. These included Sir Trevor Phillips, former chairman of the Equality and Human Rights Commission, Islamism expert Ed Husain and the world's largest Muslim organisation, Nahdlatul Ulama. Respected voices like these should have been heeded from the start rather than left to condemn its conclusions.

Instead, the report's authors relied upon the help of Asim Qureshi, the activist who in 2015 described Islamic State executioner Jihadi John as a 'beautiful young man', as well as a group called Muslim Engagement and Development (Mend), which in 2024 denounced the Home Office's proposed blacklisting of terrorist group Hizb ut-Tahrir. Sir William Shawcross's 2023 review of Prevent, the government's counter-extremism programme, said that Mend had 'a well-established track record of working alongside extremists'. Also involved was the Muslim Council of Britain, which has been subjected to a non-engagement policy by successive governments since 2009. Were these really the best people to influence policy on 'Islamophobia'? Or had soggy centrist fundamentalism begun to act as a Trojan horse for the new radicalism? It is clear that the thousands of targets of child rape gangs were among the victims of such cultural folly. Seen through Jewish eyes, the advance of a repressive Islamist agenda through the statute books with the help of naïve politicians can only evoke a sense of foreboding.

The rest is radicalism

There is a certain gentle affection that surrounds the 'centrist dad'. Here is a middle-class, well-educated and ultimately harmless man who may be a little too keen on the sound of his own voice and the display of his own intellect but is generally mild and moderate in all things, and thus both an object of light-hearted fun and grudging respect. Such figures now wield great influence in society. Millions tune in to *The Rest Is Politics*, presented by the former Conservative minister Rory Stewart and former Labour spin doctor Alastair Campbell, and millions more to similar offerings from the likes of faded centrist politicos Ed Balls and George Osborne. This relentlessly feeds what the *Guardian* has described as 'the ravenous appetite of centrist commuting blokes of a certain age to listen to – be *in the room with* – two sensible Remainer men who wish they were still in charge'.[14]

In the light of the sort of deep social harms we have seen, however, the purveyance of centrist fundamentalism lends these people a rather more troubling significance. Consider Stewart, who with his patrician credentials has risen to prominence as a prince of the tribe. Over the years, the former international development minister, who in 2000 took leave from his position at the Foreign Office to traverse the Middle East on foot, has often allowed his ideology to eclipse such common sense as he may possess. In the run-up to the last American election, he predicted that 'Kamala Harris will win comfortably', adding, 'ignore the polls – they're herding, after past misses'. It is hard to know which was worse, the original misjudgement or the decision to make it public. Either way, both seemed to stem from the hubris typical of the centrist fundamentalist, who feels so entitled to imprint his ideology upon the world that he gapes when it resists his signet ring.

It gets darker. In February 2025, after the former Islamic State and al-Qaeda jihadi Abu Mohammad al-Jolani rampaged through Syria with Turkish backing and toppled the tyrannical Bashar al-Assad, Western liberals fell over themselves to embrace him as a revolutionary hero. Riding this wave, Stewart travelled to Syria and interviewed the newly besuited Islamist with his co-presenter Alastair Campbell, who described the man as a 'fighter turned president' who was basically fine. One could only wonder at the irony of these two former British officials, both of whom had been heavily involved in the 2003 invasion and subsequent occupation of Iraq, conducting fawning interviews with a man who had fought a campaign of terror against them under the banner of al-Qaeda, crimes for which he had served five years in a United States prison. It didn't take long for the pair's poor judgment to be exposed. Just a month later, Jolani's men embarked upon a killing spree, butchering hundreds of civilians from the Alawite, Christian and Druze minorities and posting gruesome footage of the executions online.

Again, the lesson was not learned. A podcast the following month found Stewart and Campbell presenting the notorious Francesca Albanese, the United Nations Special Rapporteur and scourge of Jews everywhere, as also basically fine. America, she had remarked in 2014, had been 'subjugated by the Jewish lobby'. Amid a storm of outrage she apologised, but it set the tone for much of her perspective since. On October 7, she posted that 'today's violence must be put in context' — even Hamas, it seems, was basically fine — but she never extended this dignity to the Israeli military campaign, which she has wrongly labelled a 'genocide'. That day, she also posted 'the victims of 7/10 were not killed because of their Judaism, but in reaction to Israel's oppression', making an argument in defence of Hamas that even Hamas itself does not make. As if that is not enough, she has compared Israel's war of self-defence with the Nazi Holocaust and equated Benjamin Netanyahu with Adolf Hitler. Albanese is no Syrian warlord, but was it necessary to launder her reputation with a soft-soap podcast? By elevating both these characters to the top of the 'basically fineism scale' (as the writer Henry George cleverly described it),[15] Stewart and Campbell offered an object lesson in the kind of moral contradictions that result from an essentially ideological approach to life.

Perhaps the most eye-popping display of centrist fundamentalism, however, came in February 2024, when Stewart appeared on the *Making Sense* podcast, presented by the philosopher and neuroscientist Sam Harris. For about twenty minutes, Harris – an atheist who is sceptical of Islam – attempted to discuss the scourge of jihadism in the Muslim world, only to have his questions deflected at every turn on the shield of Stewart's basically fineism. 'I think people don't like foreigners trying to boss them around and they will reach for religion when it suits them,' the former Conservative minister said at one point. 'I think these phenomena are much broader and I don't think they're limited to Muslims.'

When it came to the conflict between Israel and Hamas, Stewart could find only equivalence, remarking: 'There are lies from both sides, there are truths from both sides and nobody is giving a fair hearing to any of it.' He went on to play down jihadi savagery by pointing out that the Vietnamese, Jews, Hindus and Buddhists had also been violent in their turn. Suicide bombing was 'a relatively small component', he argued, comparing it to the Germans who had killed themselves upon hearing of Hitler's death in 1945. 'Effective armies, great militaristic nations, are full of young men in particular who are comfortable dying,' he said, effectively relativising jihadism out of existence.

The son of a senior British spy, who was a private tutor to Prince William and Prince Harry while he was studying at Oxford, even found a way to dilute the crimes of the young Muslim men who left the West to fight for the barbaric Islamic State.

'The idea of educated, young men and a few women wanting to go off and do something crazy and idealistic and dangerous at the other end of the world is not that unusual,' he pointed out. He even equated these people, who included the likes of Jihadi John – the terrorist from Queen's Park in London who became notorious for beheading journalists and aid workers in Syria – to his own younger self, who had left Oxford and governed a province in Iraq. Whether serving Britain overseas or travelling illegally to join the world's most savage jihadi state, the impulse was the same, Stewart suggested: 'a combination of adventure, excitement, idealism, missionary zeal.' So basically fine.

As soon as the conversation turned to the United States, however, all traces of Stewart's basically fineism evaporated. 'It never struck me that you're particularly empathetic towards or interested in the manners of other people's cultures,' he sniped. 'You give the impression that the US has the right system and everybody should be following an American model, and therefore you don't really have the patience for the twenty, thirty years of work that would be involved to actually enable and midwife and facilitate and bring along people on a journey of development.'[16] How this squared with the fact that the United States obviously had the patience to remain in Afghanistan for two decades was unclear.

All of this seems little more than irritating when considered in the bubble of the podcasting universe, where the main inhabitant is the commuting dad. It is beyond doubt, after all, that Stewart and his fellow travellers have benign intentions; they are simply articulating the accepted worldview of their class of centrist fundamentalists, all of whom are convinced of its morality. But their influence is significant. Between them, Stewart and Campbell alone have almost 1.6 million followers on X and their podcast has attracted more than 700,000 audio downloads per episode.[17] This largely AB1 audience is educated, wealthy and influential in its own right, helping to cascade these views through society. Here lies its danger. One wonders how the frothy centrist dad contribution to the culture may have affected the mindset of Kyle Lawler, the security guard who failed to stop the Manchester suicide bomber in 2017 because he worried that he was being Islamophobic.

There was a coda. As we have seen, a prime characteristic of the centrist fundamentalist is to deride anybody who questions his ideology, often condemning them as a racist. Sure enough, soon afterwards, Stewart suggested that Harris was bigoted because he did not indulge the basically fineism that can allow jihadis a free pass. In a discussion about 'Islamophobia' on his own podcast, Stewart said: 'One of the things that I've noticed recently, particularly since October 7, is an increase in people making stereotypical comments about Muslims. I just did an interview with an American podcaster, a guy called Sam Harris, who was hammering me for nearly an hour, saying, "yes, but surely Rory, you have to admit there's a connection between Muslims and suicide bombers and Muslims and terrorists". He just wouldn't let it go.' When he was later challenged by Harris, Stewart offered a qualified apology.[18]

Centrist mum

It was a revealing moment. In March 2025, a study found that more than a third of German millionaires were considering leaving the country. Forty-seven per cent of those surveyed said that they were planning to relocate because of concerns about immigration. This was understandable: between 2013 and 2023, an influx of immigration had swelled Germany's population by six and a half million people, more than four times the size of Munich. This was largely the result of centrist mum Angela Merkel's open-door policy of 2015 onwards, which established the country as one of the world's most welcoming to newcomers. The problems were as inevitable as they were predictable. More than 60 per cent of those receiving welfare are now first- or second-generation migrants, and though foreigners comprise just 15 per cent of the population, they commit 41 per cent of all crime.

Tom Holland has argued that it was Merkel's Christian background – her father was a pastor and her childhood home was a hostel for the disabled – that led her to embrace this disastrous policy in a steroidal fit of basically fineism. Yet as a true centrist fundamentalist, she vehemently denied that this was the case, disguising her principles as universal humanitarian values. For this to work, the chancellor was required to extend her ideological steamroller to Islam, flattening it into the cultural landscape of the West. 'Islam, in its essentials, was little different from Christianity,' Holland writes. 'Both might equally be framed within the bounds of a liberal, secular state. Islam, the chancellor insisted – slapping down any members of her own party who dared suggest otherwise – belonged in Germany . . . As in the nineteenth century, when Jews had won citizenship of Prussia, Muslims who wished to integrate into German society had no choice but to become practitioners of that decadently Christian concept: a "religion",' to be practised in private under the umbrella of a secular state.

Of course, this was entirely alien to traditional Muslim culture. But for centrist fundamentalism to be possible, 'Islam – which traditionally had signified to those who practised it merely the activity of submission – had to be moulded, and twisted, and transmuted into something very different'. Holland concludes: 'Merkel, when she insisted that Islam belonged in Germany just as much as Christianity, was only appearing to be even-handed. To hail a religion for its compatibility with a secular society was decidedly not a neutral gesture.'[19] Muslims are surely not immune to assimilation, but such a volume of young men from poor, religiously conservative, corrupt and undemocratic countries? Over such a condensed period? With no plan? What could possibly go wrong?

Once again, the betrayal of Western selfhood constituted a betrayal of the Jews. In the years since, antisemitism – more painful for Germany than any other country – has skyrocketed. Hours after the October 7 attacks, Muslims in Berlin were handing out sweets and openly telling reporters in Hamburg that they were celebrating. Before the month was out, the headquarters of the Kahal Adass Jisroel Jewish community in central Berlin, which had been rebuilt after the Holocaust and ran an interfaith dialogue programme, was firebombed. A rabbi's house was strafed with bullets. There were several assaults; just days after October 7, Ido Moran, a grandson of Holocaust survivors living in Berlin, was attacked near Checkpoint Charlie after he was overheard speaking Hebrew. 'He came up to us and started spitting at us, shouting "Jews, Jews" in Arabic,' Moran recalled. '[The police] tell us to basically hide our identity instead of tackling the problem . . . I can't start a family in a place where my neighbours hate me.'[20] The ruins of the formerly spectacular Neue Synagoge in Berlin, which was almost completely destroyed in the war and has since been converted into a small and poignant museum, are now under twenty-four-hour police guard. The shame of such scenes in the epicentre of Never Again can hardly be believed.

In the wake of the unrest, the late Henry Kissinger, the German-born American diplomat who had fled as a child in 1938, told Germany's Welt TV: 'It was a grave mistake to let in so many people of a totally different culture and religion and concepts.'[21] Many Germans agree, with almost four in five supporting immigration reforms. But reversing the trend is no easy matter. As a Statistica report observed: 'Germany remains a popular choice for immigrants . . . Welfare benefits, healthcare, and various support initiatives for those moving to or arriving in the country are on the list of selling points.'[22] In autumn 2024, the country reintroduced border controls and started deporting Afghan refugees to Kabul, but many Germans – including almost half of the millionaires packing their bags – clearly felt this was too little, too late.

Yet although immigration is driving Germans away from their own country, that is hardly the whole story. Forty-seven per cent of the wealthy emigrants may have left for that reason, but another 42 per cent said they were fleeing the rise of nationalist chauvinism, which has been thriving. In February, Alternative für Deutschland (AfD), an anti-establishment party that holds a pro-Putin stance, won an unprecedented second place in the national elections. The leader, Alice Weidel, has described Holocaust remembrance as a *Schuldkult*, or 'guilt cult', shrugging off the term's neo-Nazi connotations. Bjorn Höcke, leader of the party's ultra faction, Der Flügel (The Wing), has twice been fined by the court for using a banned Nazi slogan, '*Alles für Deutschland*', or 'Everything for Germany', which used to be engraved on stormtrooper service daggers. He has also poured scorn on the Holocaust memorial in Berlin.

AfD lawmakers in Bavaria walked out of a tribute to Holocaust victims after the president of the Munich Jewish Community condemned politicians that trivialised Nazi crimes. AfD leaders criticised arms sales to Israel and supported Iran and Assad's Syria.[23] At the same time, however, it is the only party expressing views on immigration shared by many frightened voters who do not have the resources to go abroad. With 68 per cent of Germans favouring fewer asylum seekers, 57 per cent demanding that they are turned away at the border and only 3 per cent desiring more refugees,[24] the AfD's hardline position is popular, in spite of its shadow side.[25]

Speaking on *The Brink*, Sir Niall Ferguson told me: 'The AfD has found itself endorsed unexpectedly by Elon Musk and Vice President JD Vance, but if one looks closely at the party, it's a strange coalition between some economic radical libertarians and some outright national socialists, including antisemites. Not the kind of people you'd particularly want to go down to a *Bierkeller* with.' The rise of such a party is a microcosm of our times. With the centrist fundamentalists rendering it taboo to voice entirely reasonable concerns about throwing open the doors to millions of Middle Eastern men without a mandate, dissent could only be found outside polite society. The absence of a credible alternative lent mass support to the radicals, fuelling the chauvinism that is also driving those with means overseas.

Merkel's basically fineism took some doing, even for a centrist mum. It was one thing to turn a blind eye to the fact that these migrants were from a civilisation that had fought the Christian West for 1,400 years, had no meaningful democratic tradition, held very different views of the proper rights of women and homosexuals, and had since the nineteenth century been increasingly in the grip of anti-imperialist and jihadi fervour, but it was quite another to ignore the reality on the ground.

Back in 2016, when it felt like the whole developing world was funnelling into Europe, I covered the story across the Continent and in parts of Africa and the Middle East. At a people-smuggling rendezvous at a petrol station near the Idomeni migrant camp in northern Greece, beside the border with Macedonia, I met Imran (not his real name), a man in his early twenties who hailed from 'peaceful' Lahore. His father enjoyed a powerful position in the security services, he told me, but after an argument, Imran decided to 'become a refugee' and 'get knowledge from other cultures'.

This adventurism had led him to repeatedly try to cross the frontier into Macedonia, from where he could journey into northern Europe, but on each occasion, he had been caught by the police and dumped back into Greece. I found him deeply objectionable, and I liked him a good deal. One night, with about a hundred other migrants, he made a further attempt and this time I accompanied him. After a couple of miles of yomping through fields and woods, some of the smugglers noticed my white face in the torchlight and grew hostile. In the darkness and chaos, Imran and I became separated. I have no idea what became of him. Perhaps he is now a German citizen.

Not all the men pouring into Europe were shysters, of course. One evening, I was sitting in a pavement café in one of the squares in Skopje, Macedonia, contemplating the imposing, Soviet-era statues. One of the nearby shadows detached and slunk up to my table. It was an emaciated Syrian in need of help. I offered him food but he told me that his 'stomach had closed' and asked for money, which I think I provided. We spoke briefly about the war and how he had escaped it by giving his life savings to human traffickers. Then he slipped back into the shadows.

Over those years, I met many different refugees in various European countries and came to know and like several. They struck me as most educated and humane. These people were served terribly by those fraudsters, jihadis and criminals who rode into Europe upon their backs and the depraved smugglers who trafficked them, not to mention the Western centrist fundamentalists who permitted such a travesty to unfold.

Such was the cultural and political climate, however, that debating the value of blindly opening the borders to men like Imran was all but silenced by the dogmas of 'refugees welcome' and 'we can do this' ('*Wir schaffen das*'). When those dealing with the problem first-hand – like Gianluca Rocco, the International Organisation for Migration's regional response coordinator in Greece – warned that many of the migrants were 'single males' who were not refugees and were 'nervous, aggressive and dangerous', Merkel and her friends put their fingers in their ears.

Before long, evidence of this moral blindness was everywhere. The following December, I found myself in Berlin, reporting on yet another terrorist atrocity. Thirteen people had been killed and fifty-six injured when a lorry was driven into a Christmas market in Breitscheidplatz by a twenty-four-year old Tunisian jihadi by the name of Amnis Amri, who had arrived in Europe on a small boat.

On New Year's Eve 2016, as many as twelve hundred women in Cologne and elsewhere were surrounded by gangs of migrants and sexually assaulted or raped in the street. The story was kryptonite to the centrist fundamentalists, who having sought to depict these men as basically fine, tried to stifle it. Initially, reports were edited or silenced, surfacing only in far-right publications. I remember the caution of British journalists as we watched the unreliable fringes of the German media. Eventually, Hans-Peter Friedrich, the country's former interior minister, issued a furious statement condemning the 'cartel of silence' and 'news blackouts', insisting that 'the consequences of uncontrolled immigration cannot be swept under the carpet'.[26] A police inquiry eventually blamed cultural differences,[27] herd mentality, intoxication, frustration and lack of social bonds with Germans.[28] Unsurprisingly, it turned out that many of these men were not basically fine after all.

At the time, I was in favour of 'refugee visas'. Europe could seal its borders – as countries like Hungary did – to stem the march of the migrants and thwart the people smugglers. Instead, member states could offer a quota of visas that would be administered at makeshift consulates in the refugee camps in countries neighbouring Syria. Applicants would be assessed and vetted, and the ones who were successful would be flown directly to Europe, whether Germany, France, Sweden or Britain. After the war, they could either be returned to their own country or apply for settled status. Although a logistical challenge, this would have been a sensible and compassionate response to genuine destitution. We could have kept the numbers manageable, vetted people thoroughly, focused on helping women, children and the elderly and provided proper support.

It is beyond question that centrist fundamentalism has made a serious contribution towards the slow collapse of our culture and the polarisation and radicalisation of our politics. The West is being subverted and the reasonable centre – the true centre, not the oyster-bar centre of the centrist fundamentalist – is being devoured along with the Jews. As if the ravening national chauvinism was not concern enough, it is mirrored in the rampage of the radical left. Four weeks after October 7, an old university friend with whom I had lost touch many years before sent me a message out of the blue. Now an academic, she had been forced to refer a number of her students to Prevent, the government's counter-terrorism programme, after they included jihadist rants in their essays. The university had sought to obstruct her at every turn.

She wrote: 'Dear Jake, I'm sorry for unfriending you on Facebook. When you went to work for the right-wing media, I thought you'd gone off the rails . . . I'm eating my words now. The left – which is where I've always positioned myself – has become extremist, not to mention, apparently, bloodthirsty? I basically bowed out a year or so ago on the issue of women's & children's rights v the trans mob but outright support for the brutal annihilation of Israel is a new fucking low.' She confessed to feeling 'politically homeless'. Make no mistake: if our culture is eating itself, it is being served on its own plate. The radicals are leading the feeding frenzy and the Jews are the first course.

Chapter Four

NAZIS OF ISLAM

The hardest task we have ever faced

Given that in much of the West, the most lethal of the three new radicalisms has been Islamist extremism, mass immigration from the Middle East is a source of deep concern for many Jews and Gentiles alike. As we will see, both past and recent history shows that there is nothing inherent in Islam that condemns its followers to harbour antisemitism or hate the West, but to ignore the soaring levels of bigotry in contemporary Muslim societies is a folly that their first victims cannot afford to indulge.

This has been particularly visible since October 7. When an elderly rabbi and parliamentary candidate was called a 'snake' and hounded by a mob as he campaigned outside a mosque in Prestwich,[1] alarm bells rang in Jewish homes across the country. In fact, those bells had been ringing loudly already: two days after the pogroms in Israel – before the IDF had mounted a military response – forty-five British Muslim groups and scholars signed a declaration rejecting the word 'terrorism' to describe the atrocities and defended acts of violence against

Israelis, calling for 'the apartheid state' to be 'completely dismantled'.[2] Precious few Islamic figures condemned Hamas.

A year later, with the war still grinding on, a study found that only three out of four British Muslims – whose growing numbers comprise almost 7 per cent of the population – doubted that Hamas had committed murder and rape on October 7, while 46 per cent expressed sympathy for the jihadi group.[3] Coincidentally, that same proportion believed that Jews had too much power over British government policy. More than half wanted to make showing a picture of Muhammad illegal, and a third wanted to see Sharia implemented in the country. Such radicalism has been dominating the community for some time. Ten years ago, after the massacre at the offices of the magazine *Charlie Hebdo* and a Jewish supermarket in Paris, nearly 80 per cent of British Muslims said depicting Muhammad was offensive and 27 per cent had 'some sympathy' for the motives of the jihadi butchers.[4]

Most Western democracies face a similar predicament. Almost half of French Muslims wrongly saw October 7 as 'an act of resistance against colonisation', while nearly one in five expressed support for the acts of savagery.[5] It is no coincidence that France, home to Europe's largest Muslim community at 10 per cent of the population, has seen a spate of gruesome antisemitic murders in recent years; or that one in ten French Jews departed for Israel between 2000 and 2017.[6]

Similarly, studies have found high levels of antisemitism among Muslims in Germany,[7] Sweden,[8] the Netherlands[9] and across the West. For Jewish people, this evokes disturbing memories; during the Second World War, Holland deported the largest proportion of Jews of any European country,[10] some seventy-seven thousand perished under French control[11] and the history of Germany speaks for itself. In the United States, meanwhile, just a few days after October 7, more than 57 per cent of Muslims surveyed said the atrocities against families were at least somewhat justified 'as part of their struggle for a Palestinian state'; 39 per cent approved of the jihadi group's leader, Ismail Haniyeh, who was later killed; and more than 31 per cent approved of Iranian tyrant Ayatollah Khamenei.[12] With attacks on Jewish targets by Islamist extremists becoming increasingly common, it is no surprise that Jewish schools, community centres and places of worship now require heavy security.

Many Jews fear that the trends are against them. The Muslim demographic group in England and Wales has increased by more than a million between 2011 and 2021 (when the last census was carried out), accounting for a remarkable 33 per cent of overall population growth during that period. It now stands at almost four million, increasing from 4.8 per cent in 2011 to nearly 7 per cent of the nation.[13] By comparison, there were about 287,000 Jews in England and Wales in 2021, accounting for just 0.5 per cent of the population. In continental Europe there are about forty-eight million Muslims[14] and 1.3 million Jews, a number that has declined by 60 per cent in the last fifty years.[15] If the problem of Islamist extremism is not tackled, the threat will only continue to grow in proportion.

This is not to ignore the moderates in Islamic communities. Neither is it to suggest that a predisposition to violence is a condition of Britain's fastest-growing religion. But as Dame Louise Casey concluded in her landmark 2016 report into opportunity and integration, 'we found a growing sense of grievance among sections of the Muslim population, and a stronger sense of identification with the plight of the "Ummah", or global Muslim community',[16] adding that 'none of the eight hundred or more people that we met, nor any of the two hundred plus written submissions to the review, said there wasn't a problem to solve'.

Similarly, Sir Trevor Phillips wrote that 'the integration of Muslims will probably be the hardest task we have ever faced'.[17] Given the proximity that these two Blairites had to the origins of multiculturalism, their warnings are even more significant. Is it any wonder that Jews are worried? When patriotic and law-abiding minorities are worried, this offers an early sign that the mainstream should be worried, too.

However we got here, the presence of tens of millions of Muslims in the West is a fact of life. The further to the right one drifts, the louder the clamour for 'mass deportation'. It is true that it is the right and duty of every society to deport some people in some circumstances. But although we cannot tolerate foreigners who abuse our laws or seek to undermine our freedoms, and although the spread of parallel societies must be urgently addressed, and although our immigration system must be made unrecognisably tougher, resorting too eagerly to draconian policies becomes impractical and illiberal.

Is there room for offering financial incentives plus a free aeroplane ticket home to anybody who has failed to integrate, as some Scandinavian countries do? Interventions by the authorities to open up some of the most insular communities? A robust deportation policy for foreigners who break the law? Probably. However, if we go too far down the road of authoritarianism, we will be in danger of losing ourselves. We need an approach towards Islamist radicalism that embraces those Muslims who have in turn embraced our way of life, while adopting a profound intolerance of those who foment hatred, divisiveness, radicalism and violence. In some ways, this is reflected by Arab states such as Saudi Arabia and the United Arab Emirates, which in recent decades have been clamping down hard on extremism. There is hope that if coupled with a sensible approach to immigration – a difficult political challenge in itself – this will create natural change over time.

This is the point at which we must depart from Samuel Huntington's notion of a 'clash of civilisations'. For one thing, there are Muslims who stand on the right side of history. For another, many are victimised by the same Islamist enemies. As the novelist Salman Rushdie wrote in his 2001 essay 'Yes, This Is About Islam': 'Whatever the public rhetoric, there's little love lost between the Taliban and Iranian regimes. Dissensions between Muslim nations run at least as deep, if not deeper, than those nations' resentment of the West. Nevertheless, it would be absurd to deny that this self-exculpatory, paranoiac Islam is an ideology with widespread appeal.'[18]

I grew up in the milieu of Orthodox Judaism, in which some of my family remain. Although my female relatives cover their hair, are married to rabbis and centre their lives around religious observance, they are fully invested in British society. Like my non-Jewish grandfather, Gramps – who admittedly was avowedly secular – served his country proudly during the war. I have never met anybody with more love for our country. As he grew older, he would tell the story of his wartime adventures repeatedly. He was hardly alone: about forty-two thousand Jews fought for Britain during the First World War and up to sixty-five thousand in the Second World War, including four thousand refugees from Nazism.[19]

Jews have a different history to Muslims, of course; but in principle, this helps inform my feeling that the wearing of the hijab and other religious traditions do not in themselves need to be a barrier to integration (though the burkha and niqab is another matter, and everything is dependent on social context). Indeed, at least four hundred thousand Muslims fought for Britain in the Great War, with more than forty-seven thousand making the ultimate sacrifice. About a million fought for this country against Hitler and his accomplices. This must mean something. In fact, it means a great deal.

Hummingbirds

Some years ago, I was with a colleague from a progressive newspaper at the Damascus Gate into the Old City of Jerusalem, interviewing Superintendent Micky Rosenfeld of Israel's police about a spate of stabbing attacks. When a man in traditional Islamic dress walked past, my left-wing companion suggested that he might be an example of a person of interest. Rosenfeld looked genuinely bewildered. 'Why?' he said. 'That man is just a conservative Muslim. That doesn't make him a threat.' Many Gulf Arabs wear robes yet oppose jihadism ferociously. The fact that a centrist fundamentalist journalist could be more judgmental than an Israeli police officer spoke volumes.

Those who doubt that Muslim integration is possible in the democracies must consider the example of the Jewish state. That country evokes more Islamist hostility than any other, but at the same time, its offer of equality in a free society, together with its confidence in its own peoplehood, are strong enough to have gained the loyalty of a significant number of its Muslim citizens. On October 7 – when fifteen Muslims were butchered alongside more than a thousand Jews – heroic Arab Israelis risked their lives to protect their Jewish compatriots.[20] As the country reeled in the aftermath, Alaa Amara, an Arab bicycle shop owner from Tayibe in central Israel, donated fifty children's bikes to evacuees from the south. When his shop was burned down by extremists in an act of retribution, a crowdfunding campaign raised more than $150,000 to rebuild it.[21]

After October 7, examples of Jewish–Muslim solidarity were hardly limited to Mr Amara and his wonderful bicycles. Three days after the atrocities, the Internet star Nuseir Yassin, founder of the 'Nas Daily' channel which has millions of followers, wrote a column headlined, 'I identified as Palestinian-Israeli but now I'm Israeli first'. The next day, the popular Arab-Israeli news anchor Lucy Aharish – who personally oversaw the rescue of two families on October 7[22] – called for national unity in a monologue to camera. 'We, the citizens of the state of Israel, all of us, left and right, secular and religious, Jews, Christians, Druze, Muslims, minorities and immigrants from all over the world, stand united together in this fight,' she said.[23] When Iman Khatib-Yasin, an Islamist member of the Knesset, publicly doubted the 'rape of women' and 'slaughtering of babies' by Hamas, she was summarily ordered to resign by Mansour Abbas, the statesmanlike leader of the United Arab List, Israel's main conservative Muslim political party.[24] Captain Ella Waweya, the most senior Arab Muslim woman in Israel's army, recorded a powerful message for social media. 'We are all together defending and protecting our homeland and our state,' she said. 'We are all Israeli, and we know why we are fighting.' She signed off with a salute: 'Long live Israel.'[25]

Such examples can only shed a sceptical light on views such as were famously expressed by General Charles de Gaulle: 'Those who advocate integration have the brains of hummingbirds, no matter how learned they are. Try mixing oil and vinegar. Shake the bottle. After a while, they'll separate again. Arabs are Arabs, the French are French. Do you think the French body can absorb ten million Muslims, who tomorrow will be twenty million and the day after tomorrow forty?' For all the great difficulties of integration, patriotic Muslim Israelis like these, and those like them in Britain and across the democracies – including the great many who have served their countries in uniform and the few who continue to do so – prove that although turning the tide may be an almost crippling challenge from where we now stand, a better future is not completely out of the question. Perhaps the hummingbird holds some wisdom.

Even if the way forward is clear, the climb is steep. Any progress we hope to make rests upon a renewed grasp of our values and the confidence to insist upon them. After all, newcomers cannot integrate if there is nothing with which to integrate. Whichever way you look at it, a strong national story is the root of a better future. How can moderate Muslims be expected to stand up to the radicals when they see hordes of leftwing Britons tacitly supporting Hamas on the streets of our capitals, our liberal broadcasters amplifying jihadi propaganda and our politicians working hand-in-hand with Islamists to outlaw 'Islamophobia' as a euphemism for blasphemy? As the writer Ed Husain, who was a committed Islamist extremist in his youth, put it: 'If British policy makers and elected officials are content to tolerate intolerance, and give a platform to those who are committed to destroying democracy and advocate religion-based separatism, why should a minority Muslim population turn on its own?'[26]

Refusing to let go of optimism is vital but we must not downplay the vast and complex scale of the task. Sir Trevor Phillips was right: this may very well be the hardest test of the West. In the long term, healing this social malaise will require little less than a cultural reformation. But the work must start now. As a matter of urgency, we must roll up our sleeves and embark upon the job of restoration in a way that combines muscular enforcement with our democratic ethos and fosters a spirit of national togetherness between Muslims and non-Muslims alike. Sceptics must tell me this: if we want to keep hold of both our way of life and our values, what is the alternative?

Muslims and Jews

History suggests that there is nothing inherent to Islam that condemns its followers to hate the Jews and their homeland. Indeed, until the twentieth century, the stories of the two peoples, which had been entwined since the very dawn of the religion of Muhammad, involved less antisemitism than sullied the Christian West. The faiths have much in common. Both root their observance in a God-given set of rules, the Sharia and Halacha, which govern every aspect of individual and communal life, from circumcision to dietary restrictions. Since the fall of the Second Temple, neither has featured ordination or the cloister, with rabbis and imams tending to be seen as the most learned among equals. Both reject the possibility of human divinity and its attendant iconography, as exemplified in the person of Christ. The formalisation of a coherent Jewish theology in the Middle Ages even carried the terroir of the Muslim lands in which it occurred; the great Jewish sage Maimonides, known to Muslims as Musa bin Maymun, who lived under Muslim rule in the Iberian Peninsula, north Africa and the Middle East – and served as court physician to Saladin, that scourge of the Crusaders in the Levant – was influenced by Islamic intellectuals like the Andalusian polymath Ibn Rushd.

Over the centuries, Jews were sometimes able to thrive and even gain prominence in Muslim lands. Several examples spring to mind. In eleventh-century Grenada, the Talmudic scholar and statesman Shmuel ha-Nagid was revered by both Arabs and Jews. For twenty years, he was the power behind the throne, first as vizier to the caliph Habbus bin Maksen al-Muzaffar and his son Badis. After Saladin conquered Jerusalem from the Crusaders in 1187, he encouraged exiled Jews to return from as far afield as Yemen, north Africa and Europe. His tolerant rule allowed the Ramban, the renowned Spanish scholar, physician, philosopher and kabbalist, to move to the Old City, where he established a synagogue that stands to this day.

In eleventh and twelfth century Egypt, 'Jews were a powerful and numerous community, led by the family of Rais al-Yahud — chief of the Jews, appointed by the caliphs — who served as royal doctors as well as advisers', records Simon Sebag Montefiore.[27] (One of these families was that of Maimonides.)

In the eighteenth century, Haim Farhi became chief advisor to the Ottoman governor Jazzar Pasha, who drove Napoleon out of Palestine in the 1799 siege of Acre, as well as the financial vizier and de facto ruler of the coastal city. In Iraq, the Jewish statesman Sir Sassoon Eskell acted as Minister of Finance under King Faisal I and was rewarded with a knighthood by George V in 1923. This group of stories is pointillistic and we must not forget the list of massacres over the centuries. Despite episodes of appalling bloodletting and deep religious prejudice in the Islamic world, however, until the nineteenth or twentieth century, antipathy towards the Jews flowed more readily from Christianity.

The fraught relationship between Jesus and the Jewish establishment formed the fulcrum of his spiritual revolution during his lifetime; his rejection ended in deicide, the tale of which is embedded in the education of every Christian child. For Christians, relations with Jews have always held an uncomfortable asymmetry. Whereas they accepted the Hebrew Bible, the compliment was not returned. If this constituted some power imbalance, it was one that the soldiers of Christ frequently sought to rectify by extracting a blood price.

As Tom Holland told me on *The Brink*, 'it's been both the privilege and the terrible misfortune of the Jews to play such an important part in Christian mythology'. Muhammad, by contrast, was not a Jew, his death had nothing to do with the Jews, and his revelation was no extension of Judaism. Emerging from pagan Arabia, Islam's encounter with the three Jewish clans of Medina, a minor chapter in Muhammad's life until modern times, ended in a decisive victory, meaning that there was never any price to be paid. The Muslim prophet ended his life a triumphant warlord – in this he was not dissimilar to the likes of Joshua, David and Solomon, though very different to Christ – and his Quran was not an appendage to an Old Testament. For many centuries, therefore, the Jews did not embody the threat or insult to Islam that they embodied towards the Church.

Is certainly true that Jews are demeaned and cursed in the Islamic scriptures, both as unbelievers and in the context of the Medina battles. Muhammad's encounter with the Jewish clans there involved the expulsion of the Banu Nadir and Banu Qainuqah, followed by the slaughter of up to nine hundred Jewish men of the Banu Qurayza. This conflict was mainly the result of power politics and betrayal during times of unrest, rather than a drive for ethnic cleansing. Holland has even doubted whether it occurred at all, pointing out that there are 'serious difficulties in accepting this tradition as true'.

He writes: 'Our only sources for the annihilation of these Jews are all suspiciously late. Not only that, but they date from the heyday of Muslim greatness: a period when the authors would have had every interest in fabricating the sanction of the Prophet for the brusque slapping down of uppity infidels.'[28] There are also passages which address the Jews benignly as the holders of an earlier iteration of God's word. Moses is honoured; the prophet's tenth wife, Safiyya, was a Jewish convert; and verses such as 17:104, give divine validation to Jewish rights to Israel. These are glossed over by countless firebrands today, who tend to give much more emphasis to notorious hadiths like 'the stone behind which a Jew will be hiding will say, "O Muslim! There is a Jew hiding behind me, so kill him".'

Most religions possess such a sprawl of scriptures that followers must elevate some while downplaying others, in accordance with prevailing sensibilities. Take Christ's statement in Matthew 10: 34–36: 'Think not that I am come to send peace on Earth: I came not to send peace, but a sword. For I am come to set a man at variance against his father, and the daughter against her mother, and the daughter-in-law against her mother-in-law.' Such is the centre of gravity of Christian culture that these verses are far less well-known than 5: 38–48 of the same Gospel, 'whosoever shall smite thee on thy right cheek, turn to him the other also'. For a thousand years, Muslims were often able to take a similar approach when it came to the Jews.

Over the centuries, the Jewish minority in Islamic lands shared something of the culture of the majority and contributed towards its destiny. Like Christians, they were not generally seen as ethnically distinct but simply Arabs who followed a lesser religion. There were periods of Jewish flourishing and periods of great oppression, with exile, mass violence and forced conversion present but not ubiquitous. Even these, however, were of a different order to Jewish suffering at Christian hands, lacking the conspiracy theories – Jews using the blood of children in their rituals, poisoning the wells, controlling the monetary system – that resulted from the Western conception of Jews as the diabolical enemies of Christ. Indeed, it wasn't until the fifteenth century that the blood libel entered the Muslim lexicon, when the Ottomans conquered Christian Greece.

It is difficult to generalise about the Jewish experience under Muslim rule, which spans fourteen centuries and many countries. It is a dual fate of both flourishing and agony.

Maimonides, that intellectual giant, was exiled from Córdoba after refusing to convert to Islam and spent a decade moving around Spain and North Africa. 'No nation has ever done more harm to Israel,' he lamented. 'None has matched it in debasing and humiliating us. None has been able to reduce us as they have.'[29] Notably, however, he ended up taking refuge in Muslim Morocco and Egypt.

The historian Sir Martin Gilbert observed: 'With its successes and achievements, its moments of pain and persecution, the 1,400-year-old story of Jews living under the rule of Islam is an integral part of the history of every Arab and Muslim nation concerned . . . It is a story of communities and individuals often under stress and facing difficult restrictions. It is the story of the Jewish contribution to the welfare and well-being of Arab and Muslim countries.'[30]

It is, however, possible to state that Jews under Muslim rule mostly occupied a place of inferiority, codified in law. They were forced to pay higher taxes, forfeit certain signs of status and wear demeaning symbols – the yellow badge began life in medieval Baghdad – but were rarely corralled into ghettoes or pursued by pogroms. In short, a measure of tolerance was offered in return for subservience. When Jews were targeted with violence, it was usually with the feeling that they had risen above their station, often amid the stress of threats from famine, pestilence or military conquest, such as during the Crusades, the Middle East historian Bernard Lewis has noted.[31] Muslim polemicists expended their main energies on refuting the religious bedrock of the great power of Christendom, which was a major military and evangelical threat, while tending to view the feeble Jewish minority in their midst with superciliousness and contempt.

On the whole, the Jews were simply too unimportant, both scripturally and martially, for Islamic luminaries to bother with the sort of antisemitism that was so common in the West.

Forbidden to carry weapons or ride horses, Jews were viewed by warlike Islamic society as cowardly and emasculated. These were the vanquished whose rebellion had been easily crushed by Muhammad, bearing little semblance to those demons of the Christian imagination who had wielded enough supernatural power to commit the cosmic sin of killing the son of God. Classical Islamic literature contains no equivalent of Protestant theologian Martin Luther's vicious antisemitic screeds; no Barabas, no Shylock, no Fagin; no Jew with devil's horns. Instead, we find jokes like the one from the end of the Ottoman Empire, which envisions a Jewish volunteer battalion so frightened of bandits that its officers request a police escort.[32]

'Their situation was never as bad as in Christendom at its worst, not ever as good as in Christendom at its best . . . [the Jews] were never free from discrimination, but only rarely subject to persecution,' summarised Bernard Lewis. 'There is nothing in Islamic history to parallel the Spanish expulsion and Inquisition, the Russian pogroms, or the Nazi Holocaust; there is also nothing to compare with the progressive emancipation and acceptance accorded to Jews in the democratic West during the last three centuries.'[33] Such a balance held for more than a thousand years. Then it changed.

Wildfire

The grim truth is that the Muslim antisemitism that forms the tip of the spear now embedded in the heart of the West was partly forged long ago by our own Christian traditions. This is not some centrist fundamentalist attempt to do our side down, nor an attempt to deprive Muslims of moral agency. Their savagery is their own. Nonetheless, that distinctive brand of conspiratorial bigotry suffered particularly by the Jews in the West first crept into the Islamic world with Christian converts from the turn of the first millennium. In 1453, when the Ottomans took Constantinople, many Greek Orthodox Christians came under Muslim imperial rule, carrying with them their predilections towards the Jews. These were among the first sparks. It wasn't until the nineteenth century, however, that the touchpaper was ignited for the explosion of Jew-hatred that is now upon us.

The taper was wielded by the Christian Arab minority in Muslim lands, who often found themselves in economic competition with the local Jews. A trend developed across the Ottoman Empire, from the Arab territories to the Greek and Turkish vilayets, which saw Arab Christians deploying the old Norwich weapon of the blood libel, using it as an excuse to demand boycotts of Jewish businesses. The flames were fanned by Western diplomatic officials and men of the cloth, giving rise to 'the beginnings of new-style antisemitism in the Middle East', as Lewis described it. 'The clergy of both the Greek and Catholic churches made great efforts to mobilise their followers among the subjects of the Ottoman Empire, the one in the interests of Russia, the other of the Catholic powers and especially of France,' he wrote. The Muslim uptake was not quick. 'Accusations against Jews of ritual murder in Middle Eastern cities for a long time continued to derive exclusively from Christian sources.'[34]

In 1840, some Capuchin monks, supported by the antisemitic French consul, brought a venomous blood libel to Ottoman Damascus by falsely accusing local Jews of killing an Italian friar, Father Thomas, and his servant, Ibrahim Amara. The Jews were tortured until they 'confessed', inciting a violent backlash. This appalled global Jewry and provoked an international outcry. The 'Damascus Affair', as it became known, prompted the emergence of organised Jewish activism and the establishment of newspapers like London's *Jewish Chronicle*, the oldest Jewish paper in the world (which I had the privilege to edit for four years, including during the October 7 atrocities and their aftermath).[35] It was not yet widespread, but Christian antisemitism had landed hard in Muslim society.

As the century wore on, the trend continued. Popular European books and pamphlets saturated with antisemitism were translated into Arabic for the first time and disseminated. By the Dreyfus Affair at the turn of the century – when a Jewish artillery officer was wrongfully convicted of treason against France and imprisoned for five years in a penal colony until his exoneration in 1906 – the outrage found supporters across the Islamic world, particularly in those parts that were under French influence, and particularly among Arab Christians.

Yet many Muslims resisted the growing hatred of Jews. Some Ottoman newspapers strongly backed the 'Dreyfusards'; the famous Salafist theologian, Rashid Rida, argued that French racial bigotry against the Jews smacked of jealousy and condemned those Egyptian writers who had supported it.[36] Ottoman officials suppressed some of the new translations of antisemitic texts and forcibly closed various newspapers that printed such rhetoric. Several intellectuals denounced the rising hatred in the strongest terms and appealed for solidarity among the Abrahamic faiths.[37] Greater forces of change were at work, however, and these would eventually stoke the flames into a conflagration.

The Christian West had been in the ascendancy since the late eighteenth century, slowly reversing the dominance of Islam – which for centuries had subjugated hundreds of millions of people, from China and Indonesia to Europe, only being turned away from France at the Battle of Tours – and routing it. The great Muslim retreat before the armies of Christendom commenced with the loss of Spain and Portugal, followed by the European menacing of North Africa. Islamic territories gradually fell to Britain, France, Russia and Holland, with Iran coming under economic and political pressure from the West. While Muslim energies flowed into fighting the Europeans, they were diverted from spiritual and intellectual pursuits, causing them to fall behind in terms of literature, the sciences, innovation and philosophy, areas in which they had previously excelled.

In the heart of the Middle East, the Christian advance was held back by the Ottoman Empire, which retained some strength despite having entered its twilight years. But the Battle of the Pyramids, when Napoleon's forces wiped out the mighty Ottoman Mamluk army in a matter of hours in the blistering summer of 1798, became a mortifying psychological blow when just a month later, fourteen ships of the Royal Navy, led by Lord Nelson, in turn routed the French to ensure British access to its imperial assets in India. Rarely had the Islamic world looked so weak.

As Western influence spread, Muslim rulers began to emulate its successful emphasis on the nation-state, leading to the Ottoman Imperial Reform Edict of 1856, in which Sultan Abdülmecid I mandated equality between his Muslim and non-Muslim subjects. This attempt at imposing Western ideals, which had few cultural precedents in the Middle East, was not a success. An Ottoman official recorded the grumblings of ordinary Muslims: 'Today we have lost our sacred national rights, won by the blood of our fathers and forefathers . . . This is a day of weeping and mourning for the people of Islam.' There were even objections from Christians. 'The government has put us together with the Jews,' some Greek subjects lamented. 'We were content with the supremacy of Islam.'[38] Finally, the First World War heralded the collapse of the six-hundred-year-old superpower and Western supremacy was assured.

This was a process of deep and traumatic humiliation for a civilisation that from its earliest days had defined itself by martial power. Moreover, it had confusing theological implications, as the Quran saw military dominance as a sign of Allah's favour. Muslim lands – which for centuries held local ethnic loyalties within an overarching Ottoman imperialism – were catapulted into an age of nation-states with little cultural understanding of the Enlightenment principles on which they rested. The repercussions extended first into economics and politics and from there into culture and society. The sight of former Ottoman territory being carved up by high-handed Britain and France after the Sykes-Picot Agreement of 1916 created scars that have yet to fully heal; almost a century later, when Islamic State jihadis dismantled the frontier between

Syria and Iraq, they did so amid chants of 'We've broken Sykes-Picot' and 'Raise your sword against the cross'.[39]

All this radically altered attitudes towards Jews in Muslim societies. As the economic crash of the thirties bit deep, the old tolerance evaporated, with Christian and Jewish minorities refigured as potential fifth columnists subverting the weakened ummah. The blood libel, which had started to emerge from Muslim agitators at the end of the nineteenth century, spread like wildfire as the traditional figure of the feeble Jew surrounded by the power of Islam gave way to a hallucination of a dangerous outsider, who – as Christian antisemitism suggested – may be possessed of a deceptive nature and dark abilities. These suspicions seemed to be confirmed when the weakest people of all emerged from the devastation of the Holocaust to reclaim their ancestral homeland in the heart of the Middle East, defeating Muslim resistance in spectacular fashion. This constituted the final insult.

Pigs of the earth

Deep Muslim resentment of imperial Britain and France contributed towards its eager embrace of Hitlerism from the thirties onwards. In some ways, it was a match of mutual interests. In a 1937 memorandum, Berlin's foreign minister, Konstantin von Neurath – later found guilty of war crimes at Nuremberg and sentenced to fifteen years in prison – outlined the Reich's opposition to a Jewish state, which he feared could be a threat to Nazism. 'Germany therefore has an interest in strengthening the Arab world as a counterweight against such a possible increase in power for world Jewry,' he concluded.[40]

Four years later, the mufti of the Arabs of Palestine, Hajj Amin al-Husseini, offered Arab allegiance to the Axis 'on the sole condition that they recognise in principle the unity, independence, and sovereignty of an Arab state of a Fascist nature, including Iraq, Syria, Palestine, and Trans-Jordan'.[41]

The alignment flowed from more than dry strategic goals. Traditionally, Arab identity tended to be a local affair, built on culture, language and blood, with ethnic political groups commonly clustered under an imperial ruler. The channelling of these forces into a pan-Arab nationalism that could compete on the global stage was largely a response to the collapse of Islamic empires and the supremacy of Western powers. The natural patriotism displayed by the British and the French, who had long ago imbibed the atmosphere of the nation-state resting on democratic institutions, the rule of law and the spirit of individual freedom, had no true parallel in the Muslim experience.

Germany, however, was different. Particularly since the nineteenth century, its territory had been parcelled out among various rulers, including foreign monarchs, which made it far closer to the style of the Middle East. The sort of identity this had fostered was more familiar to Arabs. Unlike in the stable democracies, where individual citizenship sat within a political entity with established borders, selfhood in the fragmented lands of Germany tended to be founded on tradition, culture, history, language and – increasingly under Hitler – blood.

Already, Prussia had blazed a trail with a successful campaign for unification. The Führer was going much further, expanding his lands to absorb millions based on their ethnicity, leaving the disgrace of the First World War behind in a blaze of glory. Although Arab liberals were appalled by Nazism, all of this provided an inspiring vision for emerging nationalists, who easily saw the Muslim ummah reflected in the German *Volk*. In his autobiography, the Syrian Ba'athist politician Sami al-Jundi recalled: 'We were racists, admiring Nazism, reading its books . . . We were the first to think of translating *Mein Kampf*. Whoever lived during this period in Damascus would appreciate the inclination of the Arab people to Nazism, for Nazism was the power which could serve as its champion, and he who is defeated will by nature love the victor.'[42]

Speaking on *The Brink*, Ed Husain told me: 'At the time, the Bolsheviks were saying, "workers of the world unite", and the Nazis were saying, "we're going to have a thousand-year Reich". Cairo was then the leader of the Arabic-speaking Muslim world. What was it that Egyptians could say to both Egyptians and the wider Arab world? It was "Muslims of the world unite". The Zeitgeist was to mobilise and organise as these units, based on nation states and loyalty to law, land, history and peoplehood.'

Until the twentieth century, the Islamic world had been dominated by the Sufi mystical tradition, in which brotherhoods of followers were led by spiritual guides, like the thirteenth-century poet Rumi, along transformative paths, or *Tariqa*, which lead to God. Under the influence of German and Soviet totalitarianism, however, 'we moved away from mysticism and love and loyalty and kindness for fellow human beings', Husain said. 'We were infected by these European ideas of nationalism and mobilising as a vigilante against your government. So that's where I think we ended up. It's this perverse concoction of atheism, social Darwinism, Marxism and Islamism.'

Then, of course, there were the Jews. The Nazi loathing for them speaks for itself. But one of the main factors that united the Third Reich and the Muslim world was their joint opposition to a Jewish state. The confused notion that 'Hitler was a Zionist', which has become popular in the dimmer corners of the left occupied by people like contemptible socialist firebrand Ken Livingstone – who made a great show of the claim in 2016 – is a gross misreading of history. For one thing, it ignores *Mein Kampf*, in which Hitler wrote: 'While the Zionists try to make the rest of the world believe that the national consciousness of the Jew finds its satisfaction in the creation of a Palestinian state, the Jews again slyly dupe the dumb Goyim. It doesn't even enter their heads to build up a Jewish state in Palestine for the purpose of living there; all they want is a central organisation for their international world swindle . . . a haven for convicted scoundrels and a university for budding crooks.'[43] At his command headquarters in 1941, the Führer told Himmler and Heydrich: 'The attempt to found a Jewish state will fail.' Looks like Hitler wasn't right. Nor was Ken Livingstone.

Although it is true that in the thirties, Nazis toyed with the idea of dumping the Jews in Palestine, this was purely a way to offload the 'problem' on somebody else. 'Palestine is a suitable place for German Jewish immigration,' wrote Hans Schwarz van Berk, the editor of the official Nazi Party newspaper *The Attack* (which was founded by Joseph Goebbels), after a trip to the region in 1937. 'They will not take root there, their fortunes will be spent and the Arabs will liquidate them.' This view was characteristic of the German establishment at the time.

Once the Peel Report of 1937 gave British backing to the creation of a Jewish state, however, making the fulfilment of Zionist dreams a realistic possibility, Reich officials were appalled and quickly abandoned the idea. 'The formation of a Jewish state or a Jewish-led political structure under British mandate is not in Germany's interest, since a Palestinian state would not absorb world Jewry, but would create an additional position of power under international law for international Jewry,' the Nazi Foreign Minister clarified shortly afterwards. Chillingly, he added: 'Even when no member of the Jewish race is settled on German soil, the Jewish problem will still not be solved for Germany.'[44]

This view has since chimed with that of many leading Arabs. It has squatted at the heart of the bloodshed for decades and finds expression to this day. 'If the Jews left Palestine to us, would we start loving them?' asked the Salafist imam Muhammad Hussein Yaqoub on Egyptian television. 'Absolutely not. The Jews are infidels . . . Our fighting with the Jews is eternal, and it will not end until the final battle . . . The curse of Allah upon you, pigs of the earth.'[45]

As we have seen, from the Arab point of view, erasing Jewish self-determination – and in many cases, erasing the Jews – had become a matter of honour, amplified by burgeoning Muslim antisemitism. 'If . . . England loses and its allies are defeated, the Jewish question, which for us constituted the greatest danger, would be finally resolved; all threats against the Arab countries would disappear, millions of Arabs would be freed, and many millions of Muslims in Asia and Africa would be saved,'[46] the Mufti made clear in a radio broadcast in 1942, showcasing the kind of conspiratorial hatred of Jews that had its roots in Europe.

Whereas Christian antisemitism had corrupted the Islamic bloodstream unsolicited, Arab leaders were the ones to court the Führer and request alliances, overlooking Nazi disdain for their own race in their eagerness for empowerment against the Jews. Indeed, when the Iraqi Christian newspaper *al-Alam al-Arabi* serialised *Mein Kampf* in Arabic, it tactfully omitted the 'racial ladder', which had the Arabs on a decidedly low rung. They adopted the antisemitic ideology of Germany without hesitation, retrofitting it into a radicalised Islamist context. When the Nuremberg Race Laws codifying Jewish racial inferiority were introduced, Muslim leaders fell over themselves to send notes of congratulations to Hitler.

Aping Adolf

From the earliest days of Nazism, countries in the Middle East started to ape its ways, finally finding a powerful ally in the fightback against the Christian West and its figurehead, the Jews. A common ditty chanted across the Middle East at the time ran: '*Bala Misou, bala Mister, bissama Allah, oria alard Hitler*', or 'No more Monsieur, no more Mister, in heaven Allah, on earth Hitler'.[47] In Iraq, schools restricted Jewish students by quota, Hebrew and Jewish history were removed from the curriculum and the three Jewish newspapers, *al-Hasid*, *Yeshurun* and *al-Misbah*, were abolished. In 1935, Aharon Sasson Nahum, the respected chairman of the Zionist Organisation in Iraq and founder of the Hebrew Literary Society in Baghdad, was deported, and 2,500 Kurdish Jews fled from their ancient homes in the north of the country. On the evening of Rosh Hashanah 1936, two Jews were shot in the street; the following day, there were further murders in Baghdad, Basra and Amarah. In Tunisia, a three-day orgy of pogroms that shared similarities with those of October 7 rocked the seaside town of Gabès in 1941. Among those who lost their lives was Afila Rakach, who was cooking for her family when the mob burst in. 'They grabbed a pot of boiling soup, poured it over her, tortured her in the house, stoned her and then killed her,' a neighbour, Yosef Huri, later recalled. Admiral Jean-Pierre Esteva, Resident-General in Tunisia for the Vichy government, explained in a telegram that the Nazi advance around the world 'leads Muslims to believe themselves to be more and more on top of the Jews'.[48]

The Palestinian Arab mufti, al-Husseini, made himself a useful Axis ally. In 1940, he helped the pro-Nazi Rashid Ali al-Gaylani seize the position of prime minister of Iraq. His supporters later carried out the first Nazi-style pogrom in Baghdad, lynching six hundred Jews and destroying more than nine hundred homes while British troops refrained from stepping in for political reasons. The mufti also contributed to the doom of countless Jews by writing to the Bulgarian, Italian, Hungarian and Romanian governments to pressure them to halt emigration, as well as creating a Bosnian Muslim division of the Waffen SS, which helped liquidate the Jews of Yugoslavia. But aside from being the first Palestinian leader to turn down the two-state solution in favour of a failed genocidal war, al-Husseini is chiefly remembered as an arch brainwasher, broadcasting hundreds of hours of hybrid Nazi-jihadist antisemitic propaganda in the Arabic language across the Middle East (which is discussed in *Israelophobia*). This was hugely influential in consolidating Arab sympathy for the very darkest aspects of Nazism.

The influence of Hitlerism upon the Islamic world cannot be underestimated. Political parties that emulated the Nazis – like the Young Egypt Society, or 'Greenshirts', whose slogan was 'one party, one state, one leader' – mushroomed across the Middle East. All the trappings of fascist kitsch were present and correct, including coloured shirts, stiff salutes, torchlight parades, paramilitary structures and a rigid discipline fetish, with aspiring dictators often at the helm. Political violence became very much the vogue. Moreover, the chemical reaction between radicalised Islam and Nazism produced a kind of euphoria. 'Just like National Socialism was propelled by a utopia which advocated salvation through destruction,' the historian Matthias Küntzel noted, 'Islamism is propelled forward by a similar utopia.' Even though the Third Reich fell in 1945, the tipping point of influence had been reached long before. In fact, in many ways the defeat, mortification and dismantlement of Nazi Germany mirrored the Western conquest of the Islamic empire, binding radical Muslim defiance more closely to the afterlife of Hitlerism. So deeply ingrained had his vicious ideology become in the Islamic world that it extends a deep influence over large swathes of it to this day.

Such was the tumultuous milieu in which jihadism truly took off. The Second World War had compounded the sense of Muslim humiliation, which was now bound to that of the Nazis; the sense of besiegement fuelled an intensification of Islamic identity; the foregrounding of suicide for the sake of the ummah represented a gratuitous celebration of the primacy of the tribe (one thinks of Hamas leader Ismail Haniyeh reacting on camera with great sanguinity after his sons were killed in 2024, later saying, 'through the blood of the martyrs and the pain of the injured, we create hope');[49] and all was glued together by a theology in which death, the ultimate sign of defeat in healthy cultures, was transfigured into a divine victory. Thus a new version of Islam arose in which all traditional injunctions against violence, even the murder of fellow believers, were overruled amid the intoxicating drive for death. 'The shedding of Muslim blood is allowed . . . in order to avoid the greater evil of disrupting jihad,' al-Qaeda's first emir in Iraq, Abu Musab al-Zarqawi, made clear.[50] With the addition of certainty in paradise for martyrs, with or without the virgins, the bloody package was complete.

No analysis of the context should be taken to downplay the evil of this depraved ideology. Without this evil, all the military defeat in the world and all the brainwashing could not have birthed the suicide bomber or those contemptible thugs who raped, murdered, mutilated and kidnapped so many innocent families on October 7, not to mention the baying hordes that gloried in it.

It is true that jihadism is hardly history's sole illustration of the human tendency towards what Douglas Murray has called the 'death cult'. Take the modern suicide bomber. The Japanese kamikaze – who did not fly his Ohka into American ships off the coast of Okinawa out of any religious fervour – can be ranked alongside him, but there were also the Chinese 'Dare-to-Die Corps' of the early twentieth century, and the Luftwaffe's '*selbstopfereinsätze*', or 'self-sacrifice missions', used against Soviet bridges in Poland during the desperate Battle of Berlin.[51] To this, Murray adds a Spanish iteration, which he described on a podcast with Sam Harris. '[The death cult] has manifested on the right and the left in history,' Murray said. 'It manifested in Spain in the 1930s with the Francoists chanting to Miguel de Unamuno, "*Viva la Muerte*", long live death; the great Spanish philosopher of his era realises his life's work is just done, it's over, because he's at a university in front of a group of young men chanting "long live death" and reason and rationalism will no longer work.'[52]

Nonetheless – despite the self-soothing of centrist dad totems like Rory Stewart – modern jihadism cannot be dismissed simply as an unfortunate quirk of human nature. When was the last time a Francoist or Dare-to-Die Chinese revolutionary blew themselves up in the middle of a bustling Western city? When did a kamikaze unit last export an ideology of death across the world that inspired countless young men to embrace a blood cult? Jihadism is a singular expression of evil. It forms the sharp end of a grave threat to the West which is ideological as well as mortal: its devotees shine a corona of deathly glamour into resentful Muslim communities around the world, magnifying hostility towards the democracies and fostering the drive to 'resist' with the cry of 'Allahu Akbar'.

The Somali-born writer and activist Ayaan Hirsi Ali told me on *The Brink*:

> As you unpack it, you're going to find that you'll feel sorry for Muslim populations, because they have been victims of despotism, victims of Islamism, victims of both the Soviet Union and even the American hemisphere. All of this is very

> serious and has had its impact. But I don't want any of it to be used as an excuse to say, 'they'll never learn, poor them, they've been victims, let them just be antisemitic'. For the last twenty-five years, we've been waiting for the silent majority of peace-loving Muslims to stand up, to organise, to get out there and say, 'The Islamists don't speak for us.' We haven't seen that. What I can, however, observe is that it's maybe not about majorities, but maybe it's just about power.

The reformist steps taken by countries like the United Arab Emirates and Saudi Arabia, Hirsi Ali added, which have taken the fight to the jihadists and made efforts to liberalise, offer some hope that strong leadership in the Islamic world may one day contribute towards a 'top down' sea-change in Muslim communities in the West. Given how embedded Islamist networks are across the democracies, however, and how determinedly they are working to subvert them, eradicating their influence will not be achieved without a bitter and protracted struggle.

Chapter Five

THE ART OF DEATH

Brothers in arms

The most influential, enduring and pernicious Islamist organisation to embody the legacy of Hitler is one of the West's principal adversaries today. Along with smaller groups like the south Asian Jamaat-e-Islami and the subversives of Iran, the sprawling and fanatical Muslim Brotherhood is now embedded throughout the democracies in sophisticated networks that work to subvert our societies from within, to a timescale measured in generations. Dedicated to the establishment of an Islamic caliphate under Sharia by way of blood and tears, the Brotherhood was founded by Egyptian schoolmaster Hassan al-Banna in 1928 and became a vehicle for the blending of Nazism and Islamism. 'There was a young man who was feeling wounded and bruised in Vienna by the loss of Germanic power, one Adolf Hitler, while in Cairo, you had Hassan al-Banna, who was feeling the same loss of the Ottoman Empire, which was now dissolved,' Ed Husain told me on *The Brink*. 'Al-Banna took it upon himself and a very small number of friends, who become his disciples, to revive that Islamic caliphate. In that pursuit, he ended up within ten years with more than two million members.'

Al-Banna's vision was a totalitarian one, including obedience to a charismatic leader, surveillance across both private and public spheres, draconian censorship of books and music, suppression of journalism and 'a campaign against harmful customs', not to mention the Islamisation of schools, the military and government.[1] The influence of the Führer was clear. Yet this was blended with the appetite for blood that has come to define the cult of jihad.

One phrase in particular encapsulated al-Banna's legacy: '*fans al-mawt*', or 'the art of death'.[2] All the Sunni jihadi organisations that have menaced the security of the West in recent decades, from Islamic State to al-Qaeda, and who menace it still, are creatures that emerged from the swamp of al-Banna's Brotherhood, with Hamas the most native of all. Even the Iranian Shia regime leaves a blood trail to the same source; the fanatical writings of Brotherhood icon Sayyid Qutb – who was hanged by the Egyptians in 1966 after ordering an attempted assassination of president Gamal Abdel Nasser – were 'read across the House of Islam by all sects, including the Shiite lecturer in philosophy and Sharia in Iran, Ruhollah Khomeini', Simon Sebag Montefiore records.[3] It is no exaggeration to say that the victims of 9/11, the Bataclan attacks in Paris, the Manchester suicide bombing, October 7 and many other atrocities all have the same twentieth-century Egyptian schoolmaster to thank.

After the Second World War, it was with the Brotherhood's help that the Palestinian mufti, al-Husseini, by now a war criminal, fled Europe. Upon his safe arrival in Egypt, he was quickly given a position in the group's hierarchy. As the foremost architect of Nazi-Islamist jihadism, who had spent years blending the two ideologies and brainwashing millions of often illiterate Arabs with his radio broadcasts, the mufti and his ideas helped magnify the Brotherhood's extremism, honing an ideology that despised the West in all its forms and fantasied about exterminating the Jews.

But even his legacy is overshadowed by the gigantic malevolence of Sayyid Qutb, the foremost Brotherhood demagogue. Described by Simon Sebag Montefiore as 'a pale, heavy-lidded bachelor who had been disgusted by American decadence during his studies in Colorado and preached jihad against the materialistic West',[4] he was born to a secular nationalist family in Musha, a village in central Egypt, in 1906. After his mother died in 1940, he turned to the Quran and quickly became bitterly resentful of every Western expression of joy, from popular music and 'obscene films' to bikinis on Alexandria beaches. Qutb hated the corrupting influence of American Christians in his country, whether missionaries running hospitals or debauched tourists on Nile cruises, and would light fires outside pubs as a warning of hell.

'How I hate and despise this European civilisation and eulogise humanity which is being tricked by its lustre, noise and sensual enjoyment in which the soul suffocates and the conscience dies down, while instincts and senses become intoxicated, quarrelsome and excited,' he wrote in 1946 in the *Arrissalah* magazine.[5] This animosity was superseded only by a loathing of Jews, whom he resented as impertinent *dhimmis* who had risen above their station. After spending time in America in the late forties, he added black people and their musical culture to his list of evils, though he absorbed warped notions of 'social justice'.

Qutb grew to become the most consequential figure in modern jihadism, his twenty-four books and hundreds of essays raising generations of butchers and leaving countless families soaked in blood. Much of his work was produced during a decade in prison, where he was held after a failed jihadi plot to assassinate the president. These writings came to rival *Mein Kampf* – which was also written in prison – in their influence. As the Syrian-German political scientist Bassam Tibi observed: 'Based on my observations of the world of Islam, I can state that militant fundamentalists are far more familiar with Sayyid Qutb's main writings than with the Quran, of which they often know only those parts selectively quoted by Qutb.'[6]

While al-Banna had been an authoritarian reformer and Husseini a nationalist propagandist, Qutb was a revolutionary. A talented writer, his work proved intoxicating to many young men. After his execution in 1966, his brother Muhammad, a co-conspirator, fled to Saudi Arabia with other senior Muslim Brotherhood figures. There he became a mentor to Osama Bin Laden, who praised one of his books on a video in 2004.[7] Matthias Küntzel, the political scientist and historian, wrote: 'Qutb's writings make pious Muslims into self-confident soldiers, who joyfully devote their lives to the war against Islam's enemies. The purpose of the programme is not education or compromise, but a radical rejection of the godless society and an orientation towards Islamic world revolution.'[8] Note that he writes in the present tense.

Daddy jihadi

Qutb relentlessly promoted jihad as the duty of every Muslim. 'The Muslim war aims at converting all humans on the entire earth,' he wrote. 'How necessary is the martial principle of Islam in the form of armed struggle . . . It is an expansionist militancy which aims at liberating the whole of mankind.'[9] Faith trumped everything, from loyalty to one's people to the closest family bonds. 'A Muslim has no country except that part of the earth where the Sharia of God is established,' he stated. 'A Muslim has no relatives except those who share the belief in God . . . A Muslim has no relationship with his mother, father, brother, wife and other family members except through their relationship with the Creator.'[10] When the going got tough, the devotee need only look to Allah. 'Brother, push ahead, for your path is soaked in blood,' he ranted. 'Do not turn your head right or left but look only up to heaven.'[11]

At the centre of this martial theology was a loathing of the Jews, whom Qutb figured as the principal antagonists in his cosmology, erasing a millennium of Jewish–Muslim relations in which, as we have seen, strife was bitter but relatively infrequent. Instead, he retrofitted a Nazified narrative to the earliest encounters between the two faiths. Referring to Muhammad's power struggles with the clans of Medina – the veracity of which, as mentioned, Tom Holland has cast into doubt – Qutb wrote: '[the Jews] have continued to scheme against Islam and the Muslim community ever since . . . In modern history, the Jews have been behind every calamity that has befallen the Muslim communities everywhere.'

In statements such as this, the voice of Nazism came through clearly, particularly slogans like Heinrich von Treitschke's *'Die Juden sind unser ungluck'*, or 'the Jews are our misfortune', which was adopted as the motto of Nazi propaganda weekly *Der Stürmer*. Indeed, Qutb referenced Hitler directly as an instrument of Allah. In his 1950 book *Our Struggle with the Jews*, he wrote: 'Allah gave to the Muslims power over them . . . Then the Jews again returned to evil-doing . . . Then Allah brought Hitler to rule over them. And once again today the Jews have returned to evil-doing, in the form of "Israel."'[12] As the historian Jeffrey Herf notes: 'In terms that his audience understood, *Our Struggle with the Jews* was a call to massacre the Jews living in Israel. It is evidence of ideological continuity with the radical Islamist propaganda coming from wartime Berlin.'[13]

In 2014, after a Brotherhood attack on a police station, an Egyptian court condemned 529 members of the group to death, described by Amnesty International as 'the largest single batch of simultaneous death sentences we've seen in recent years'.[14] From one point of view, this brutal response was an expression of how Middle Eastern strongmen tend to do business. At the same time, however, it represented the fear among Arab rulers of the subversive power of the Brotherhood, which has long been bent on nurturing a jihadi revolution by way of brainwashing, rabble rousing, attempted coups and the judicious use of assassins. Just three weeks after Egyptian prime minister Nokrashy Pasha outlawed the group in 1948, for instance, he was shot dead by a trainee vet working for the Brotherhood.

The Egyptian branch of the group supposedly renounced violence in the seventies – while continuing to support Hamas

– but in 1980, after two Brotherhood agents attempted to assassinate Hafez al-Assad in Syria amid Islamist disturbances across the country, al-Assad and his brother Rifaat massacred a thousand Brotherhood inmates at Palmyra prison. Two years later, after the jihadi murder of Egyptian president Anwar Sadat, who had made peace with Israel, the Syrians sought to liquidate the problem with an assault on the Brotherhood stronghold in Hama that claimed forty thousand lives. Clearly, Arab countries with an intimate knowledge of the organisation take it most seriously.

It was not for nothing that the historian Serge Trifkovic argued that 'the most potent heirs to the Nazi worldview in our own time as regards the Jews are not skinheads and Aryan National survivalists. They are schools, religious leaders, and mainstream intellectuals in the Muslim, meaning primarily Arab, world.'[15] Yet this is the ideology that has subtly spread its tentacles into Muslim communities in the West. For all its spectacular ambitions, one of the Brotherhood's characteristics is its slowly-slowly approach. Al-Banna believed that a jihadi revolution could be achieved by building grassroots influence over several generations, quietly encouraging a popular demand for Sharia until a weakened government had no choice but to fold. That strategy is pursued to this day. In 2015, the British government asked Sir John Jenkins, His Majesty's former ambassador to Riyadh, and the late Sir Charles Farr, former chairman of the Joint Intelligence Committee and Director of the Office for Security and Counter-Terrorism, to produce a report on the Brotherhood's activities in Britain. Although it was secret, a shorter version was made public. It said: 'From its foundation the Muslim Brotherhood organised itself into a secretive "cell" structure, with an elaborate induction and education programme for new members. It relied heavily on group solidarity and peer pressure to maintain discipline. This clandestine, centralised and hierarchical structure persists to this day.'[16]

As the Jenkins-Farr report made clear, 'Brotherhood organisations and associates in the UK have neither openly nor consistently refuted the literature of Brotherhood member Sayyid Qutb, which is known to have inspired people (including in this country) to engage in terrorism . . . Their public narrative – notably in the West – emphasised engagement not violence. But there have been significant differences between Muslim Brotherhood communications in English and Arabic.'

Such habitual duplicity is one of the ways the group has passed under the radar in the democracies. According to political scientist Dr Carrie Rosefsky Wickham, on social media the Brotherhood has even mistranslated 'Sharia' as 'democracy' to hoodwink English speakers. 'Brotherhood leaders have grafted ideas of popular sovereignty, pluralism, citizenship rights, and the rule of law into a pre-existing discursive framework that prioritises ideological outreach as a means to prepare society for the eventual establishment of a system based on the full application of Sharia,' she wrote.[17]

This secretive, devious and determined group – outlawed as terrorists in Egypt, Saudi Arabia, the United Arab Emirates, Bahrain, Jordan and Austria, yet allowed by centrist fundamentalist governments to dominate thousands of mosques across the West – has spent decades quietly cultivating the seeds of fanaticism and blocking Islamic integration. 'For the most part, the Muslim Brotherhood have preferred non-violent incremental change on the grounds of expediency, often on the basis that political opposition will disappear when the process of Islamisation is complete,' the Jenkins-Farr report said. 'But they are prepared to countenance violence – including, from time to time, terrorism – where gradualism is ineffective.' Its doctrine, he added, permits 'the use of extreme violence in the pursuit of the perfect Islamic society'.

In Britain, the first Brotherhood clubs opened sixty years ago, mainly run by exiles and overseas students who kept their distance from the corruption of secular society. 'It gave them, as it gave my generation here in Britain, worth, meaning, identity, purpose, network and even access to women,' Ed Husain said on *The Brink*. 'In the mosque, women and men pray separately. But in Muslim Brotherhood organisations, women and men study together, work together and share a common goal. So for the young Egyptian then, as for the young Muslim in the West today, there was an appeal that the more mystical, loving, Sufi forms of Islam – which remain popular from Indonesia to Morocco – could not offer, because they couldn't adjust to the modern realities.'

In the late eighties and early nineties, however, the Brotherhood established a network of public groups to push jihadi ideology on ordinary Muslims. 'None were openly identified with the Muslim Brotherhood and membership of the Muslim Brotherhood remained (and still remains) a secret,' the Jenkins-Farr report said. According to a recent briefing by the Counter-Extremism Project,[18] these groups include mosques, think tanks, sports clubs and education centres. 'None will ever willingly reveal any connection to the Brotherhood, while even employees and volunteers may not be aware of the true political nature of the organisations they serve,' the briefing said. 'Company directors – likely members of the Muslim Brotherhood themselves – will hold multiple positions in these organisations simultaneously, and often appoint relatives, from siblings to sons and daughters, to similar positions within the ecosystem. They may subtly change the spelling of a name or include middle names to make it harder to connect the dots.'[19]

Under this system, seemingly innocent sports coaches or counsellors who share Brotherhood ideology work to create an insular subculture for Muslims which cuts them off from wider society, a strategy that Emmanuel Macron, the president of France, has denounced as 'Islamist separatism'.[20] Brotherhood front charities, meanwhile, raise funds which find their way to jihadis through a labyrinth of intermediaries. Hamas has been heavily supported by the Brotherhood in Britain, both ideologically and financially, Sir John Jenkins confirmed.[21] As in Britain, so across the West. The French anthropologist Florence Bergeaud-Blackler – who now requires police protection – put it pithily: 'Their goal isn't to adapt Islam to Europe but to adapt Europe to Islam.'

Speaking on *The Brink*, Ayaan Hirsi Ali said:

> The irony is that when Saudi Arabia, the UAE, Egypt, Jordan and others proscribed the Muslim Brotherhood and took their leaders down, the Brotherhood decided to headquarter themselves in Europe and in America. Why? Because in America and in Europe, constitutionally, we have the freedom of religion, freedom of speech and freedom of association. So that's the paradox . . . The big conundrum for Western governments is how can we ban them and at the same time retain our freedoms. Arab countries don't wrestle with that.'

The dogs

Another subversive Muslim group is the Islamic Revolutionary Guard Corps, a fanatical branch of Tehran's armed forces that often works covertly overseas, using intimidation, assassination and military operations. It is banned in the United States, Canada, Sweden, Saudi Arabia, Bahrain and other countries, yet faces no such measures in Britain or elsewhere in the West. In 2022, the director general of MI5, Ken McCallum, revealed that the group had attempted ten assassinations of British residents that year alone. 'Iran projects threat to the UK directly, through its aggressive intelligence services,' he said. 'At its sharpest, this includes ambitions to kidnap or even kill British or UK-based individuals perceived as enemies of the regime.'

As ever, whenever there exists a hatred of the West, there will be found a particular hatred of the Jews. In recent years, Iran was discovered to be 'mapping' prominent Jews in Britain and elsewhere in the West for 'future lethal operations', in order to create leverage against Israel. One British domestic security official told me: 'The one issue that really stops me sleeping is Iran. If you knew what I know, it would stop you sleeping as well.' Yet despite concerted campaigning, the government has refused to take decisive action against the terrorist group.

Above all other groups, however, the Brotherhood exerts the greatest power in Muslim communities. As a further measure of its ability to exploit democratic freedoms, it has developed aggressive strategies to defend itself against any attempt to expose it. A 2024 report by the French intelligence services highlighted how the group had built a 'vast network of lawyers . . . committed to the cause'.[22] As any journalist will confirm, whenever a group is accused of having links to the secretive Brotherhood, in France or elsewhere in the West, or extremist sympathies in general, a chorus of denials are inevitably followed by threats of legal action. Moreover, the French Interior Minister Gérald Darmanin has said that the Brotherhood was behind attempts to legislate against 'Islamophobia', thus weaponising society's tolerance to silence dissent and enable their extremist agenda to proceed. 'This is their word, and it covers their primary strategy, that of victimisation,' Darmanin said.

For this reason, Ayaan Hirsi Ali denounces the centrist fundamentalist habit of bracketing 'Islamophobia' with antisemitism. Appearing on *The Brink*, she told me: 'Islamophobia is a ploy to silence any criticism of the Islamist agenda. Number one on the Islamist agenda is to annihilate Jews and to destroy the state of Israel. So when people say they oppose Islamophobia and antisemitism in one breath, it's like they're scratching their nails on a board. I cringe. I want to scream, either they are ignorant and have no clue what they're saying, or they're doing it deliberately.' It must be noted that the list of groups and individuals who were instrumental in creating Britain's 'Islamophobia' definition, which was discussed above, included those accused of links to the Muslim Brotherhood, though such allegations have been vehemently denied.

In April 2025, the *Telegraph* newspaper was censured by the independent press regulator, Ipso, after it accurately quoted a parliamentary speech made the year before by Michael Gove – then the Communities Secretary – in which he had accused a British Islamic organisation of being 'dominated by the Brotherhood and clearly linked to other Brotherhood-associated groups'. In a column about the scandal, Gove wrote:

> Islamists in the UK have long exploited libel and other laws to silence critics and evade scrutiny. When, as a government minister, I argued we must name and expose extremist organisations, there were multiple excuses offered to stymie me. But the most consistent was always the risk of losing libel actions against these groups, allowing them to secure damages from the taxpayer and thus fund even more extremist activity . . . I never thought that an organisation named in Parliament as giving rise to concern for its Islamist orientation and views would be able to persuade our press regulator – whose job is to uphold free speech – to demand an apology from a newspaper for accurate reporting.[23]

It is true that those Arab states that have clamped down on the Brotherhood do not operate within the norms of democracy, so are able to take action without concern for newspaper regulators and activist lawyers. But it is equally true that they do not suffer from the 'down with us' brainwashing of centrist fundamentalism. In January 2025, the Emirati government issued a statement sanctioning a number of individuals and groups which allegedly belonged to the Brotherhood. Eight turned out to be based in Britain, all under innocuous names. The Emirati counter-extremism analyst Amjad Taja said: '[The Brotherhood] operate schools, gyms, universities and charities freely. These groups can turn a son against his mother, instil hatred for one's own people, burn national flags, incite religious conversion and encourage attacks on teachers . . . their goal is moral collapse.'[24] Britain, he added, was becoming a 'global power base' for Islamist radicals. 'All this is happening while Gulf countries are rolling back ultra-conservatism.'[25]

Ever since the 2023 war in Gaza commenced, I have maintained regular contact with an old Palestinian journalist contact in the Strip. He loathes Hamas and the Brotherhood – he sees them as two ends of the same Kalashnikov, so to speak – and from the beginning, he secretly wanted Hamas to lose. When we spoke on the phone, at first he would refer to the jihadis as 'the dogs' in case he was overheard by terrorist thugs. Later, as their power waned, he would speak more freely from his tent in Deir al-Balah in central Gaza. 'If you want to destroy the Muslim Brotherhood, you have to start in London,' he told me recently on a WhatsApp call. 'Why have they not been arrested? How can they fly around between Qatar, Cairo and Turkey? Western countries want to arrest Netanyahu more than they want to arrest the Brotherhood. What a joke.'

Immediately after October 7, long-established Brotherhood networks were activated across the West, with spectacular results. Appearing on *The Brink*, Sir Niall Ferguson questioned how such volumes of Muslim and progressive radicals were so quickly galvanised to join marches, bully Jews and set up encampments in universities. Indeed, the first rallies were held on October 7 itself, while the butchery was still going on. 'I think part of the reason is that the resources are there. The resources are there because the Muslim Brotherhood has been carefully preparing the way for organised anti-Israel protests and it has established the points of contact with the woke left,' he said. 'So the mobilisation takes place with amazing speed. The most remarkable thing about what happened after October

7, 2023, was how fast these demonstrations took place, how quickly they were organised. That speaks to the role that the Muslim Brotherhood and its various affiliates have played.'

In the conclusion to their report, the two distinguished public servants could not have been clearer. 'Aspects of Muslim Brotherhood ideology and tactics, in this country and overseas, are contrary to our values and have been contrary to our national interests and our national security,' they wrote. Over the decades, however, the West has singularly failed to act against this recognised national security threat. In the meantime, the Brotherhood has been preventing Muslim integration by enforcing insularity and fostering anti-Western sentiment. Today, it forms a cage of radicalism around many Islamic communities, dragging Muslims into its ideological orbit with the threat of social and even physical consequences for dissenters. As Ed Husain, who has experienced this first hand, told me on *The Brink*: 'I just think these people are in our midst here in Britain and we're too soft on them.' It seems obvious that if the West is to fully integrate minorities, root out extremism and beef up national security, banning the Brotherhood – and other subversive Islamist groups such as Jamaat-e-Islami and Iran's terrorist Guards – must be the first step.

The origin of the specious

The Islam Channel, Britain's most successful Muslim TV channel, has been accused of glorifying jihadism and inciting hostility against the West. A complaint submitted in March 2025 by liberal Muslim scholar Dr Taj Hargey said it had repeatedly broadcast praise of October 7, compared Israel to the Nazis and given airtime to extremists. Constitutionally, he said, the channel portrays Islam as under siege from an oppressive West and views Iran, Hamas and other jihadis as 'resistance' movements against the democracies. This wasn't the first time the channel has been at the centre of such scandals; in 2023, it was fined £400,000 after airing a documentary that regurgitated a neo-Nazi conspiracy theory that Israel was trying to take over part of Argentina and Chile, and earlier that year it had hosted former Malaysian prime minister Mahathir Mohamad, who said he was 'glad to be labelled antisemitic'. In 2020, meanwhile, the channel was forced to pay £20,000 after broadcasting a religious education series that contained 'antisemitic hate speech'.[26] With two million viewers daily, the Islam Channel is watched by 60 per cent of British Muslims.[27]

As we have seen, antisemitism is not inherent to Islam. Yet in addition to the Nazi poison that has been injected into so many Muslim societies, and in addition to the pernicious role played by the Brotherhood in subverting society from within, we need to accept a simple truth: in recent decades, the pace and volume of immigration into many Western countries has been so relentless that assimilation has been simply impossible. The evidence is all around us. Many parts of Britain, particularly in the Midlands and the north, are now home to parallel communities of first- and second-generation immigrants in conditions of widespread welfare dependency. In one especially vivid example, in two dozen streets in North Evington, Leicester – where two mosques cater to 1,670 people – about 40 per cent of residents are economically inactive and

43 per cent of adults speak little or no English, according to census records.[28]

How can nationhood survive in such circumstances? Nearly a million people in Britain either cannot speak the native language well or cannot speak it at all, which obviously affects their ability to become employed, while the government funds translation when they use public services. Frequent viewing of foreign language programmes on television has increased by 24 per cent in the last five years.[29] In March, British government figures revealed that taxpayer-funded welfare was being claimed by over a million foreigners; forty nationalities were receiving greater benefits per capita than Britons, with Congolese, Iraqis and Afghans claiming four times as much.[30] Travel across Europe, as I have done in my time as a foreign correspondent, and you will find similar scenes everywhere from the banlieues of Paris to the sprawling suburbs of Stockholm and Brussels.

The huge cultural upheaval this has heralded – which has neither historical precedent nor democratic mandate – is still playing out. On the one hand, the white British population in Dagenham has fallen by over half in the last quarter of a century, and on the other, almost half of mothers from the Pakistani community of inner-city wards in Bradford were married to a cousin. There are almost a hundred Sharia councils in Britain, and it is unlikely that the Brotherhood is unaware of this. Reportedly, many such councils turn a blind eye to marital coercion, wife beating and rape in certain circumstances. As parallel minority communities grow, the Western instinct to denigrate its own Christian heritage while elevating Islam is accelerating the collapse.

Although the Palestinian victims of Israeli attacks in Gaza brought hundreds of thousands of activists onto the streets of democratic capitals across the world, the erasure of Christians in the Middle East has gone almost completely unnoticed. This has been one of the great global outrages of our times, doubly so on account of our indifference towards it. In 1894, up to a quarter of Turks were Christians. Today, after the massacres of Armenians ordered by the Ottomans and the Islamisation of the country, that number stands at just 2 per cent. Between 1955 and 2005, up to two million Christians and animists in southern Sudan were butchered by the country's Muslim Arab government, without a single placard being raised in the West. The population of Bethlehem was 85 per cent Christian in 1948; by 2016, that number stood at a mere 16 per cent and is probably smaller today, as Christians continue to emigrate amid higher Muslim birth rates. Thousands of Christians and Yazidis were killed by Islamic State in the years leading up to 2020. In 2025, many Christians were slaughtered by jihadi mobs alongside the Druze in southern Syria. Yet these outrages and many more have stirred few hearts in Christendom.

This has created a dark mirroring. Western Christians both turn a blind eye to the suffering of their coreligionists overseas and enthusiastically denigrate themselves at home. Many Muslim states, meanwhile, persecute Christians with impunity in their own lands as they watch their cousins in Western societies enjoy increasing prominence and respect. One party has made a virtue out of weakness and self-loathing while the other pursues strength and dominance.

In his book *Among the Mosques*, Ed Husain, who remains a devout Muslim, visits places of Islamic worship all over Britain, providing a startling account of the norms behind closed doors. As if the Brotherhood wasn't enough, an ultra-conservative sect called the Deobandis – the group that spawned the Taliban – control almost half of all Britain's mosques, he reveals. They believe that women should leave the house as little as possible and frown upon listening to music. In one such mosque in Dewsbury, there is no area for women to pray. 'This would be a temptation for many,' is the explanation he is offered.

In Bradford, he meets parents who ban their children from drama classes, while in Manchester a local imam refuses to condemn men who would kill anyone who 'insults the Prophet'. This, he says, is a parallel society, a world within a world, populated by people who may live physically in Britain but culturally exist elsewhere. In an Islamic bookshop in Blackburn, he even finds writings by none other than Sayyid Qutb and a text telling woman it was a sin to 'enjoy dancing and listening to music' or to partake in the '*kuffar*' way of life. Is it any surprise that – at least when he wrote the book in 2021 – 95 per cent of leadership positions in British mosques were occupied by men? 'In Gulf Arab states, you don't find Qutb's books being sold, and therefore you don't have the propagation of those ideas of destroying Israel and destroying every Arab Muslim government,' Husain told me on *The Brink*. 'You don't find the Muslim Brotherhood there because they're banned, unlike in Britain.'

Allah sees everything

The last general election provided a grim watershed: for the first time, seats were won in Parliament based on a sectarian agenda. This was largely down to an insurgent force called the Muslim Vote, a pressure group that told Muslims around the country how to vote tactically. It stood candidates in vulnerable constituencies, all of whom owed their allegiances purely to religious and ethnic interests and had a single set of demands, all related to Gaza. With no manifesto or pretence of appealing to the wider electorate, this was a non-party; yet in numbers, its five 'independent' MPs were equal to Reform UK. In its biggest achievement, shadow paymaster general Jonathan Ashworth – who did not support suspending arms sales to Israel or the International Criminal Court case against Benjamin Netanyahu – was ousted in Leicester South by Shockat Adam, who was backed by the Muslim Vote. He reacted with the war cry: 'This is for Gaza.'

Campaigning by these candidates was accompanied by intimidation, abuse and dirty tricks, all on the theme of Gaza. At one point, Ashworth was forced to hide in a vicarage from a mob of 'screaming' Palestine supporters. He had never known a campaign of 'such vitriol, bullying and intimidation,' he said.[31] Shadow health secretary Wes Streeting – who managed to cling on to his seat with a majority of just 528 – was targeted by a fabricated recording in which he appeared to say, 'I don't fucking care', about the deaths of Palestinians. His Labour colleagues Jess Phillips and Shabana Mahmood likewise narrowly survived the onslaught and used their victory speeches to decry the harassment they had faced. Phillips's address was almost derailed by heckling from pro-Palestine thugs[32] and had to be paused several times. 'This election has been the worst election I have ever stood in,' she said. Her campaign had been forced to make regular calls to the police, she revealed, speaking of party volunteers being filmed in the street and having their tyres slashed. Mahmood, meanwhile, described masked men disrupting a community meeting. This was 'an assault on democracy itself', she concluded.

There were signs that the intimidation was working. In May 2024, a leaked video of Labour's deputy leader, Angela Rayner, showed her pleading for votes with a group of Muslim men. 'If me resigning as an MP now would bring a ceasefire, I would do it. I would do it,' she begged. Should it be any surprise that in the eyes of the Muslim Vote, those five seats were only the beginning? Disclosing its ambitions on X after the results were declared, it vowed that Labour would suffer greater losses at its hands in 2029. 'In Muslim-heavy seats, the seeds of our community's future have been sown,' the group wrote. 'It will not be a landslide in the coming elections – and that is when the message sent today will really resonate.'

This is only the beginning. Eight months after the general election, Noor Jahan Begum was elected as a councillor in Ilford South, near where the MP David Amess was stabbed to death by an Islamic State jihadi in 2021, under the slogan 'I stand with Palestine'. A few weeks later, a campaign video declaring that 'Allah sees everything' suggested which local candidates voters in Wycombe should support based on whether they would back a boycott of Israeli goods, ignoring the fact that exerting 'undue spiritual interference' before a vote is a criminal offence. The video was condemned by Conservative leader Kemi Badenoch as 'Islamist sectarianism' that had no place in Britain.

For a subset of citizens to set aside all domestic concerns in favour of a foreign war three thousand miles distant, and to organise behind it along ethnic lines, is not just a profound indictment of our fraying social cohesion but a red flag about choppy waters ahead for Britain. One cannot help but wonder whether this would have been possible had the Brotherhood been banned. As things stand, however, the continued rise of radical Islam in Parliament appears almost inevitable, raising the spectre of a sectarian influence upon our country's leadership and policymaking. Once again, this is a worrying development for the vast majority of Britons and is especially concerning for the Jews.

Chapter Six

WHITE RUSSIANS

Bread and friendship

During the long decades in which the Brotherhood was quietly building its networks and it was rendered taboo to complain about the soaring levels of immigration, anti-establishment political movements came to fill the gap. Some, like Reform UK, arose in reaction to a climate of centrist fundamentalism, while others, like the Brothers of Italy, were reformed versions of fascist outfits established in previous decades. Today, they span a bewildering range of ideological positions.

'We're talking about a really complex and heterogeneous group of parties and organisations,' Sir Niall Ferguson told me on *The Brink*. 'Even within the United States, the term "far right" covers a multitude of different movements or ideas. In Europe, as might be expected of nationalist movements, there are dozens. Each nation state has its own far right. The Dutch far right, and the German far right, and the Italian far right don't have much in common, really.' Yet even the new parties of the left, such as the Worker's Party of Belgium or Syriza in Greece, find a common denominator in their anti-establishment flavour, and those of the right – from Marine Le Pen's Rassemblement National, which shook off its openly fascist origins to become the largest opposition party in France's parliament in 2022, to the neoconservative Vox party in Spain – contain a popular reaction against centrist fundamentalism's message of 'down with us'. In many countries, they are on the brink of permanently upending the old political order.

The economic crash of 2008, when many ordinary people felt that the pain that should have been felt by the bankers was directed into their pockets, added fuel to the trend. By 2014, I found myself in Malmö, Sweden, reporting for the *Telegraph* on the rise of the Sweden Democrats in advance of the European Union elections. Although founded in 1988 as a white supremacist outfit, with Nazi uniforms worn to meetings, by 2014, its logo had been changed to a blue-and-yellow daisy. Alongside a concern for 'preserving traditional culture', the party was campaigning on a platform of law and order and rights for the elderly.

In a place like Malmö, the appeal was obvious. While the centrist fundamentalists were deriding all expressions of concern about migration as racist, Sweden's third-largest city had become unrecognisable. In 2014, it already had one of the largest foreign-born communities in the country, with 40 per cent of the population from a foreign background; in the years since, that number has swollen to 54 per cent. In suburbs like Rosengård, known for its gang violence, immigrants now account for almost 90 per cent of residents.

When I interviewed the Sweden Democrat leader, Jimmie Åkesson, outside the local Bread and Friendship café, I remember him struggling to be heard above the leftist demonstrators yelling their lungs out nearby. 'Malmö is a good example of an irresponsible immigration policy,' he said, bowing to my ear. 'Everyone who thinks immigration is a good thing should take a good look at this city.'

Åkesson's party may have had Nazi roots, but it was now squarely in touch with the concerns of the people. The following year, the open-door policy of 2015 saw hundreds of thousands of Middle Eastern migrants enter the country amid an outpouring of basically fineism. By 2024, the Sweden Democrats were a mighty force, the largest member of the country's conservative bloc and the second-largest party in the Riksdag, wielding great influence over the ruling coalition by way of a confidence-and-supply arrangement.

Partly because of their pressure, Sweden's formerly generous immigration policy was in reverse. Deportations were back in vogue, with payouts of more than 350,000 kronor, or around £25,000, for families who volunteer to leave, and citizenship was being stripped from dual nationals who commit serious crimes. The country now boasted a 'net negative' migration tally. Åkesson must feel some satisfaction. His hopes for the 2026 election are high.

For Sweden's tiny Jewish population, the fall in Middle Eastern migration – which had coincided with a surge in hostility towards Jews – can only provide some relief. As I recall from my visits, Swedish synagogues sit behind the sort of security normally seen only at airports, and since October 7, antisemitism has soared by 450 per cent.[1] Yet it is hard for them to stomach a party whose members were wearing Nazi uniforms as recently as the eighties.

The radicals found lurking within the ranks of the Sweden Democrats have included the likes of Per Olsson, who was thrown out after buying Nazi memorabilia, praising Hitler on Facebook and calling Anne Frank 'the coolest Jew in the shower room';[2] and a cell of fourteen party officials who were secretly backing the neo-Nazi Nordic Resistance Movement.[3] This pattern repeats across the West. In Germany, the AfD has had members like Christian Lüth, who described himself as a 'fascist' and praised his 'Aryan grandfather'.[4] In France, a spate of 'black sheep' candidates were exposed running for the anti-establishment Rassemblement National in 2024's elections, including Ludivine Daoudi, who had been photographed in a Nazi cap.[5]

Anti-establishment parties vary widely in their proximity to radicalism. But how comfortable can mainstream voters feel as they try to drive immigration and social policy? This question may confront Jewish minorities first, but the rest of the electorate quickly thereafter. Moreover, in recent years, the unpleasant currents in these waters have been strengthened, whether intentionally or unwittingly, by two very different strongmen: Vladimir Putin and Donald Trump.

The Nazis of America

One of the darker aspects of the Land of the Free has been its long preoccupation with race. In the twenties, eugenics was popular among the establishment, with Harry Laughlin, one of its foremost exponents – whose work influenced Nazi policies – appointed as an adviser to the House Committee on Immigration and Naturalisation. Amid forced sterilisations, laws in twenty-seven states targeted the 'genetically unfit', including black Americans, those with mental illnesses and Jews.

In *Mein Kampf*, Hitler expressed his admiration for the country where the Ku Klux Klan had been active since 1865. 'The racially pure and still unmixed German has risen to become master of the American continent,' he enthused, 'and he will remain the master, as long as he does not fall victim to racial pollution.'

In February 1939, on George Washington's birthday, more than twenty thousand homegrown Nazis rallied in Madison Square Garden. Holding placards with slogans like, 'Wake up America, smash Jewish communism' and 'Stop Jewish domination of Christian Americans', they were overshadowed by a three-storey banner of George Washington, flanked by the swastikas of the fascist German American Bund. The event ended with a speech by 'Bundesführer' Fritz Kuhn, who had fought for Germany in the Great War before gaining American citizenship and developing ambitions as a dictator. When Kuhn demanded a 'white, Gentile-ruled United States' free from 'Jewish domination', the crowd responded with mass renditions of the Sieg Heil and chants of 'Free America'. Any mentions of President Roosevelt were jeered.

After the United States entered the war and Nazism was beaten into submission, such nativism was repressed. Although the American Nazi Party was created by George Lincoln Rockwell – who coined the term 'White Power' – in the late fifties, it never attracted more than a few hundred followers and the Civil Rights Act of 1964 dealt it a blow. But as the American political scientist Leo Strauss observed, 'it would not be the first time that a nation, defeated on the battlefield and, as it were, annihilated as a political being, has deprived its conquerors of the most sublime fruit of victory by imposing on them the yoke of its own thought'.[6]

Thankfully, the United States has firmly maintained the spirit of freedom and democracy; but it has incubated in its shadow something far darker. In 1974, the physicist and fascist novelist William Luther Pierce founded the National Alliance, an influential neo-Nazi organisation with an annual income of a million dollars. His books, particularly *The Turner Diaries*, which he published in 1978 under a pseudonym, inspired numerous atrocities, including the 1995 Oklahoma City bombing, and his organisation radicalised thousands. Despite his singular influence, he was far from the only such cult figure.

In 1978, a pastor from Idaho called Richard Butler founded Aryan Nations, a radical group subscribing to the Christian Identity doctrine, which figured Christians as the true chosen people and foresaw a race war between Aryans and Jews and blacks. Six years later, after the group's terrorist offshoot, The Order, was defeated in a gun battle with police on Whidbey Island, off the coast of Seattle, its leader, Robert Mathews, was elevated in death to supremacist martyrdom; a few years after that, further martyrs were added when a shootout between police and Aryan Nations activist Randy Weaver claimed the lives of his wife and son.

In 1988, fourteen supremacists connected to The Order were acquitted by an all-white jury after being accused of plotting to overthrow the 'Zionist Occupied Government' and conspiring to assassinate officials. One of the accused, Louis Beam, a former Klan chief and Aryan Nations member, promoted the 'leaderless resistance' strategy, which envisioned a white supremacist revolution being achieved with small cells and lone wolves. The massacre of nine black Americans by twenty-one-year-old Dylann Roof at a church in Charleston in 2015, and the butchery of eleven Jews at the Tree of Life synagogue in Pittsburgh in 2018 – discussed in *How to Fight Antisemitism* by the journalist Bari Weiss, who had celebrated her bat mitzvah there – were both gruesome examples of 'leaderless resistance' in action.

The Anti-Defamation League has recorded that between 2005 and 2007, white radicals attempted seven terrorist attacks. In a dramatic rise, however, between 2020 and 2022, forty such attempts were recorded. Fifty-eight people were murdered in supremacist atrocities between 2017 and 2022, the highest in any comparable period since the 1995 Oklahoma City bombing; 72 per cent of these, whether arsonists targeting abortion clinics or armed white supremacists storming synagogues, followed the 'leaderless resistance' model.[7] According to the 2024 Global Terrorism Index, produced by an Australian think tank, 'in the US since 2007, there have been sixty politically motivated attacks compared to fourteen religiously motivated attacks. Five out of seven attacks in 2023 were linked to people with far-right sympathies or connections'.[8]

In his recent book about antisemitism in America, Senator Chuck Schumer, the first Jewish Senate leader in history, wrote: 'For our entire lives, American Jews of my generation have known that if someone was going to walk into our homes or synagogues with a gun, it was more likely to be someone from the far-right. It was something we felt intuitively, if abstract. In the last ten years, that feeling has become stronger.'[9]

As was seen at the 2017 'Unite the Right' march at Charlottesville, Virginia, when a fatal car-ramming emerged from a febrile environment, lone-wolf attacks tend to be eruptions of a growing ideological volcano that extends some way beneath the surface of mainstream society. In 2022, the political scientist Gary Jacobson claimed that 'twenty to twenty-five per cent of the Republican electorate can be considered extremists'; he based this assessment on studies like an *Economist*/YouGov poll finding that 20 per cent of Republicans thought it was 'definitely true' that 'top Democrats are involved in elite child sex-trafficking rings', as well as his own research showing that a quarter had 'positive things to say' about the insurrectionists of 6 January.[10] Other studies have found that up to 60 per cent of Republicans believed that Jews were importing non-white migrants into America to 'replace' the native population.[11] Last year, a report by the Southern Poverty Law Centre suggested that almost fifteen hundred radical-right groups were active in the country.[12]

In a replication of the funhouse mirror effect, the march of the nationalist chauvinists has coincided with the creeping advance of centrist fundamentalism on the American left, alienating the mainstream. The Black Lives Matter protests of 2020 accelerated the transformation of the Democratic Party into a vehicle for progressive radicalism. Culture warriors with vast influence, such as the activist Ibrahim X. Kendi, argued that certain types of racism – against white people, to be exact – were to be commended. 'The defining question is whether the discrimination is creating equity or inequity,' he mused in the bestselling *How to Be an Antiracist*. 'If discrimination is creating equity, then it is antiracist.'[13] What happened to judging people by the content of their character? This is a question to which we shall return.

In that overheated cultural moment, Nancy Pelosi and other Democrats 'took the knee' on Capitol Hill wearing Covid masks and, for some reason, Ghanian kente scarves. State governors and mayors responded to demands to 'defund the police' by cutting back forces now viewed as beyond the pale. After taking office in 2021, Joe Biden ordered 'racial equity' reviews across all government departments and said that transgender girls should be allowed to compete against biological ones in sports.

Meanwhile, the concerns of ordinary citizens were nowhere. In fact, in an expression of brute centrist fundamentalism, for years they had been treated with contempt. In 2016, just as the British electorate responded to a rain of patronising insults by voting for Brexit, weary American voters looked at the outlandish proposition of Donald Trump – the obnoxiousness, the braggadocio, the allegations of racism and financial irregularities, the misogynistic audio tapes, the rumours of Russian collusion, the lack of political experience and total disregard of the norms of professional society – and decided that if it meant an end to the condescending merry-go-round of politics as usual, the man would be worth a gamble.

As with the British left, inevitably the Democrats had also betrayed the Jews. In an extended mirroring of the shameful antisemitism of the Corbyn years in Britain, the party had long become infested with the kind of Israelophobia embodied by the 'Squad'. Among countless outrages, three of its principal activists, Rashida Tlaib, Ilhan Omar and Cori Bush, voted *against* a House resolution condemning the global rise of antisemitism in 2024.[14]

With these people in its ranks, the administration proved itself unable to stand strong behind Israel as it battled Hamas, did nothing to confront the open antisemitism at Ivy League universities after October 7, and pursued a laughable policy of appeasement towards Iran. Although Israel was not a core concern for most voters, this contributed towards an impression of the party as anti-American and weak. From soccer moms to black voters, Latinos and Hispanics to conservatives and evangelicals, the country seethed. In the shadowy corners, an obsession with race and identity matching that of the progressive left was growing, leading the movement to be branded 'woke right'. Further betrayals were in store.

WWG1WGA

The Donald's landslide victory of 2024 was nothing if not a ruthless rebuke to the naval-gazing radicalism of the Democrats. Some of his actions in his frenetic first hundred days revealed just why they deserved it. Examples of Biden-era spending that went straight into the trash included $70,000 to fund a musical pushing progressive values in Ireland, $32,000 for a transgender comic book in Peru, $1.5 million to 'advance diversity, equity and inclusion' in Serbia, $2 million for sex changes in Guatemala and bucketloads more cash to produce 'personalised' condoms for poor countries.

It wasn't only about the money. Also into the garbage went 'disparate-impact theory', a principle which had been embedded in American law since the seventies. This had meant that whenever an institutional standard might be felt to affect minorities disproportionately – mostly black people – it would be held to violate civil rights legislation. Over the years, it had been used to abolish credit-based mortgage lending; prosecutions for turnstile-jumping, shoplifting and resisting arrest; stop-and-search; literacy and numeracy tests for police officers and firemen; general-knowledge tests for teachers and disciplinary measures for unruly pupils; criminal background checks for tenants; and speed cameras. In other words, it obscured the causes of these maladies among black Americans by passing them off as symptoms of racism. As a result, the maladies were allowed to fester, society was forced to bite its tongue and the country got worse for everyone. Such was the pit of madness into which the Democrats had descended.

As ever, the Jews had been one of the groups most affected. The president's furious war on diversity, equity and inclusion, which ranged from removing the vast Black Lives Matter slogan painted on the road leading to the White House to forcing all federal employees to remove gender pronouns from their email signatures, crippled one of the biggest Trojan horses for antisemitism of modern times. Indeed, Trump took particular aim at measures that target Jews explicitly. Also on his list of bad ideas to be killed off, for example, was the legal immunity granted by Biden to the United Nations agency for Palestinian refugees, or UNRWA. What possible reason could there have been to protect the agency from justice? Both weapons and hostages had been held in its facilities, terrorists had been found in its schools and its aid had turned up in the hands of Hamas. To Israeli intelligence, this was no surprise; 10 per cent of its staff, about twelve hundred people, belonged to Hamas or Palestinian Islamic Jihad, and at least twelve had taken part in the butchery of October 7.

These included men like Mohammad Abu Itiwi, who murdered sixteen unarmed Israelis as they cowered in a bomb shelter near Kibbutz Re'im before kidnapping a further four. Among his hostages was Hersh Goldberg-Polin, who lost his arm in the attack and, after eleven appalling months of captivity in the catacombs of Gaza, was executed at point-blank range. It couldn't have been clearer: through its ideologically driven moral blindness, the Biden administration had been working to protect the interests of the enemy. Trump's reversal of the policy allowed bereaved families and former hostages to hold the agency to account by way of a powerful class action lawsuit.

Similarly, the new president went to war with America's most prestigious universities, which had inexcusably become hotbeds of radicalism, progressive activism and brazen antisemitism. Harvard – the world's richest school, which sits on a $50 billion endowment fund equivalent to the GDP of Jordan – put up a particularly ferocious fight. The institution had disgraced itself after October 7 by indulging brazen displays of Israelophobia and turning a blind eye to the bullying of Jewish students. This shame was compounded when its then president, Claudine Gay, was asked at a congressional hearing whether calls for the genocide of Jews constituted harassment under university policy and was only able to say that it 'depended on the context'.

Once elected, Trump demanded that the college, which had enforced a 'Jewish quota' within living memory, 'cease all preferences based on race, colour, religion, sex, or national origin', enshrined 'viewpoint diversity' and reformed those programmes which 'most fuel antisemitic harassment'. This seemed entirely reasonable. Indeed, the very fact that these basic measures required enforcement was deeply shameful. Harvard refused, however, choosing instead to put up a fight in the name of inequality, after which $2.2 billion of its federal funding was frozen. Leaving aside the question of why government cash was being provided in the first place, the gap between the narcissistic Shangri-La of the Ivy League and the universe of the ordinary American, who labours under an average salary of $66,622, could not have been clearer.

Inevitably, after years of this cultural suicide, the Democrats peered into the funhouse mirror and the warped reflection that started back at them had an orange sheen. As Trump himself told thousands of supporters at a rally in March 2023: 'I am your retribution.' Yet many Jews remained wary of his support. His cult of personality – which runs contrary to the instincts of the founding fathers, who deplored idolatrous 'Caesarism' and designed the Constitution to enshrine 'a government of laws and not of men' – was unsettling enough, but the voluminous Maga movement contained deeply mixed messages.

Although the unlikely coalition that returned the president to power comprised blue-collar workers, conservatives, Latinos and Hispanics, redneck hillbillies, black voters, Gen Z men, female Democrats, evangelicals and Catholics, it also included a motley collection of white supremacists, anti-government radicals, pro-life extremists, religious fanatics and basement conspiracy theorists who had traditionally been shunned by the Republicans. Convinced that the establishment tells nothing but lies, many of them believe in a conspiracy theory known as 'Pizzagate', which holds that Trump is secretly fighting a cabal of Satan-worshipping paedophiles headquartered in a pizza parlour, including Joe Biden, Hillary Clinton and Barack Obama, as well as Oprah Winfrey, Tom Hanks and the Dalai Lama. This bizarre idea lies at the heart of the 'QAnon' movement, devotees of which believe in a coming 'storm', code for Trump's final victory, when he will regain power and his opponents will be tried and even executed live on television. As we have seen, about one in five Republicans now take this stuff seriously.

This phenomenon reflected the startling rise to dominance of social media. This deep cultural change, which was accelerated greatly by the Covid lockdowns, freed people to express views that a sense of shame would surely have restricted in real life. The new option of a secret self allowed widespread psychological splitting and the cost-free indulgence of disturbing passions. As the 'attention economy' and the tyranny of the algorithm rewarded the most extreme statements and ideas, a culture of nihilism and purposeless mockery emerged which would have been impossible without the distancing effects of anonymity. The sudden availability of information outside education ecosystems, combined with the betrayal of centrist fundamentalism, led to the wholesale denial of expertise and a flattening of authority; this opened the door for malign actors to sell snake oil to hordes of followers. Gradually, radical doctrines and discourse were incubated until the great rebellion was able to filter back into mainstream society.

As for Trump himself, he began by claiming that although he didn't know much about QAnon beliefs, he could not disprove them. By 2022, however, he began to feed the beast. On social media, he posted a picture of himself wearing a 'Q' lapel pin accompanied by the slogan 'The storm is coming', and republished dozens of Q-related posts. One of his rallies in Pennsylvania ended with a QAnon song entitled 'WWG1WGA', or 'Where We Go One, We Go All'.[15]

Perhaps he was doing what many politicians would have done, faced with such a deep wellspring of votes. Either way, after each ambiguous acknowledgement from their idol, the QAnon internet lit up with jubilation. But it overlapped with a much more widespread and lethal conspiracy, one that was an existential threat to Jews.

The ultimate saviour

Whenever madness takes hold of the masses, it doesn't take long for a particular minority to be dragged in. According to a 2022 study, 60 per cent of Republicans – and a larger portion of QAnon devotees[16] – now subscribe to a belief in the supremacist 'great replacement theory', which transmutes Renaud Camus's observation about population change into the conspiracy that Jews are supposedly using their 'power' to funnel immigrants into America as part of a 'genocide' of white people. This madness has inspired acts of terrorism, claiming many lives. The theory was behind the 2018 Tree of Life synagogue shooting in Pittsburgh; neo-Nazi Robert Bowers chose it as a target because its congregants had raised money to help refugees settle in America. Trump may never have endorsed this dangerous rubbish, but neither has he explicitly disavowed it. In the meantime, it has taken its place alongside the QAnon cult in continuing to buoy the Maga movement.

Once again, Jewish eyes provide a sharper version of the worries of the majority. The president's muscular support for Israel, which has seen the undoing of much Biden-era progressive radicalism and antisemitism on campus, not to mention the bombing of Iran's nuclear facilities, has been a great relief, but it is difficult to ignore his flirtation with extremists, conspiracy theorists and Holocaust deniers. These include Nick Fuentes ('I love you, and I love Hitler'),[17] Candace Owens (Judaism is a 'paedophile-centric religion that believes in demons'),[18] Dan Bilzerian ('I believe that Jewish supremacy is the greatest threat to America, and I think it's the greatest threat to the world today')[19] and Kanye West ('Heil Hitler').[20] This flirtation is rarely explicit, always ambiguous and often belatedly denied.

The most notorious display of such strategic ambiguity came on 6 January 2021, when after his defeat a Trumpist mob attempted a coup on Capitol Hill. In his book, Senator Schumer – who had to be evacuated from Congress by security – gave an account of the experience. 'Rioters were seen to have made the Nazi salute outside the building, swastikas were displayed on flags and other totems, stickers were placed on clothing that identified some of the rioters as members of the NSC, or Nationalist Social Club, a reference to the Nazi party,' he wrote. In addition, slogans on shirts included '6MWE', which stands for 'Six million wasn't enough', and 'Camp Auschwitz: Work Brings Freedom', with 'Staff' on the back. Schumer vividly recalled the reaction of fellow Republican senators. 'They seemed furious with President Trump for inciting the riot,' he revealed, 'and especially his unwillingness to help get it under control, his disregard for the scenes of utter mayhem on Capitol Hill and for the safety of his own vice president.' He concluded: 'Let me state unequivocally,

I do not believe Donald Trump is an antisemite. But he all too frequently has created the feeling of safe harbour for far-Right elements who unabashedly or in coded language express antisemitic sentiments.'[21]

These fanatical Trumpists may be cranks, but the point has long passed where they may have been dismissed. In different forms, their digital tribunes reach audiences in the tens, even hundreds of millions around the world. Between 2012 and 2017, white nationalist accounts on X saw a 600 per cent increase in followers.[22] Several white supremacists command particularly large numbers of followers, ranging from Richard Spencer, who has advocated the enslavement of non-whites and rose to fame in 2016 when his cry of 'Hail Trump' prompted the Sieg Heil from his audience; to the former Ku Klux Klan Grand Wizard David Duke; to Holocaust denier Augustus Sol Invictus; to Anthime 'Baked Alaska' Gionet, an internet prankster and rapper who became an evangelist for racist nationalism. All in different ways have pushed elements of the great replacement theory. But among the most pernicious is Andrew Anglin, a former 9/11 truther who has been described as 'the alt-right's most vicious troll and propagandist'.[23]

Anglin, a thuggish yet oddly elfin man in his forties, with ginger hair and melancholy blue eyes, is the founder of the world's biggest neo-Nazi website, *The Daily Stormer*, whose name echoes the Third Reich tabloid *Der Stürmer*, and which peddles a similar style of antisemitism. In a profile of the white radical, the Anti-Defamation League notes: 'In the "Jewish Problem" section of *The Daily Stormer*, he accuses Jews of all sorts of societal ills. Anglin also lauds Hitler and promotes

Holocaust denial. His hatred extends to other minorities, particularly blacks, and he frequently uses news items as a launching pad for his racist tirades.' In his own words, Anglin has stated that his goal was 'to normalise our ideas, to get to the point where you can say these things that we believe in the open . . . that is not far out of our reach. All we have to do is hit a critical mass point'.

As well as encouraging his followers to learn martial arts and train with pellet guns, the former heavy drug user commands a venomous army of online trolls. These can be directed at enemy targets, usually Jews. In 2014, *The Daily Stormer* encouraged its acolytes to bombard the British Jewish politician Luciana Berger with antisemitism, and in 2016, it subjected the community in Montana to a ferocious assault described as 'domestic terrorism' by police, for which a US federal magistrate recommended $14 million in damages. Some would argue that Anglin has blood on his hands. Thomas Mair, the unemployed gardener who murdered British MP Jo Cox in 2016, was a devotee of *The Daily Stormer*, and Dylann Roof, the Charleston church killer, reportedly left comments on the site. After the massacre, his hairstyle became popular among readers, for whom he was a hero.

Anglin is also overtly misogynist, banning women from writing for his site and attending 'Stormer Book Clubs', and popularising the bizarre term 'white Sharia', an ironic vision of women as chattels with the sole purpose of childbearing and satisfying men.[24] In a further measure of American white extremism, Anglin is despised by some of his peers; he has reportedly had relationships with Asian and Filipino women, which was condemned as 'traitorous to the white race'.

Anglin – and many others like him – are examples of the lieutenants of white radicals who back Trump to the hilt. According to the investigative journalist Luke O'Brien, by 2015, '*The Daily Stormer* had become arguably the leading hate site on the internet, far surpassing *Stormfront*, whose message boards had brought white nationalism into the digital age back in the 1990s'.[25] That year, Anglin 'immediately put all his resources toward willing a Trump presidency into reality. He churned out cheerleader posts and deployed his trolls on behalf of Trump, directing several of his nastiest attacks at Jewish journalists who were critical of the candidate or his associates'. While on the campaign trail, Trump was asked directly about antisemitic death threats sent by Anglin's troll army to the journalist Julia Ioffe, who had written a disobliging profile of his wife. 'I don't have a message to the fans,' Trump responded. When approached by a reporter afterwards, Anglin said: 'We interpret that as an endorsement.'[26]

In the years since, Anglin has come to refer to the president as the 'Glorious Leader', the 'Humble Philosopher', and even the 'Ultimate Saviour'. For Jews, as for tens of millions of ordinary people, this could not be more confusing. The long and repugnant tradition of American Nazism has taken as its champion a man who has made bold moves in support of Israel and the Jews. In addition to big-picture concerns like the betrayal of Ukraine and disruptive tariffs, such is the swirling instability with which most Jewish Americans are forced to contend.

'I used to feel that antisemitism had no home in America. But if we move away from the values that made us exceptional and allow lies and violence to be normalised, it could have a home here after all,' Bari Weiss told me on *The Brink*. 'I'm not saying that the United States hasn't given us the most exceptional diasporic experience in Jewish history. But I'd be lying if I didn't tell you that we are going through a shattering of that faith.' Ultimately, people all over the world, whether Jewish or not, can only resent the rampant centrist fundamentalism, followed by the progressive radicalism, that raised Donald Trump into the funhouse mirror in the first place.

Russia is our friend

Speaking to me on *The Brink*, Bernard-Henri Lévy identified what he described as 'the two biggest geopolitical catastrophes' of our times. The first was 'radical Islam gaining more and more ground, both outside the West and in the West', he said, while the second was 'Putin becoming what he is today'.

On the face of it, the very different ideologies of Putinism and Islamist radicalism seem to defy comparison. Yet there are troubling overlaps that tug on the nervous system of America and the West. At the heart of the malevolence is Aleksandr Dugin, the firebrand philosopher with a sweeping grey beard who has been variously nicknamed 'Putin's Rasputin' and 'Putin's brain' on account of his great influence upon the Kremlin. The ideology he propounds is nothing if not convoluted, but it is based on a 'Fourth Political Theory', supposedly beyond communism, fascism and liberalism, and boils down to support for a kind of Hulk Russian empire that will stomp to victory over the democracies. This he describes as a 'tellurocracy', or a power extended over land, which will vanquish the 'thalassocracies', or seaborne powers, meaning the United States, Europe and the West, and establish Eurasian supremacy from Vladivostok to Dublin.

The process of imperial expansion is intended to be heralded by the breakdown of the Pax Americana into a world of multipolar power relationships, which will remove individual rights, suffrage and limited government and replace them with Russian chauvinistic illiberalism. Of course, in the light of this doctrine, the notion that Putin's thirst for Ukraine may be slaked by appeasement and territory, and that he would refrain from later advancing into the rest of the country and its neighbours, is for the birds.

Worship of power lies at the heart of Dugin's thinking. His best-known book, *The Fourth Political Theory*, even contains some admiration for the neoconservatives of the United States for their strength in enforcing the 'American century'. In Dugin's universe, 'the higher up and more authoritarian the ruler, the closer he is to the masses and the more stable his rule'.[27] In this vision, under the control of Putin, whom he dubs the new 'czar', the tellurocracy would usher in 'Finis Mundi', or the finishing of the world as we know it, overturning what he charmingly terms 'Pax Judaica'.

Ever since Putin's landmark speech at the 2007 Munich Security Conference, when he derided the global order and announced a more muscular Russia, the despot has all but parroted his pet ideologue. Indeed, Putin's notorious 2021 essay justifying his invasion of Ukraine, which hankered after the return of a Novorossiya-style empire, could have been written by Dugin. As retired KGB Major General Oleg Danilovich Kalugin pointed out in his book *Spymaster*: 'When Putin came to power in 2000, he stated publicly, "Over the years we fell prey to an illusion that we had no enemies. We paid dearly for that." That's Putin. And those who believe that he converted to Western values are simply misled by Russian propaganda. Putin is a virtual democrat, just as he is a virtual Christian. He sees the world through his KGB prism and acts accordingly. Under him, Russia will remain on the edge of the abyss.'[28]

The parallels with jihadism, with its bloody and utopian desire for a caliphate and fanatical hatred of the democracies, are obvious. Indeed, in this Manichaean worldview, anything that stands on the other side of Dugin's 'eschatological line' from the West, from Orthodox Christianity to any Muslim power that opposes the democracies, is embraced. *The Fourth Political Theory* lavishes praise upon the 'conservative revolutionist' Osama Bin Laden, who supposedly offered hope that 'those values that were gathered into a heap and taken to the junkyard at the very start of modernity can still arise'.[29]

Meanwhile, the avowedly anti-Western radicals within the Iranian regime believe that an Armageddon involving the destruction of Israel will herald the coming of the Mahdi, an invisible messianic figure, after which the most loyal soldiers of Allah will rule the world in 313 provinces. This is only marginally more bizarre than Dugin's binary struggle and he aligns them on the 'right' side of it, in an unadulterated celebration of all types of hostility towards the West.[30] Although Dugin is less saturated with antisemitism than his jihadi firebrand allies, his dogma can only be especially disturbing for Jews.

In this way, the radical forces of jihadism and nationalist chauvinism, Nazism and Soviet-inspired gangsterism, converge behind the figurehead of Vladimir Putin. 'Dugin promotes an alliance between Orthodox Christianity and Islam,' Lévy told me. 'When he says Orthodoxy, he does not mean the nice, brilliant and glorious Orthodoxy, which I admire myself, but he means the messianic Orthodoxy, matching with ultranationalism. And when he says Islam, he does not mean the moderate, bright Islam which I know exists in the world, but he's speaking of the Islam of Isis, or Al-Qaeda, or Hamas.' Soberingly, the Frenchman added: 'The responsibility of men and women of goodwill is to oppose this bloc of foolishness, of craziness, which is attacking us.'

By 2015, Andrew Anglin hadn't cast a vote for years. But he was not going to miss the opportunity to contribute towards a victory for Trump. As he was living overseas, he voted by absentee ballot; according to records kept by his hometown of Franklin County, Ohio, the envelope arrived from Krasnodar, a major economic hub in southern Russia, not far from the Black Sea.[31] At the time, *The Daily Stormer* was engaged in a frantic influence operation in support of the Glorious Leader – by which it meant Trump – reaching huge numbers of people with its potent blend of brazen racism, extremist nationalism, fanaticism and cultish utopianism. It would appear that this poison was being brewed under the nose of Putin.

Whether the Russian authorities played any part in this propaganda effort is unknown. But as O'Brien observes, 'Anglin worshipped Putin, and seemed like exactly the type of online agitator Russia might use to sow chaos during the US election'. Anglin later denied 'under penalty of perjury' that he had received any support from the Kremlin. Yet a data analysis of *The Daily Stormer*'s traffic, cited by O'Brien, found that its content was being shared by a network of bots and sock puppets that traded in divisive political material and operated in the hours of daylight in Moscow.

Setting the neo-Nazis aside, it is depressing how far sympathy for Putin now travels into the further reaches of the right, where he finds himself re-imagined as a kind of culture wars figure, a nuclear-armed Jordan Peterson. 'The West can become wildly deranged through woke ideology, but the answer doesn't have to be Putinism,' Douglas Murray pointed out on *The Brink*. 'I think some people find that hard. I think they want the strongest possible inoculation against the leftist diseases of their time.'

A very modern Nazi

Support for Putin's authoritarianism is now endemic across the American far-right. A landmark moment came in February 2024, while the war raged in Ukraine and *Wall Street Journal* journalist Evan Gershkovich languished in a Kremlin prison, when the American broadcaster Tucker Carlson travelled to Russia to conduct a cosy interview with the tyrant. With almost twenty-five million followers on social media, Carlson is both one of Trump's most valuable supporters and a leading voice in the unhinged world of white radicalism.

Moreover, his erstwhile mainstream credentials – he rose to fame on Fox News before ideological drift, a massive libel case and allegations of sexism got him fired – has made him a pinup for those even deeper in the swamp. Predictably enough, Anglin is a fan of Carlson; after watching one of his video monologues on the great replacement conspiracy theory, for example, the neo-Nazi posted: 'Tucker Carlson finally struck back against the Jews on Monday, dropping the ultimate truth bomb on his audience.'[32]

Now master of his own online platform, Carlson has interviewed the likes of Alex Jones, who went bankrupt after families of schoolchildren murdered at Sandy Hook elementary school in 2012 won a $1.5 billion lawsuit against him – he had repeatedly claimed it was a hoax and the parents were actors – and Representative Marjorie Taylor Greene, a QAnon fan who once suggested that Californian wildfires were caused by a Jewish space laser. In addition to a preoccupation with the usual conspiracies and a loyalty to Trump, Carlson has long harboured a great fondness for Putin, that other juju of the nationalist chauvinist scene. He has become well known for parroting Kremlin *dezinformatsia*, describing Volodymyr Zelensky as a 'dictator' and suggesting, without credible evidence, that secret American laboratories were producing biological weapons in Ukraine. True to form, the interview with Putin – which lasted more than two hours – was a soft-soap affair, with the Russian leader given free rein to range across his revisionist version of history that blamed Kiev for the war and gave his country entitlement to Ukraine. On YouTube, the interview has been viewed more than twenty-one million times.

The propaganda did not end there. Carlson also made a short and jaw-droppingly naïve film about life in Russia, marvelling at the clean subway, absence of beggars and attractive interior of Kievskaya Station. In 1989, when Boris Yeltsin visited the United States and experienced the abundance of a supermarket, he became convinced of the bankruptcy of Soviet ideology. In 2024, during a visit to a Moscow supermarket, Carlson rejoiced in the shopping trolleys, low prices and well-stocked shelves, without stopping to consider how much poorer Russians are than Americans, how much weaker their currency and how much smaller their economy. He concluded that he had been 'radicalised' against Russia by his American overlords and that it was actually a pretty decent place, leveraging viewers away from the truth. Once again, this brainwashing influenced millions.

William Faulkner famously observed that although we think the past is dead, in truth 'it's not even past'. Nowhere is this more apposite than in the case of Carlson, who in parallel with his Russophilia has also been pushing a new wave of Second World War revisionism that seeks to rehabilitate Hitler and denigrate Churchill. In 2024, he introduced the podcaster Darryl Cooper to his huge audience by way of a long and meandering interview on his YouTube channel. In an episode entitled 'Winston Churchill Ruined Europe', Cooper – who admits to being no historian yet has built a career upon making the most radical historical claims – offered viewers a ridiculous account of the struggle against Nazism in which Churchill was 'the chief villain', rather than the hero who stood alone against fascism and almost single-handedly changed the course of history. This disgraceful falsification was presented as an act of rebellious truth-seeking in an era dominated by establishment lies. 'There are just certain things you're not allowed to question,' Cooper says at one point.

'Literally, it's a crime to ask questions?' Carlson replies, appalled.

'You might absolutely go to jail in this country.'

This execrable discussion has since been viewed more than 1.2 million times.

The following year, in an appearance which 'broke the internet' on the world's biggest podcast, the *Joe Rogan Experience*, Douglas Murray lambasted those who showcase the revisionism of Cooper and his ilk. Speaking to me on *The Brink*, Murray said: 'A nasty bit of the swamp is the people who have been doing this counterfactual history where they say America shouldn't have entered World War Two. Then the fascists and the communists could have fought it out and America wouldn't have needed to lose any soldiers.' The denigration of Churchill and elevation of Hitler is the gateway to Holocaust denial, he said. This, Murray added, appeals to 'the ones who believe the Nazis screwed up ethno-nationalism for everyone. So instead of contending with the Nazis, we will try to buff the edges of Nazi fascism. That's a really dark, dark, game to be playing'. Happily, the episode in which Murray took the revisionists to task has been watched nearly 4.5 million times.

This revisionism makes more sense – as I argued to Murray on *The Brink* – when it is placed in the context of the radical right's affections for Putin. When influencers construct an argument whereby Hitler wasn't so bad, Churchill wasn't so good and America shouldn't have got involved, what they are really arguing is that Putin isn't so bad, Zelensky isn't so good and America should stay out of it. It is a strange reprise of Neville Chamberlain's 1938 argument that Britain should steer clear of 'a quarrel in a faraway country between people of whom we know nothing'.

Whitewashing the bullying of a despot, as if both sides may be at fault, is the first step in the direction of appeasement, and appeasement is the first step in the direction of sympathy. These are clear examples of the new radicalism making a bid for cultural dominance by eschewing the old moral certainty that led those before us to sacrifice so much in the struggle for freedom. After decades of centrist fundamentalism, few have the backbone to oppose such radicals. Democracy is on the descent and the Nazis, in some strange way, are back.

Ninety years ago, communists and fascists were doing battle in the streets of Berlin. Fast forward to today, however, and their bastard progeny are finding common cause in opposition to liberal democracy, sharpened by hatred of the Jews. In a sign of the degeneracy of the times, this is articulated using the buzzwords of the culture wars, with white nationalist rhetoric casting Putin as the scourge of 'wokesters', represented by Ukraine and the American left.

For unabashed American Nazis, the inheritors of a long and ignominious tradition, the core of Putin's attraction clearly lies in his brute authoritarianism, especially after so many years of emasculating centrist fundamentalism. Their admiration for the Russian leader is a form of wish fulfilment, as they long to be able to dispense with the pettiness of democracy that has given a voice to their weakling enemies. Embedded within this, of course, is bestial antisemitism; when *The Daily Stormer* reported that 'Russia and Iran Sign Landmark Partnership Agreement', the standfirst read, 'Bad news for the Jews', and the story pushed the bizarre conspiracy theory that Jewish Americans had instigated the war in Ukraine in an attempt to 'force people to become gay' in Russia. The sorry truth, however, is that for great swathes of the myopic radical right, the war between Russia and Ukraine, which has claimed hundreds of thousands of lives, seen twenty thousand children kidnapped by Moscow, ushered in a disturbing new era of drone warfare and has prompted acts of astonishing human bravery, has been reduced to the digital culture wars. Putin, in other words, has become a very modern Nazi.

Unhumans

In 2011, Pat Buchanan, a 'paleoconservative' Republican demagogue – whose ideology is built of nationalism, hardline Christianity and isolationism – published *Suicide of a Superpower: Will America Survive to 2025?* The correct answer, of course, was yes, despite the radicalism of the author. Typically, Buchanan's four-hundred-page polemic presented the world through the prism of tribalism. White people, it argued, must unite to hold down the rise of non-whites. They must reclaim a country of heterosexual Christianity, cleansed of liberalism and minorities. They must make common cause with Russia, which, Buchanan claimed, had 'implored the white nations to unite'. The centrality of race to this doctrine prefigured the rise of the radical progressive movement towards the end of the Obama years and formed the template for the radical conservative response to it. Fast forward to the year about which Buchanan's book speculated, and a strapline on *The Daily Stormer* website described itself as 'the world's number one woke right website'. Buchanan was the daddy of this movement.

Like other elements of his dogma, this emphasis on a muscular Christianity has since taken on a life of its own. Unsurprisingly, Tucker Carlson, who in many ways can be seen as the heir to Buchanan, also taps into the stream of religious fervour on the American right. For years, Christianity has been in decline across the West. Britain and America are perhaps the two poles of this overall trend. In the United States, among the most religious of the democracies, the share of those declaring themselves as Christians has stabilised at 62 per cent in the past five years, a reduction from 78 per cent since 2007.[33]

In Britain, meanwhile, the number of native Christians fell by 5.3 million between 2001 and 2011, which equates to a loss of about ten thousand a week. Just over 46 per cent of the population admits to being Christian today,[34] with church membership declining from 30 per cent in 1930 to just over 8 per cent in 2025.[35] In a clearer illustration of the divergence of the two cultures, just 28 per cent of Britons believe in either God or a higher spiritual power,[36] compared to 90 per cent of Americans.[37]

Although Christianity in the United States is smaller than in previous decades, it has grown more radical, with an increasing spread of beliefs that are not shared by many in the mainstream. A significant number of churchgoers – 40 per cent, according to one survey,[38] though the true number may be lower[39] – now hold the beliefs of a loose, Pentecostal version of 'dominionism', sometimes known as the New Apostolic Reformation, a movement that developed in the fifties and sixties as a conservative riposte to the progressive Pentecostalism then found in Latin America.

In 2024, Carlson told a documentary maker that he was 'physically mauled' by a 'demon' while sleeping and awoke with claw-marks on his back. As delusional as this may seem, it reflects one of the most prominent characteristics of this brand of belief: its preoccupation with fighting the forces of Satan.

Whole cities are 'demon-mapped' by pastors, with sectors supposedly controlled by beings like Greed, Rebellion and Lust and battle joined with prayer and ritual. But the war is not limited to the spiritual realm. At the heart of the movement's theology is the 'Seven Mountain Mandate', abbreviated to '7M'. This amounts to a plan to 'take dominion' of seven spheres of society: media, government, education, economy, family, religion and the arts, in a drive to undo the Enlightenment principle of the separation of church and state.

As the religious commentator Mark Oppenheimer writes, '[they believe that] a Christian theocracy under Old Testament law is the best form of government, and a radically libertarian one. Biblical law, they believe, presupposes total government decentralisation, with the family and church providing order'.[40] They are fanatical supporters of Trump.

This way of thinking influences many on the radical right, even if they do not subscribe to the movement wholesale. And it is being taken in authoritarian directions.

In 2024, a book called *Unhumans: The Secret History of Communist Revolutions (And How to Crush Them)* became a *New York Times* bestseller. Written by Jack Posobiec – who has heavily promoted both the great replacement theory and the 'Pizzagate' conspiracy – and ghostwriter Joshua Lisec, it cast the left as 'unhumans', arguing that as they were 'opposed to humanity itself', they deserved to be placed 'outside of the category completely, in an entirely new misery-driven subdivision'. These 'unhumans' were said to 'run operations in media, government, education, economy, family, religion, and arts and entertainment', which corresponded to the seven mountains that must be wrested from the devil.

It was time, they argued, to replace democracy with something stronger. 'Our study of history has brought us to this conclusion: Democracy has never worked to protect innocents from the unhumans,' they wrote. As a suggestion of where this might be headed, they praised the Spanish dictator Francisco Franco as a 'great man of history' comparable to George Washington, and lauded the brutal Chilean ruler Augusto Pinochet. Not only was this paean to authoritarianism graced with a foreword by former Trump strategist Steve Bannon, it received an enthusiastic endorsement from the vice president himself. 'In the past, communists marched in the streets waving red flags,' JD Vance wrote. 'Today, they march through HR, college campuses, and courtrooms to wage lawfare against good, honest people. In *Unhumans*, Jack Posobiec and Joshua Lisec reveal their plans and show us what to do to fight back.'[41]

The question that has haunted this discussion, as it haunts many Jews, has been the nature and extent of Trump's sympathies for white radicalism. But we will never know and, in the final analysis, it does not matter. This is not about Trump so much as it is about Trumpistan. What must be indisputable by now is that the Maga movement has breathed great quantities of oxygen into the lungs of anti-establishment demagogues around the world, ranging from nationalists to downright Nazis. It is also indisputable that under the planetary influence of the forty-seventh president, many disruptive forces across the West have become emboldened in their pro-Russia stances. Both the AfD in Germany and the Rassemblement National in France, two of Europe's most powerful new political storms which threaten to blow away conventional politics permanently, have been openly supported by Trump and his team. Both are enthusiastic supporters of Putin. It is no coincidence that they also have had something of a problem with Jews.

In *On Tyranny*, written as the world staggered after the Second World War, Leo Strauss reflected: 'The analysis of tyranny that was made by the first political scientists was so clear, so comprehensive, and so unforgettably expressed that it was remembered and understood by generations which did not have any direct experience of actual tyranny. On the other hand, when we were brought face to face with tyranny – with a kind of tyranny that surpassed the boldest imagination of the most powerful thinkers of the past – our political science failed to recognise it.'[42] The way in which so many in the West so readily indulge a species of basically fineism towards the Kremlin today, in spite of the bitter experience of previous generations, and in spite of Putin's stated aim of authoritarian imperial expansion, underlines once again that the past is not even past.

In his notorious 2007 Munich speech heralding the rise of an assertive new Russia, Putin lambasted the democratic hegemony of the Pax Americana. 'A unipolar world means one centre of power, one centre of force, one centre of decision-making,' he said. 'This is unacceptable for the world. It is destructive, even for the hegemon itself.'[43]

Running through his address was the unmistakable voice of Dugin, who wrote: 'If you are in favour of global liberal hegemony, you are the enemy.'[44] The drain on American resources which the period of hegemony entailed was dramatic and there is a strong argument that the forces of history and economics made some realignment unavoidable. Today we can only watch as Putin's vision of multipolarity is ushered in, bringing with it the erosion of democratic norms, the collapse of Western security and the threat of global war.

In the year following October 7, the number of American Jews applying to emigrate to Israel surged by 84 per cent, part of a global trend amid rising antisemitism in the diaspora.[45] Meanwhile, there was a 50 per cent rise in Israelis leaving the country, some in response to the assault by jihadism, others in despair at Israel's chauvinist political insurgency. The overall picture is one of anxiety in the face of the new radicalism. The only solution, for the Jews as for the West, is to remedy the state of the democracies by stepping back from the brink. Without such cultural restoration, the best we can hope for is the paradox of Trumpistan: even as the president defends the Jews in so many significant ways, under his leadership the United States has made an enemy of itself.

Chapter Seven

YOUNG STALINS

Back in the USSR

Whether they are found dyeing their hair on university campuses or tapping lanyards in the corridors of the BBC, politically correct progressives appear to have little in common with nationalist chauvinists. Such is the horseshoe of radicalism, however, that their respective journeys to the opposite extremes of the political spectrum often lead them to very similar conclusions. Both end up seeing the world primarily through the prism of race. Both are possessed of an intolerance, sometimes verging on totalitarian in spirit, towards those with dissenting views. Both may have rather a soft spot for Russia, whether as the fiefdom of a white ruler or as a hollow emblem of socialism; there is a reason, after all, why radicals of both left and right have now been given the label of 'woke'.

As we have seen, jihadism, the third tribe, also tends to hold many of these characteristics, though like the others it contains its own unique evils, and even those that it shares will differ in particularities, means of expression, emphasis and lethality. But the most enduring incantation of these three dissonant voices invokes a hostility towards Jews. Show me a fanatical transgender campaigner, climate change campaigner or decolonisation campaigner, and chances are I'll show you an antisemite as easily as I may in Charlottesville or Islamabad.

After all, it was not people from the woke right who sat back and watched as Lior Tibet was dragged out of that memorial service in Dublin, and it was not a Muslim politician who delivered the Gaza speech that caused her to stand in protest in the first place. Rather, that evening in Dublin, the man who hijacked the Holocaust ceremony had been previously condemned for eulogising socialist despots like Fidel Castro[1] and Hugo Chavez[2] and has been described by a fellow politician as 'completely blinded by his archaic far left Marxist ideology'.[3] Step forward President Michael D. Higgins. The rotund, five-foot-two octogenarian, whose gleaming pate is rimmed by a cascade of candyfloss hair, might have a vaguely comical air, but like Jeremy Corbyn in Britain, he represents a bastion of hard-left thought upon which younger and trendier forms continue to be built.

Cast an eye across the left today and it is evident that the old Soviet animosity towards the Jews and the West remains in rude health. Indeed, it is rare these days to find an old-fashioned socialist who stands in support of the Jewish national home, as was the norm in past generations. For this, as well as the broader movement of progressive radicalism that benights our societies, we have the second great totalitarian power of the twentieth century largely to thank.

Consider Corbyn, who has joined Higgins at events to mark Bloody Sunday in Londonderry[4] and publicly urged the Irish president not to join Nato after Russia's invasion of Ukraine.[5] His political awakening took place against a backdrop of the Cold War amid Lenin caps, little round CND badges and rallies on rainy Saturdays. The Soviet hand reached deep into his milieu; he was a longtime columnist for the *Morning Star* newspaper, which was funded by the Kremlin and remains aligned to the manifesto of the Communist Party of Britain, and had friends at *Soviet Weekly*, the propaganda paper published from the Soviet Embassy in London by Sovinformburo, the USSR's news agency. Not only have the politics of his generation of leftists changed little over the decades but their risible agenda has come to win over masses of impressionable youngsters.

In the leadup to Putin's invasion of Ukraine in 2022, Corbyn parroted Kremlin talking points by wrongly blaming the massing of Russian forces on the border upon historic provocations by the democracies;[6] this was hardly a surprise given that in 2009, he had described Nato as 'a military Frankenstein', adding that 'Nato's influence has been malevolent, to say the least'.[7] A few months after the T-62 tanks rolled in, he urged Western countries to stop arming the courageous defenders of Kyiv[8] and argued that military alliances like Nato should be disbanded.[9]

Similarly, in 2018, the old socialist, who had briefly been launched via a quirk of fate into the unhappy role of Labour leader, failed to condemn the Kremlin for poisoning double agent Sergei Skripal and his daughter Yulia in Salisbury, calling instead for a 'robust dialogue with Russia on all the issues currently dividing our countries, rather than simply cutting off contact'. But the most distasteful sign of Cold War influence upon Corbyn and his fellow travellers, young and old alike, lies in their persistent fondness for jihadis. Since October 7, this has gone from a poisonous flick of hypocrisy to a widespread and disturbing movement that is eating away at the already depleted values of our society.

We have been forced to become accustomed to thousands of people marching through our capital cities expressing their support, either overtly or by association, with the very jihadis who would have them killed. Yet when considered from a distance, the leftist love affair with the cause of Palestinian militancy is not an obvious one. Both in the West Bank and Gaza, democracy is at best a sham, and corruption and tribalism is rife, not to mention internecine violence, the incitement of terrorism, misogyny, homophobia and religious fanaticism. All this, however, was given a phoney revolutionary facelift during the Cold War, when the Kremlin gripped the Palestinians as a lever against the West, thereby succeeding Nazi Germany as the most important ally of the Arab world.

The former Romanian intelligence officer Ion Mihai Pacepa, the highest-ranking defector from the former communist bloc, attested that in the sixties, the father of Palestinian nationalism, the Cairo-born Yasser Arafat, and the terrorist group the Palestine Liberation Organisation (PLO), became clients of the KGB. 'I was responsible for giving Arafat about $200,000 in laundered cash every month throughout the 1970s,' Pacepa recalled. 'I was given the KGB's "personal file" on Arafat. He was an Egyptian bourgeois turned into a devoted Marxist by KGB foreign intelligence. The KGB had trained him at its Balashikha special-ops school east of Moscow and in the mid-1960s decided to groom him as the future PLO leader.'[10] He duly secured this position in 1969.

In his speeches, including the notorious 1974 'gun and olive branch' address to the UN General Assembly, Arafat shamelessly ventriloquised Israelophobic KGB propaganda, railing against 'imperialism, colonialism, neo-colonialism and racism, the chief form of which is Zionism'.[11] The Russian bearhug continued after Arafat's death in 2004; his successor, Mahmoud Abbas, who extended his leadership indefinitely despite his four-year term officially expiring in 2009, studied for his PhD at Patrice Lumumba University in Moscow, now People's Friendship University of Russia. In his thesis, he argued that Zionists had engineered the Holocaust as a pretext to establish Israel and that the number of Jewish dead had been exaggerated sixfold for political gain.

Sly alignment

The alliance between the Palestinians and the Kremlin was forged by way of Algeria. In 1962, the militants of the Front de Libération Nationale (FLN) drove the imperial French helter-skelter out of their lands after a bloody guerrilla campaign. This landmark victory for decolonisation was equally a victory for the Kremlin, which had given political, diplomatic and military assistance to the FLN, which in turn had used this backing to inflict a death by a thousand cuts upon the mighty French Republic. The humiliation of Paris showed how Islamic grievances could be instrumentalised by a Soviet agenda. The achievement brought deep satisfaction to both parties: the Algerian Muslims had succeeded in reversing the dominance of Christendom, which had rankled deeply ever since the collapse of the Ottoman Empire, while the Kremlin had succeeded in dealing a heavy blow to the West.

The Palestinians were deeply impressed by the Algerian model. The FLN campaign had been bloody and relentless, sapping the morale of colonial France. Moreover, the guerrillas had multiplied their strength with backing from a growing number of countries that were opposed to the West. Whereas the United Nations had fifty-one member states when it was founded after the Second World War, this number had more than doubled by 1965, as new states broke out of territories that were formerly under the colonial rule of Britain and France. This created a naturally anti-Western, revolutionary bloc that was all too happy to embrace the Algerian cause.

When, on 1 November 1954, the FLN launched its campaign with a series of attacks on military and civilian targets across the country, accompanied by a call to arms on Egyptian radio, sympathetic foreign broadcasters drew attention to the struggle. Within a matter of months, the first summit of Asian and African states, many of which were newly arisen, had recognised the legitimacy of the FLN's claim to Algeria at the Bandung conference in Indonesia. This group of twenty-nine countries, including China, Libya, Pakistan and Turkey, represented more than half the global population and was explicitly opposed to colonialism.

From then on, Third World countries formed a wellspring of support for the FLN at the United Nations, choking off support for France. Moreover, as the guerrilla campaign wore on, the shock and awe of Paris's response – the Battle of Algiers of 1956–7 was won with crushing force, martial rule and torture – alienated both ordinary Algerians and the metropolitan French, causing international support to collapse and contributing towards the ignominious French defeat in 1962.

A certain diminutive Palestinian-Egyptian had been following the FLN's progress for years as he plotted a terror campaign of his own. The triumph in Algeria convinced Yasser Arafat that a similar course of action would work against the Jews. He must have hoped it would be easy; after all, the vanquished French had ruled the north African territory since 1830, whereas the modern state of Israel was only born in 1947. It must have seemed to him like the next domino to fall.

In 1964, the PLO launched its first assaults on Israelis. Over the decades that followed, different Palestinian terror groups – some overtly Marxist–Leninist, others harnessing the force multiplier of jihadism – continued to draw inspiration from the Algerian story, attacking Israel at home while developing alliances with the USSR and Third World countries to suffocate it on the international stage. This pattern persists to this day. Indeed, when asked about Palestinian deaths on Lebanese television two weeks after October 7, the former Hamas leader Khaled Mashal remarked: 'The Algerian people sacrificed six million martyrs over 130 years . . . No nation is liberated without sacrifices.' Unsurprisingly, Hamas does all it can to manipulate Israel into killing civilians, as the French had done to their ultimate cost.

Arafat's sleight of hand in eliding the Palestinian struggle with decolonisation was a stroke of genius, as it opened the door both to full Soviet backing and an existing body of international support. In 1974, in his famous 'gun and olive branch' address to the UN General Assembly, these influences converged. The PLO leader began by congratulating its new

Algerian president, Abdelaziz Bouteflika. 'We have known you also to be in the vanguard of the freedom fighters in their heroic Algerian war of national liberation,' Arafat said. The tirade that followed was taken straight from the Kremlin's propaganda playbook: 'The world is in need of tremendous efforts if its aspirations to peace, freedom justice, equality and development are to be realised, if its struggle is to be victorious over colonialism, imperialism, neo-colonialism and racism in all its forms, including Zionism.'

As anybody with the lightest general knowledge knows, 'Zionism' simply refers to the Jewish desire for self-determination in their homeland, a goal that was achieved after a thoroughly anti-colonial struggle against imperial Britain in 1947. Falsifying it as a form of 'colonialism' and 'racism' akin to 'Nazism' was a core Soviet propaganda message. The contemporary ubiquity of those patent untruths, thirty-five years after the collapse of communism, demonstrates both the remarkable skill of Kremlin spin doctors, who had adapted material from *The Protocols of the Elders of Zion* and Hitler's *Mein Kampf*, and the fearsome influence of the USSR's propaganda machinery. It also illustrates the number of sympathisers that still occupy positions of power in the West.

But although it immersed the world in lies, covered itself in gore and dismembered the dove of peace, Arafat's strategy of decolonisation was always doomed to failure. Whereas the French had been driven out of Algeria after eight gruesome years, Israel only grew stronger during five decades of Palestinian terror, despite suffering frequent atrocities and several genocidal invasions launched by the Arab world. The reason should have been obvious to the wily leader: Israel was not a colonial project, so the methods of decolonisation could never work.

The Jews have a more ancient bond to their land than that of any other people, one of an entirely different order to the thin ties between the French and Algerian soil. The first Jewish kingdom was born on that stretch of land between the Mediterranean and the Jordan a millennia before the birth of Christ, and more than 1,500 years before that of Muhammad. Jews know it as their homeland in their souls. In May 2025, a friend posted a video of a wedding he had attended near the Western Wall in Jerusalem that was interrupted by an air raid alarm on account of a Houthi rocket attack. The bride, groom and guests were seen dancing into the bunker amid the blare of the siren, singing the 2,600-year-old words of Jeremiah during the Babylonian exile: 'Again it will be heard in the hills of Judah and in the streets of Jerusalem: the sound of joy and the sound of revelry, the sound of the groom and the sound of the bride.' Where are the Babylonians now? Yet the Jews remain.

Secondly, as Arafat adjusted his gunsights, he ignored the fact that most Israeli Jews had either been born in that land or had arrived there as destitute refugees, often approaching the point of death. Most could hardly be mistaken for white, and they had no equivalent of the French motherland to which to flee. Where were they supposed to go? All of this bequeathed the Jews a defiant determination to survive against all odds, moored in conviction in themselves and their bond to their ancestral land. They could not be so easily defeated. Yet this misconception of Israeli being-in-the-world as mere colonialism fires Palestinian militancy to this day, despite it heralding disaster after disaster for the Arabs themselves.

Indeed, the seven-front war that commenced on October 7 has resulted only in the destruction of Hamas and Hezbollah as meaningful fighting forces, the deaths of the entire leadership hierarchy of both and the abject humiliation of their puppet masters in Tehran. Rather than bringing death, as it did to the French in Algeria, a thousand, two thousand, ten thousand or any number of cuts has only burnished the resilience of the Jewish state. The sooner its enemies learn that Israel cannot be beaten by pseudo-colonial 'resistance', the sooner they may accept that the Jews are there to stay, which remains the untrodden first step along the path of peace.

One battle that was won by Arafat's sly alignment with Algeria and the Soviets, however, was for the heart of the left. The decolonisation movement produced a generation of radical intellectuals and revolutionaries that energised progressives with revolutionary fervour; the Palestinian cause was now fraudulently placed at the heart of that struggle.

Frantz Fanon was a Martiniquais psychiatrist and Marxist intellectual, who worked in Algeria during the uprising against the French. He joined the FLN and became their most powerful spokesman. In *The Wretched of the Earth*, his seminal work inspired by his time in Algeria, he psychoanalysed the effects of colonialisation on the colonised and argued for violent resistance. 'The native who decides to put the programme into practice, and to become its moving force, is ready for violence at all times,' he wrote. 'From birth it is clear to him that this narrow world, strewn with prohibitions, can only be called in question by absolute violence.'[12]

The popular chant, 'Resistance is justified when people are occupied', which is often heard at rallies in support of Gaza, shows how the Palestinian cause has been cleverly shoehorned into this alluring account of decolonisation. But there are facts. Israelis are no imperialists. Gaza has not been 'occupied' since 2005, when Israel unilaterally pulled out. October 7 was not an act of 'resistance' but an eruption of depraved and gratuitous jihadi butchery, of a piece with the bloodletting in Iraq and Syria under Islamic State, not to mention the atrocities in Paris, Berlin, London and New York, many of which I saw with my own eyes as a reporter.

Reading Fanon's elegant prose brings home how his model never held relevance to Israel. 'The settler makes history and is conscious of making it,' he wrote. 'And because he constantly refers to the history of his mother country, he clearly indicates that he himself is the extension of that mother country. Thus the history which he writes is not the history of the country which he plunders but the history of his own nation in regard to all that she skims off, all that she violates and starves.' This may very well have been true of the colonial French, but the 'mother country' of the Jews is none other than the land of Israel. The Palestine activists at Ivy League universities may like to chant for Jews to 'go back to Poland'; but they fled that country for a reason, and it was never 'theirs' in the first place.

Nonetheless, shit has a habit of sticking, especially when it has been flung with an agenda. The way Fanonesque terms like 'settlers' and 'settler colonialism' are now associated with Israel is testament to the success of Soviet myth-making, as well as the extent to which a crude version of radical decolonisation theory has contaminated public discourse in the West, to the great detriment of us all.

Orientalism

Fanon himself never addressed the matter of the Jewish state in his writings. That dishonour was left to Edward Saïd, a Palestinian-American intellectual ten years his junior, upon whom Fanon was an influence. Saïd, who was anointed as one of the fathers of 'post-colonial studies' when he was a professor of literature at Columbia University in the sixties, also counted among his influences the Italian Marxist Antonio Gramsci, who is famously associated with the concept of the 'long march through the institutions', to be undertaken by quiet revolutionaries as a means of toppling the bourgeoisie; and the radical theorist (and paedophile) Michel Foucault, who pioneered poststructuralism alongside the Algerian philosopher Jacques Derrida and the French essayist Roland Barthes.

During the sixties and seventies, humanities departments at many of the major universities were rife with attempts to overturn all our old assumptions, challenging concepts of objective truth, unassailable moral values and even the existence of meaning itself. Under the rubric of 'critical theory', literature was hijacked to confirm the beliefs of Marxism, postcolonialism, feminism, deconstruction and 'queer theory', rather than cherished as a current that flows from human hearts of the past to our own in the present. Of course, there was never a 'conservative theory' or 'liberal theory' of literature. In different ways, all these thinkers – and many others of the same scene – rooted their authority in a contempt for authority and their beliefs in a contempt for belief. According to these schools of thought, culture may be divorced from its roots and hijacked as a metaphor for radical politics.

This was achieved by way of a crafty little shimmy known as 'the death of the author', an extrapolation of Friedrich Nietzsche's famous assertion that 'God is dead'. Invented by Roland Barthes in 1967, this is the idea that the author's intention is supposedly unknowable, and meaning is projected by the reader, so a text can be taken to mean anything you like (so long as it is radical). At any time, a critic can pop up and suggest that Shakespeare's *King Lear* is an allegory about patriarchal power and European colonisation, or Bram Stoker's 1897 novel *Dracula* is a metaphor for sexual deviancy and fear of homosexuality, and the vampire should be seen as a queer liberator, and nobody can do anything about it.

By the time I went up to Oxford to read English in 1999, 'critical theory' was starting to spread. One undergraduate class, for instance, focussed on the Aretha Franklin lyric, 'you make me feel like a natural woman'. Provided with the lens of 'queer theory', we were taught that there was no such thing as a 'natural woman'; the song was suggesting that people may only 'feel like' one in response to the gendered gaze. The fact the songwriter, Jerry Wexler, said he was playing with the African-American idea of a 'natural man', meaning someone with a bond to his ancestral heritage, made zero difference. At the time, we had no idea where all this would lead.

From his intellectual perch on the corpse of the author, Saïd made everything about colonialism. The titles of his essays, which seem almost like spoofs outside the university world today, speak for themselves: 'Yeats and Decolonisation' (1988); 'Jane Austen and Empire' (1990). But his more indelible achievement was a political one: the act of hitching his intellectual antecedents like Fanon to the Palestinian issue, and seating this within the vehicle of postmodernism, which was fast gaining ground in the academy. In the same breath, he perniciously elided Israel with the imperial West.

Like his essays on literature, Saïd's writing on Israel often feels like an exercise in wish-fulfilment, as he distorts the history of the Jewish state to conform to an irrelevant postcolonial model and makes it a figurehead of the hated democracies. 'Although it coincided with an era of the most virulent Western antisemitism, Zionism also coincided . . . with the period of unparalleled European territorial acquisition in Africa and Asia,'[13] he wrote in his 1979 book *The Question of Palestine*. Here he wilfully overlooked the basic fact that the state of Israel was actually a *post*colonial state, arising after Jewish militia drove imperial Britain out of Palestine. Rather than expanding, Western powers were relinquishing their old Ottoman and colonial territories at the time of Israel's birth, giving rise to a range of new nation-states, from Algeria, Syria, Lebanon, Jordan and Iraq to India and Pakistan. Israel was simply another among them.

Saïd's most famous work, *Orientalism*, argued that the West viewed Muslims patronisingly, as two-dimensional caricatures, second-order problems to be solved. It expanded on his 1968 essay 'The Arab Portrayed'. 'If the Arab occupies space enough for attention, it is a negative value,' Saïd wrote. 'He is seen as a disrupter of Israel's and the West's existence.'[14] After its publication in 1978, *Orientalism* was derided by the great Arabist Bernard Lewis as 'outrageous', not just for its thesis but its scholarship. 'Mr Saïd's knowledge of Arabic and Islam shows surprising gaps,' he wrote in the *New York Review of Books* in 1982. 'The one Arabic phrase which he quotes is misspelled and mistranslated and several of the few other

Arabic words which appear on Mr Saïd's pages are similarly misrepresented.'[15] Saïd had made similar errors in translating German, Lewis pointed out, and often displayed a contempt towards Arabic scholarship that was more egregious than that of the Westerners he was attacking.

Nonetheless, *Orientalism* was embraced by the left – or, as Lewis put it, by 'brainwashed university students who ought to know better' – and its influence was profound. From the humanities to social science departments, in history, anthropology, sociology, political science, philosophy, art history and literature, academics began to think in terms of difference and the politics of representation. *Orientalism* provided the semiotics for minorities to articulate their resentment of white dominance. Sometimes, of course, not least in the case of segregation in the United States, this resentment was well justified. Yet the Jews were seized upon from the start.

Our friends from Hamas

In the afterword to *Orientalism*, Saïd wrote that his Palestinian origins made the book a 'history of personal loss and national disintegration', which aimed to 'liberate intellectuals from the shackles of systems of thought like Orientalism'. Israel's victory in the Six Day War had exacerbated his sense of national bereavement, he said, as the comprehensive Arab defeat had ushered an Israeli presence into much of the West Bank and Gaza (from where Israel unilaterally withdrew in 2005). But Saïd failed to appreciate that the short, sharp war of 1967, which had resulted in that stunning Israeli triumph, had only commenced after Arab armies massed on Israel's borders in a prelude to a repeat of the genocidal invasion they had attempted in 1948. Indeed, Israel's Arab neighbours tried the same thing six years later and were once again beaten back.

It is hard to avoid the conclusion that *Orientalism* was little more than a convoluted way of softening up Western selfhood. As usual, Israel was taken as the voodoo doll. But why should the victors atone for a victory? After all, it was the Arab world that tried to wipe Israel out, not the other way round. If they didn't like the taste of defeat, they might have considered not launching a war of extermination in the first place. Rather than pull apart subtle Western prejudices towards the 'Orient', Saïd's talents might have been put to better use in analysing the hatred of Jews among Palestinian leaders, which prompted the Six Day War in the first place and fuels the conflict to this day. Instead, he offered the world an abstrusely packaged bundle of malice towards the West which was sold to generations of students as enlightened thinking in an effort to turn them against themselves.

Saïd's politicisation of academia must have been catnip to the Kremlin, as it helped to undermine the self-confidence, coherence, happiness and might of the democracies. His binary conception of the world, which placed Jews and the West on one side and all people of conscience on the other, reflected that of the Soviets, who saw capitalist imperialism as the epitome of evil. To the USSR, anybody opposing the West was to be embraced as revolutionaries, whatever their motivation and the brutality of their methods. As progressives adopted Saïd's worldview, and that of other radical intellectuals, they gradually came to support their own enemies. Beginning in academia, this movement slowly spread outwards into society.

'Whatever its intellectual merits, academic "post-colonialism" is not just of academic importance,' the ethicist Nigel Biggar argued:

> It is politically important, too, insofar as its world-view is absorbed by student citizens and moves them to repudiate the dominance of the West. Thus, academic post-colonialism is an ally – no doubt, inadvertent – of Vladimir Putin's regime in Russia and the Chinese Communist Party, which are determined to expand their own (respectively) authoritarian and totalitarian power at the expense of the West. In effect, if not by intent, they are supported by the West's own hard-Left, whose British branch would have the United Kingdom withdraw from NATO, surrender its nuclear weapons, renounce global policing and retire to free-ride on the moral high ground alongside neutral Switzerland.[16]

John Rees, a leading figure in both the British Stop the War Coalition and the Socialist Workers Party, trumpeted this hypocrisy in his book, *The ABC of Socialism*, thirty years ago. 'Socialists should unconditionally stand with the oppressed against the oppressor, even if [the oppressed] are undemocratic and persecute minorities, as Saddam Hussein persecutes Kurds and Castro persecutes gays,' he wrote.[17] Particularly after the Six Day War of 1967, Israel became a totem of democracy in the Middle East, on account of its friendship with the United States. In the eyes of the Kremlin and hordes of progressive radicals, therefore, this meant that Israel's terrorist enemies, from Marxist–Leninist outfits like the Popular Front for the Liberation of Palestine to the most depraved jihadi butchers, were automatically to be seen as resistance heroes. After all, what's a bit of rape, kidnap, murder and mutilation in the cause of 'decolonisation' and overturning democracy?

This is the lens through which we can understand how Rees's more famous friend and colleague could have come to speak so warmly of the future perpetrators of October 7 at an infamous meeting in Parliament in 2009. 'It will be my pleasure and honour to host an event in Parliament where our friends from Hezbollah will be speaking,' Jeremy Corbyn said. 'I've also invited our friends from Hamas to come and speak as well . . . So far as I'm concerned, that is absolutely the right function of using Parliamentary facilities.'[18] He went on to meet leaders from both jihadi groups during visits to the Middle East.

In 2018, Corbyn took to the stage at Glastonbury to a deafening chorus of 'Oh, Jeremy Corbyn' from an adoring young crowd. This became the emblem of the strange synergy between the faded old cold warrior and an up-and-coming generation of TikTokers, for whom the notion of 'resistance' provided a thrill of authenticity in a secular world saturated with disposable corporatism. Even though Corbyn was roundly dumped by the electorate in 2019, the youthquake he energised had taken on a life of its own. Since October 7, it has gone into overdrive.

In Simon Sebag Montefiore's *Young Stalin*, he describes how the tyrant's 'prolonged youth has always been a mystery, in many senses', adding that 'before 1917, he cultivated the mystique of obscurity but also specialised in the "black work" of underground revolution'.[19] Indeed, Stalin himself is said to have coined the term '*dezinformatsiya*' or 'disinformation', to name a KGB black propaganda department in 1923.

It should have been no surprise, perhaps, that more than a century later, even the most depraved frenzy of murder, kidnap, rape, mutilation and necrophilia of October 7, all of which was openly motivated by jihadism rather than any notion of social justice, was sanitised as a symbol of revolution by young progressive radicals.

From within their pampered societies, many of these youngsters seemed to take especial titillation from cosplaying terrorists and throwing about disgraceful slogans like 'Rape is resistance',[20] 'Globalise the Intifada' and 'Death to the IDF'. As my old colleague in Gaza, who was demonstrating against Hamas while youngsters in the West did the opposite, told me on the phone: 'The keffiyeh people in the West can come to replace me. They can stay here a few weeks, or even one day will be enough. They can come live in a tent for a week and see how they like Hamas. But they won't find a transgender bathroom.' In a tangible way, this betrayal of Israel was a Soviet-inspired betrayal of the activists' own inheritance, the result of their own betrayal by an increasingly empty society.

Active measures

Explicit, state sponsored brainwashing was also in full flow in the sixties. Although rarely remembered, the Soviet manipulation of the Western mind during the Cold War took place on such an astonishing scale that it should perhaps be no surprise that it continues to bear bitter fruit today. In evidence supported by many other defectors, Oleg Danilovich Kalugin attested that the KGB – which had almost half a million employees at its peak – infiltrated the West to set up 'all sorts of congresses, peace congresses, youth congresses, festivals, women's movements, trade union movements, campaigns against US missiles in Europe, campaigns against neutron weapons'. He added: 'It was really a worldwide campaign, often not only sponsored and funded, but conducted and manipulated by the KGB. And this was again part and parcel of this campaign to weaken [the] military, economic and psychological climate in the West.'[21]

Given that the dismantlement of the Jewish state was a key strategic objective for the Soviet Union in its attempt to push back the frontiers of democracy, spreading Israelophobia was a major part of the KGB's 'active measures'. Indeed, according to some estimates, this messaging occupied 85 per cent of its resources.[22] As I explored in *Israelophobia*, Soviet propagandists doctored older antisemitic material to churn out all the false propaganda claims – that Israel is a genocidal, apartheid state akin to Nazi Germany, that 'Zionism is racism', that Israel is bent on 'settler colonialism' and so forth – that continue to haunt the left today.

In addition to huge numbers of Israelophobic books and thousands of hours of monthly radio broadcasts, tens of millions of copies of bilious magazines and newspapers were printed annually in eighty languages and pamphlets were disseminated worldwide, with titles like *Deceived by Zionism* and *Criminal Alliance of Zionism and Nazism*. This material was spread by front organisations across the West, funded by Moscow and run by Soviet sympathisers. These made a significant contribution towards poisoning the minds of progressives in the democracies, who long after the collapse of the Soviet Union passed the dogma on through the generations as they took on positions of responsibility at universities, in the public sector and in the media. So steeped had they become in this ideology that they did so not with cynicism but in earnest.

Israelophobia was far from the only theme that the Soviet spy agency pursued. Glancing at a selection of the hundreds of fake stories successfully planted by the KGB in Western media makes clear the bewildering spread of disinformation that was injected into our culture during that period. Examples listed by Kalugin include: 'The CIA ousted President Nixon; the CIA arranged the 1978 mass suicide and murder of more than nine hundred people of the Jonestown cult; the U.S. was developing an ethnic weapon that would kill blacks and spare whites; the CIA was behind the assassinations of Olof Palme in Sweden, Indira Gandhi in India, and Aldo Moro in Italy, and an attempt on the pope's life; the US military planned to use tactical nuclear weapons in Italy in case the left parties came to power; US Army scientists developed the AIDS virus; and Americans steal foreign babies to use their organs for transplant.'[23]

Active measures were levelled at our societies at a time of vulnerability. The West was in a state of cultural upheaval, as the postwar generation railed against the rigid mindset of the fifties and experimented with alternative ways of living. This was an impulsive and chaotic era of counterculture and subculture, hippies and free love, civil rights and feminism, Woodstock and miniskirts, the Beatles and the Vietnam war, not to mention the advent of colour television and the space race. People were taking drugs and looking for new ideas, both of which the Soviets were only too happy to provide. While the Cold War ground on and a nuclear shadow fell across the world, the West was experiencing a kind of collective adolescence; and like all adolescents, our societies became rebellious and impressionable. While hormones raged in the democracies, the sordid uncle of the Kremlin came to play a decisive role in shaping the coming-of-age of the Western Left.

In a chilling interview in 1983, Yuri Bezmenov, a KGB propagandist who had defected some years before, said: 'It takes from fifteen to twenty years to demoralise a nation. Why that many years? Because this is the minimum number of years it requires to educate one generation of students in the country of your enemy, exposed to the ideology of the enemy. In other words, Marxism–Leninism ideology is being pumped into the soft heads of at least three generations of American students without being challenged or counter-balanced by the basic values of Americanism, American patriotism. The result? The result you can see.'[24]

Today, with the sudden dominance of social media, the rapid ascent of artificial intelligence, the headwinds of mass immigration, mismanaged economies, the widespread distrust of politics and the media and the chaotic global uprising against decades of centrist fundamentalism, society feels similarly vulnerable. In addition, the elites have saddled us with an inability to 'challenge or counter-balance' the various tides of subversive radicalism that have been developing for decades with the 'basic values' of the West. Once again, the result you can see.

For whom the Bell tolls

The Soviet project may have drawn its final breath in 1991, but its ghost lives on in the bodies of modern progressives. Nowhere is this seen more vividly than among those preoccupied with race. Particularly since the global unrest that accompanied the rise of Black Lives Matter in 2020, radical doctrines have been accepted by mainstream institutions. Concepts such as 'unconscious bias', 'microaggressions', 'structural racism', 'white privilege' and 'anti-racism training' are now widely promoted by corporations, institutions and celebrities.

From the nineteenth-century abolitionist Frederick Douglass to Martin Luther King, the aims of the civil rights movement were as simple as they were noble: to embrace African Americans in the principle enshrined in the Declaration of Independence that 'all men are created equal' and reform society accordingly. Here was a campaign that all right-minded people came to support and few would question today. The way in which this goal was subverted to focus again on racial difference, returning society to a mirror image of the original bigotry and opening the door to progressive antisemitism, is a story of many villains. One of the foremost, however, is the late legal academic Derrick Bell, the father of 'critical race theory'.

Bell was a softly spoken scholar, with spectacles and a small afro, who had served in the US Air Force in Korea before taking a job at the Justice Department in the sixties. Assigned to the civil rights division, his job was to help desegregate America's school system now that equality had been mandated. Bell quickly became disillusioned by the dream of Dr King. In his work, he saw how many affluent white parents reacted to desegregation by sending their children to prestigious private schools, condemning black children to poor facilities and replicating segregation informally.

His solution, which later became expanded into the doctrine of critical race theory, was a radical one: to dispense with the civil rights ideals of 'colour blindness' and equality, arguing instead that race should form the heart of policymaking and black people should be given special privileges. 'Bell's scepticism about the ability of the civil rights movement to achieve real progress also had a key implication for politics, one that would eventually come to exert an unexpected influence on American public policy over the course of the 2010s', wrote the political scientist Yascha Mounk in his 2023 book *The Identity Trap*. 'In an effort to achieve "racial equity", [Bell sought to] make the treatment citizens received from state institutions depend on the colour of their skin.' By the time Covid struck, the State of New York was bumping black people to the front of the queue for vaccines and medication even when white senior citizens were at greater risk. Thanks to the global dominance of American culture, this attitude was exported internationally. Racism, in other words, was back.

Here lies the tell. This new bigotry, which disguised itself as its opposite, was wrapped up in a vision of the capitalist imperialism as the greatest threat to the world. Clearly, Bell's revolutionary thinking had not come from nowhere. Indeed, although he sometimes dismissed the ideology, Marxist influence was woven throughout his work – 'as I see it, critical race theory recognises that revolutionising a culture begins with the radical assessment of it,' he wrote[25] – and two years before his death, he became a member of the Communist Party.

These instincts can be seen in an interview he gave to the *New York Observer* in 1994. 'The new crop of leaders are going to be a lot more dangerous and radical,' he said, 'and the next phase will probably be led by charismatic individuals, maybe teenagers, who urge that instead of killing each other, they should go out in gangs and kill a whole lot of white people.'[26]

During the civil rights struggle, the Jewish community had stood shoulder to shoulder with Martin Luther King, even being attacked by the Ku Klux Klan. The solidarity was reciprocal. In 1966, Dr King delivered a speech to an audience of fifty thousand Americans in which he demanded justice for persecuted Jews in the Soviet Union.

However, with ethnic struggle once again in the engine room of America, and Dr King's approach and the West facing radical challengers, the old antisemitic tropes also returned. Bell was an admirer of the firebrand Nation of Islam leader Louis Farrakhan, whose back catalogue includes countless inflammatory comments about 'the powerful Jews', whom he described unequivocally as 'my enemy';[27] Bell saw him as 'the best living example of a black man, ready, willing and able to tell it like it is'. He also held Farrakhan's right-hand man, Khalid Muhammad, who called the Jews 'bloodsuckers' whose 'father was the devil', in high regard.[28]

Given the endemic racism in America in the sixties, the global socialist uprising had an understandable appeal to black people suffering under appalling conditions. It is no exaggeration to state that all the activists that birthed the awakening that became Black Lives Matter, from the intellectual giant WEB Du Bois, whose death was greeted with sadness by the Russian leader Nikita Khrushchev, to Stokely Carmichael, a disciple of Martin Luther King who ushered in the era of 'Black Power', floated deep inside the Soviet orbit. The speeches of Malcolm

X, which long ago eclipsed the wisdom of Dr King, showed overt Kremlin influence on top of their antisemitism. 'You show me a capitalist, I'll show you a bloodsucker,'[29] he ranted, and 'you can't have capitalism without racism'.[30]

This synergy allowed an entry point for poisonous ideas to enter the bloodstream of social justice activists. Bestselling contemporary race ideologues like Reni Eddo-Lodge, author of *Why I'm No Longer Talking to White People About Race*, and Afua Hirsch, author of *Decolonising My Body*, and Robin DiAngelo, author of *White Fragility*, are united not by colour but politics. Eddo-Lodge is of Nigerian extraction; Hirsch is half-Ghanaian and half-Jewish; DiAngelo is white. But all are radical leftists, products of the Western socialist tradition rather than any ideas found in Africa or the Caribbean.

In 2017, when privately educated Hirsch, for example, used her *Guardian* column to call for Nelson's Column in Trafalgar Square to be torn down, hers was an expression of the revolutionary impulse of a hundred years before, when the Bolsheviks toppled the great monument to Tsar Alexander III in central Moscow, only expressed in the language of race and empire. Unsurprisingly, she is also hyper-critical of Israel. In August 2025, for example, she posted a display on Instagram of her holiday pictures from Crete. There was nothing but photographs of Israelophobic graffiti – including support for a boycott of the Jewish state and a sinister poster smearing Israeli soldiers as 'occupiers, racists, murderers' and declaring 'we don't want you here' in English and Hebrew – all set to chilled techno music.

Despite dissenting black voices, from the civil rights icon James Baldwin to the contemporary writers Tomiwa Owolade and Coleman Hughes, leftism now dominates the scene and race is taken as a vehicle for radical politics. This ends with such depravities as a Chicago group affiliated to Black Lives Matter posting 'I stand with Palestine' on social media after October 7, accompanied by a picture of one of the jihadi murderers borne on a paraglider.

One struggle

Ever since 2023, Gaza has ascended to replace race – which had occupied the pinnacle of intersectional convergence since the death of George Floyd in 2020 – as the primary cause for progressives of all stripes, elevating Israelophobia from simply one of the shades of the progressive rainbow to the weather that formed the very conditions for the alliance. Take the 'Queers for Palestine' movement, which bizarrely aligns the gay and trans movements with Islamic ultra-conservatism.

Given that in Gaza, women live very restricted lives and sex before marriage is forbidden, let alone homosexuality, or even transsexuality, the chances of real-life Palestinians embracing that cause seemed rather remote. In fact, the fate of gay Palestinians like Ahmad Abu Marhia, who in 2022 was kidnapped from his refuge in Israel before being taken to Hebron on the West Bank and decapitated, might suggest that 'Palestine' and 'trans rights' are perhaps not seen by everybody as 'one struggle, one fight'.[31] The fact that such dehumanisation of the Palestinians can be shown by those who ostensibly campaign against the dehumanisation of the Palestinians is both breathtakingly hypocritical and breathtakingly obvious, as well as quite amusing. It is another example of the profoundly Western nature of Western movements against the West.

The instinct shared by a range of progressives to unite in solidarity behind a single cause has roots in another aspect of the American left. Derrick Bell may have birthed critical race theory, but it was his protégée, Kimberlé Crenshaw, who inadvertently named the new discipline when she used the phrase for the title of a workshop at the University of Wisconsin-Madison in 1989. But Crenshaw's most significant contribution came when she invented the idea of 'intersectionality'.

To start with, this was an esoteric concept to remedy a blind spot in the law for people at the overlap in the Venn diagram of two minority characteristics, like black women, who might occasionally be disadvantaged by quirks of the rules in a way that black men and white women were not. Over the years, however, this idea was coarsened and blended with other strands of progressive thought. Soon, 'intersectionality' was taken to imply that no outsider could ever possibly comprehend the 'lived experience' of someone who laboured under specific minority labels. The revolutionary imperative thus became explicit: as trans activists were constitutionally unable to understand the plight of Gazans, for example, they owed them blind solidarity. Before long, intersectionality became a kind of purity test. If you wanted to join a feminist group, you were required to commit without question to a suite of positions on race, gender, climate and Palestine. Here, of course, there were echoes of the old socialist solidarity. Progressives of the world were called upon to unite behind the keffiyeh.

In the months after October 7, as Gaza protesters blocked the traffic on Brooklyn Bridge and intimidated worshippers at synagogues in London, the various radical causes locked together more seamlessly than ever before. Greta Thunberg began wearing a keffiyeh, tried to break into Gaza and led chants of 'No climate justice on occupied land'.[32] Black Lives Matter organised marches for Gaza.[33] The Palestinian flag became a rallying symbol for all radical factions, turning it from an emblem of nationhood for a people thousands of miles away to an expression of disruptive progressive sentiment in the West; the keffiyeh was appropriated as a fashionable gesture of rebellion, produced in a variety of colours, often paired with blue hair and crop tops that the vast majority of actual Palestinians would treat with bewilderment at best. Bafflingly, women even protested topless on behalf of jihadis.

Yet despite their many problems and injustices, the democracies – including Israel – are the richest, freest, happiest and safest nations the world has ever known. Indeed, the radicals on the streets could only make their voices heard because of the liberties of the West, something for which millions of migrants from despotic regimes risk their lives each year, and something which certainly cannot be found under Palestinian rule.

It has often been remarked that the zealous blindness shown by the activists towards their own contradictions resembles a sublimated faith, devoted through cultural emptiness to the unquenchable ego rather than God. This is hardly a new observation. Shortly before he passed away in 1662, the French philosopher Blaise Pascal wrote: 'What else does this craving, and this helplessness, proclaim but that there was once in man a true happiness, of which all that now remains is the empty print and trace? This he tries in vain to fill with everything around him, seeking in things that are not there the help he cannot find in those that are, though none can help, since this infinite abyss can be filled only with an infinite and immutable object; in other words, by God Himself.'[34]

At the same time, it must be acknowledged that much of the momentum is rather more quotidian. Sir Niall Ferguson told me on *The Brink*:

> The different ideas that we've been talking about are part of a package that is really designed to make thought unnecessary. You don't need to read and engage in debate because you have supplied to you the straightforward components of a Manichaean worldview in which you know what's good and bad – white men bad, women of colour good; Palestinians good, Jews bad – and you don't really need to think.

Depressingly, he argued, many young people, who are steeped in social media and buffeted by peer pressure, end up making themselves amanuenses for these radical currents for the most trifling of reasons. Sir Niall concluded: 'If you're one of the young women who don the Palestinian scarf and participate in these protests, often disrupting university life and heckling speakers, this is your social life. It's not based on a profound understanding of the Middle East, because most of those people have never been there. They've never been to Israel and they'd struggle to name the river and the sea. No: this is your social life.'

All eyes on Rafah

With this worldview imposed from all sides, young people are often ill-equipped to cope with the onslaught of digital propaganda to which they are regularly subjected. As 'intersectionality' does its thing, the most potent of these trends now concerns Israel. One vivid example came in February 2024, when the war in Gaza was at an impasse. Hamas had regrouped in the southern town of Rafah, on the Egyptian border, where scores of smuggling tunnels allowed them to be resupplied with weapons, ammunition, food, personnel and cash. Yahya Sinwar, the mastermind of October 7, was among them. It was clear that if Israel was to defeat Hamas, conquering the town was essential. As a result, an intense global disinformation campaign was mounted to block this objective, exerting a great influence upon public opinion and stalling the Israeli advance for four months.

Every group with vested interests in the survival of Hamas – from fanatically Israelophobic NGOs and UN agencies to corrupt Middle Eastern leaders and Western elites – weaponised the language of humanitarian concern to frustrate the Israeli goal. Egypt stopped aid from entering Gaza, exacerbating deprivation in the Strip in a crude attempt to pile more pressure onto Israel. Revealingly, it was based on the correct assumption that the international community would blame only one country for the dwindling aid, and not the country responsible. This was depressingly successful, providing social media with the material it needed to weave an even more Israelophobic narrative.

At the time, the population of Rafah had swelled to 1.4 million, as displaced people took refuge from fighting in the north. Rather than help Israel solve this problem, however, the Americans insisted publicly that evacuating them all from the town was impossible. To avoid a 'humanitarian catastrophe', the Biden administration said, Rafah must be left untouched. In

March, Kamala Harris assured journalists that she had 'studied the maps' and concluded that 'there's nowhere for those folks to go'. On the phone to Benjamin Netanyahu, Biden delivered his notorious catchphrase: 'Don't.'

In response, however, Israel did. In a mere ten days, the IDF successfully evacuated a million Palestinians to an 'expanded humanitarian area' stretching from al-Mawasi, north-west of the town, to the southern city of Khan Younis and the central Deir al-Balah. Relying on lessons learned from the early phase of the war, Israeli troops then launched the military operation, very slowly and methodically, with limited air support, resulting in historically low civilian casualties. One by one, Hamas cells and terror tunnels were neutralised. On October 16, Yahya Sinwar was hunted down and killed.

Social media plays a dominant role in every modern propaganda campaign of this type. On this occasion, however, it was particularly overt. At the height of the frenzy, an image of thousands of tents forming the words 'all eyes on Rafah' went viral, clocking up almost fifty million views in a matter of days on Instagram alone. The ubiquity was astonishing. One of my teenage daughters asked me if I could send her a pro-Israel meme that she could post on Instagram to stand against the wave of disinformation. She hadn't been able to find one.

This is a salutary example of the global propaganda campaign that erupts whenever Israel approaches a military victory. It unfolds like clockwork, with the United Nations, doctors and aid workers, the broadcast media, political leaders, celebrities and activists uniting to persuade the world that Israel is indulging in an affront to decency and is relishing the wanton massacre of children. The same playbook is dragged out every time; gradually, common sense is eroded and social norms are established based on lies. Foremost among these has been the campaign to stamp 'genocide' upon Israel's war of self-defence, despite the fact that it had the firepower to have wiped out Gaza entirely in a matter of hours if it had wanted to, warned civilians to evacuate before operations and facilitated the delivery of more than 1.7 million tons of aid in two and a half years.

Attacks on Israel invariably form part of a wider assault on the West. As Scott Galloway, clinical professor of marketing at New York University, has noted, since October 7, on TikTok there have been 'fifty-two videos that are pro-Hamas or pro-Palestine for every one served on Israel'.[35] Young people infatuated with the new radicalism have developed sympathies for the jihadi 'resistance'. In a disturbing example of the effectiveness of such algorithmically driven brainwashing, in November 2023, Osama Bin Laden's anti-West manifesto *Letter to America*, which sought to justify the 9/11 attacks, went viral on the platform, with millions of gullible youngsters coming to believe that the mass murderer had a point, turning against the very democracies that had afforded them such unprecedented levels of freedom, affluence, opportunity and security.

As long ago as 2013, China's President Xi Jinping called the Internet 'the main battlefield in the battle for public opinion'.[36] He added: 'Many people, especially young people, do not read mainstream media and get most of their information from the Internet. We must face up to this fact, increase investment, and seize the initiative.' If this was not clear enough, comparing TikTok with the original Chinese version, Douyin, suggests an underlying agenda. For one thing, under-fourteens on Douyin are only allowed access for forty minutes a day and there are automatic delays of five seconds if they scroll for too long. The algorithm used on TikTok, meanwhile, encourages users to remain on the app for as long as possible. Similarly, while the Douyin algorithm promotes 'inspiring' videos promoting patriotism and social cohesion, along with scientific, educational and historical content, not to mention academic and athletic achievement, on TikTok, cretinism and narcissism are rewarded. Such is the resulting dopamine hit that in 2023, Ofcom found that TikTok was the number one source of news for young teenagers.[37]

As the American technology ethicist and former Google employee Tristan Harris put it: 'It's almost like [the Chinese] recognise that technology is influencing kids' development, and they make their domestic version a spinach version of TikTok, while they ship the opium version to the rest of the world.'[38] It's easy to see how this ends. After fifteen years of TikTok, would young people heed the call to fight for their country, as their great-grandparents did? Or would they join a campus protest for Gaza, despite the fact that the leaders of Iran, Hezbollah and Hamas have openly applauded them?

Of course, it is not just the progressive movement that is juiced up by social media. The same is true of Islamist and nationalist radicals, as all of these ideologies undermine the soul of the West. Russia, post-communist China and other hostile regimes have jumped at the opportunity, using social media to stoke our domestic 'culture wars'. Iran, for example, has set up numerous English-language 'news' websites that have boosted firebrand troublemakers like George Galloway, attempted to undermine the royal family and carried anti-Western cartoons showing British missiles being fired at children in Yemen.[39] The internet is awash with this stuff, and much of it is aimed at the destruction of the Jews and the West.

If we are to leave this dystopian world and make our way back to sanity, tackling the problem of social media must be an urgent priority. Given the depth of our addiction, as well as debates over freedom of expression, the elusiveness of consensus, the challenges of enforcement and the tension between state regulation and private companies, this is hardly an easy task; and that is before we even consider artificial intelligence. But while we lapse into inaction, the civilisation that was built so devotedly and at such great cost by our forebears is being progressively hacked apart. It cannot withstand such an assault forever. It is incumbent upon all people of conscience to heed the plea with which the American social psychologist Jonathan Haidt concluded his bestselling book *The Anxious Generation*: 'New technologies are going to be disrupting our lives at a faster rate every year. Please join us in the quest to understand what is happening, what it's doing to us, and how to raise flourishing children amid the confusion.'[40]

Chapter Eight

WHO ARE WE ANYWAY?

The dying of the light

Ibn Khaldun, one of the greatest Arab intellectuals of the Middle Ages, who forms a presiding character in Simon Sebag Montefiore's masterpiece *The World*, wrote: 'Many nations suffered a physical defeat, but that's never marked their end. Yet when a nation becomes the victim of psychological defeat, that marks the end.'[1] Reading those lines, many people in the West may experience a chill of recognition. Although countries may differ quite widely, signs of defeat are everywhere. This is the case whether one uses subjective markers like unhappiness, poor life satisfaction, social incoherence, decaying trust in institutions, pessimism, and lack of purpose, national pride and shared culture; or social metrics like rising numbers of deaths of despair, deteriorating mental health, levels of immigration and integration, crime rates, obesity, welfare dependency, plummeting birth rates, addiction and decaying family bonds; or economic measures like poor productivity, deindustrialisation, soaring levels of national debt, high taxation, crippling health and welfare spending, uncontrolled rates of inflation and unemployment and trade imbalances; or geopolitical factors like the rising threat of war (combined with poor defence preparedness), the continued blight of terrorism, the fall in numbers of world democracies and increase in authoritarian regimes, political instability, degenerating quality of governance and fraying international alliances. Despite positive trends that can be found in areas like infant mortality and scientific and medical advances, there are simply too many symptoms of an underlying malaise.

As I have argued, to this long list of measures of ill health we may add the intensity of hatred towards the Jews. This oldest bigotry is so fundamental because it flows from our most primordial fears and prejudices, and arises with greater virulence when these become agitated and unchecked. Disinformation; poor education, in the broadest sense; an ebbing of our sense of the nation's place in the world; cultural impoverishment; social resentment; economic hardship; fear of conflict; ethical rudderlessness; an absence of beauty; tribalism; fanaticism; the rise of demagogues; under such afflictions, our long muscle memory of antisemitism naturally targets the Jew as a way of explaining things, a howl of anguish and consternation, a kind of therapy.

Other stars of foreboding are coming into alignment. The advent of new communications technology has always fed the hatred of Jews. The invention of the printing press enabled the Protestant reformation triggered by the antisemitic demagogue Martin Luther, who also catalysed the banishment of Jews from many German cities in their largest expulsion in medieval history. The Dreyfus Affair in France dovetailed with the wide availability of newspapers. The Nazis brainwashed their population by relying upon the new medium of radio. The antisemitic conspiracy theories that multiplied after the 9/11 attacks were enabled by the emergence of the internet. The mania of hatred that followed October 7 rests in large part upon the sudden dominance of social media.

Moreover, many fear that Jews have never in history enjoyed stability for more than eighty years before the oldest hatred reawakens. That is the period that has elapsed since Auschwitz; as the passing of the last survivor approaches, half of Americans under the age of thirty think that the Holocaust was either definitely or possibly a myth,[2] 46 per cent of young people in France have never heard of it and a third of young Britons could not name a single death camp.[3] Antisemitism is soaring worldwide. Israel's eightieth birthday, meanwhile, falls in 2028.

Antisemitism, and its latest incarnation of Israelophobia, are signs of the 'psychological defeat' of a nation. When people are confused by the overwhelming evils threatening their families, their communities, their nation and their world, and feel on a deep level a lack of control over their lives, and have lost touch with the social norms of decency and consideration that previously acted as the glue that held their society harmoniously together, the conditions are ripe for the pogrom. On several occasions since October 7, most notoriously in Amsterdam in November 2024, we have seen that bloody tradition breaking through once again in the West, though the perpetrators had largely imported their prejudices into our culture from elsewhere. If Ibn Khaldun identified *asabiyya*, or social cohesion, as a vital ingredient for wellbeing, we find ourselves in some trouble.[4]

Given the scale of the challenge, it is all too easy to lapse into pessimism. In a moving column in April 2025, the Conservative politician and writer Daniel Hannan observed that 'liberal individualism has never had a mass following. Human beings have a tendency to categorise, to tribalise and, indeed, to moralise – that is, to tell others what is good for them'.[5] Arguing that 'the golden age of free speech and free association looks increasingly like an interregnum', he concluded that 'the emphasis on personal autonomy that elevated and ennobled Western civilisation is being lost. We're going to miss it more than we know'. This may very well be true. But it seems to me that choosing to go gentle into that good night will only bring down the blinds far more quickly. Let us test the inexorability of decline by raging against it.

Turnip seeds

At its heart, the problem is how society can change in order to conserve itself. Or to put it another way, to change in order to remain the same, in a rapidly changing world. The way forward can only lie in finding proper answers to two important questions. Firstly, what changes do we wish to see in society if we are to avoid the final defeat? Secondly, how can we go about effecting such changes? The first may be answered by drawing upon the wisdom that informed the founding principles of the West, while for the second we must turn to behavioural science. Before we look at those things, however, let's get one subject out of the way: immigration.

In his famous essay *The Lion and the Unicorn*, famously written during the Blitz when 'highly civilized human beings are flying overhead, trying to kill me', George Orwell grappled with the idea of a nation's resilience in the face of generational change. English civilisation, he wrote, 'is continuous, it stretches into the future and the past, there is something in it that persists, as in a living creature. What can the England of 1940 have in common with the England of 1840? But then, what have you in common with the child of five whose photograph your mother keeps on the mantelpiece? Nothing, except that you happen to be the same person'. The world of 1940, he added, was far more volatile than ever before. 'England, together with the rest of the world, is changing,' he wrote. 'And like everything else it can change only in certain directions, which up to a point can be foreseen. That is not to say that the future is fixed, merely that certain alternatives are possible and others not. A seed may grow or not grow, but at any rate a turnip seed never grows into a parsnip. It is therefore of the deepest importance to try and determine what England *is*, before guessing what part England *can play* in the huge events that are happening.'

The difficulty today is defining what England, or Britain, or Europe, or the United States, or the West, *are*, before we consider how we would like them restored. Above all, uncertainty on this point has been imposed upon us by successive centrist fundamentalist governments, who have opened the doors to the world without properly considering the consequences and have dismantled the building blocks of our culture. Most egregiously, they did all this while silencing naysayers as 'racist' and selling the public supposed benefits of immigration that never materialised.

As the journalist Allister Heath remarked in the *Daily Telegraph* in May 2025: 'We were told that largescale immigration was necessary to boost productivity, and yet its rate of growth has diminished; we were assured it would save the NHS, and yet it is in crisis; we were told we needed workers, and yet, of the 956,000 visas issued in the year to December 2024, only 210,000 went to main applicants in all work categories.'[6] More than anything else, this disdain for the bond of trust between citizens and their government is responsible for the widespread rage and disillusionment with politics that dominates in Britain today.

A similar story can be told in countries across the Continent and further afield. One of the deep consequences of such rapid population change is that the glue which coheres our pluralistic, free and flourishing society – the very thing that allows for the successful integration of new arrivals in the first place – is being dissolved. Britain's secular system of government allows a home to people of different faiths, with different family lives and festivals, so long as they share and respect our common language, national religion, values and social norms. For such harmony to arise between people, wherever they were born, these demands must be non-negotiable. Under the influence of centrist fundamentalism, however, we didn't even negotiate them. We gave them away. Over time, the effect was a fading of what we may unfashionably call our 'traditions', which are not, as Sir Roger Scruton pointed out, 'arbitrary rules and conventions' but 'answers that have been discovered to enduring questions'.

Traditions, and their broader family of customs, are vital to the elusive experience of us-ness that Orwell was seeking to pin down in *The Lion and the Unicorn*. 'Yes, there *is* something distinctive and recognisable in English civilisation,' he wrote. 'It is somehow bound up with solid breakfasts and gloomy

Sundays, smoky towns and winding roads, green fields and red pillar-boxes. It has a flavour of its own.'

But it is much more than that. The traditions and customs of honouring our dead on Remembrance Sunday, and celebrating the failure of the 1605 Gunpowder Plot on November 5, and the monarchy, and Christmas, and Boxing Day, and knowing which clothes are appropriate for which occasion, and 'ladies first', and queuing, and rooting for the underdog, and the principle of fair play, and self-effacing irony, and mickey-taking, and pubs, and a preoccupation with the weather, and jumble sales, and putting the kettle on in a crisis, are more than just quirks. They are what make us us. Often, customs are absorbed from newcomers; adopting foreign dishes, such as curry, as part of our national cuisine is in itself a wonderful example of how the invisible hand of tradition resolves the potential tension of people of different cultures living together.

'Only if people are held together by stronger bonds than the bond of free choice can free choice be raised to the prominence that the new political order promised,' Sir Roger wrote. 'And those stronger bonds are buried deep in the community, woven by custom, ceremony, language and religious need. Political order, in short, requires cultural unity, something that politics itself can never provide.'

A similar story can be told about other countries, of course. In America, it may be pledging allegiance to the flag, guns and rock 'n' roll; in France, it may be *laïcité*, extramarital sex and public intellectuals; in Australia, it may be 'mateship', boomerangs and barbecues. Our traditions, Sir Roger argued, are 'tacit, shared, embodied in social practices and inarticulate expressions. Those who adopt them are not necessarily able to explain them, still less to justify them . . . these are things we acquire by immersion in society'. It goes without saying that newcomers cannot share in our customs if they cannot speak the language. As the rate of immigration has outstripped our capacity for assimilation, our traditions have become overwhelmed and begun to recede, giving many people the sense of being adrift in their old communities. A poll by the More in Common think tank in May 2025 found that half of British adults felt a sense of disconnection, while 44 per cent testified to sometimes feeling like a 'stranger' in their own country.[7] Remove our customs and this is the result: slow defeat. As Sir Roger summarises: 'Political order, in short, requires cultural unity.'[8]

This is an insight with a heritage. Edmund Burke offered a similar warning in his 1790 masterwork *Reflections on the Revolution in France*. Without the invisible wisdom of tradition, he wrote, 'the commonwealth itself would, in a few generations, crumble away, be disconnected into the dust and powder of individuality, and at length dispersed to all the winds of heaven'. Almost 250 years later, aside from the waiting lists, the overcrowding, the sectarianism, the crime rates, the straining public services and the housing crisis, the most deleterious consequence of the endless waves of immigration conjured by Blair and welcomed by his heirs are the mounds of dust and powder about our knees.

Join the club

So we are returned to the question: what *is* Britain? What is the West? Earlier in this book, we considered the enduring characteristics of our civilisation and found them to be rooted in Greek, Roman and Christian culture, containing such principles as the separation of powers and of church and state, individual rights, free association and so on. However imperfectly, these things continue to hold. But they are under great strain.

Britain and the other Western states that have opened the doors to all comers must accept that we are facing a new challenge and an uncharted future. How will the migration waves of the centrist fundamentalist period change us as a people? How positive will that be? A great many newcomers do not come from democratic cultures and as a share of the population their numbers are far greater than the Romans, Vikings or Normans. They may be economic migrants rather than conquerors, but their addition to the body politic may have equally profound consequences as the generations unfold. At this stage, all we know is that the West is in one of the greatest periods of flux that it has ever known.

Given this instability, we need to form a determined resolution to guide our future journey along the tramlines laid down by previous generations – whether codified, as in the Constitution of the United States, or rooted in precedent, as in Britain – that have given the world such extraordinary human flourishing.

At this point, we must begin to stake out a claim for what we would like our societies to become. Already we have examined in some detail the values, political culture and customs of the West, which range across the different countries but are united in spirit. For these to be conserved, we must suppress the potency of centrist fundamentalism, Islamist fanaticism, nationalist chauvinism and progressive radicalism, the four horsemen of our apocalypse. This would require a shift in norms and attitudes, which may be achieved both by robust government action and an awakening of the 'silent majority' who cherish their civilisation and desire to see it flourish once again.

To create the space for this restoration, however, it may be wise to consider calls for a halt – or at least a pause – to this decades-long experiment with the elastic limits of our culture. In the column cited above, Allister Heath proposed: 'We need a five-year moratorium on net migration – in other words, zero net migration until 2030, before returning to 1990s volumes. Given annual departures – 450,000 in 2023 – this would still at first allow a large number of arrivals, diminishing rapidly over the next few years, allowing the economy to adapt. This would allow the country to take stock, trust to be rebuilt and our creaking infrastructure and housing to catch up.' This may require unshackling ourselves from the European Convention of Human Rights and various other international treaties. Refugees, however, should be the exception; I would suggest that a programme of refugee visas, as I described earlier, properly managed, vetted and controlled, would be an advisable accompaniment to this policy. We cannot turn our backs on places like Hong Kong and Ukraine.

After so many years of helter-skelter immigration and the dulling effects of centrist fundamentalism, if we are to regain some control over our society's future, Heath's ideas deserve serious thought. The British tradition of tolerance and generosity, which is mirrored in other countries across the West, is not going anywhere. It has been abused for so long, however, that we are in danger of losing the very things that attract newcomers to our shores in the first place. We need time to allow the population to settle and for problems of integration and infrastructure to be resolved before we commence a new conversation about how much further we are prepared to allow our populations to expand, and how quickly. We must also develop a much more rigorous process by which foreigners may be granted citizenship, one that allows them to be welcomed 'into our culture, and not beside or against it', as Sir Roger put it.[9] We need to get ourselves back on our feet.

As Heath explains: 'Becoming British ought to become a lot more like joining a club: race or religion must not matter, but the applicant should need to show commitment, demonstrate how he or she will contribute, and explicitly pledge support to our democratic institutions and rule of law. Those who can't or won't make the commitment should either be given temporary visas or rejected. Citizenship ceremonies and the current vacuous "British values" are insufficient.'[10]

These are measures, of course, that lie within the purview of government rather than the individual. Although – as we will see – there is much that can be achieved by Burke's 'little platoons' of society if they rally behind a common goal, national leadership has a vital role to play. Britain provides an example of the broader ailments that dog the West; our attitude towards immigration in recent decades has led to a devaluing of citizenship that corresponds to the degradation of our culture and heritage led by the elites.

Consider our approach towards expelling those who should not be here. Over the last year, eye-catching cases have included an Iraqi asylum seeker who avoided deportation after pleading for time to 'make up a reason' why he should be allowed to remain;[11] an Iranian criminal who was permitted to stay so that he could cut his son's hair;[12] an Albanian convict who received leniency because video calls would be 'harsh' on his stepson; another who argued that his son had an aversion to foreign chicken nuggets; a Pakistani drug dealer who was allowed to stay so he could teach his son about Islam;[13] and a paedophile of the same nationality who avoided deportation as it would be 'unduly harsh' on his own children.[14] There are many, many more.

Combined with our habit of granting illegal arrivals hotel rooms, mobile phones, healthcare and an allowance, at a cost of £4.6 million a day last year, equivalent to fifteen new hospitals over a decade, an impression is created of profound gullibility. Foreign-born residents occupy 48 per cent of London's social housing and 72 per cent of Somalis in Britain live at the taxpayers' expense.[15] How has this benefitted us? In May 2025, the government agreed to support a dog that had entered Britain illegally on a small boat.[16] Our country is becoming an international joke.

The demoralising effects upon the existing population, and the resentment that it stokes, cannot be underestimated. If this is to change, the government must show that it understands the preciousness of its citizens and their heritage by taking legal, diplomatic and policing steps to deport foreign criminals without prevarication. This includes, of course, Islamist radicals who incite hatred against Jews and the West, towards whom there must be absolute intolerance. Rather than being treated to hotel rooms funded by the taxpayer, those who choose to arrive in this country illegally, rather than using a safe route provided for refugees, should be held securely and without luxuries and deprived of the ability to work in the black market until they too are deported.

It would also be wise to consider the example of liberal Denmark, which has become the toughest European country on immigration in recent years. In the belief that open borders harm the poorest in society the most, its leftwing leader has implemented a hardline approach towards illegal arrivals, accompanied by strict laws on integration for those allowed to stay. As long ago as 2016, Danish border police started confiscating money and jewellery from newcomers to contribute towards the cost of their upkeep. This created a powerful deterrent.

Fast forward to today and residence permits are typically for short periods only; applicants must show a proficiency in Danish within six months; and their dress is tightly controlled. Parallel societies may be forcibly broken up, even if that means the physical destruction of social housing. Criminals are barred from citizenship. Those who don't pass muster are expelled, asylum seekers are repatriated and since 2021 the country has followed a 'zero refugee' policy.[17]

Particular measures may suit some countries better than others in the short term, but what matters are the longer-term results. One measure of success is that levels of antisemitism in the West die down, even – if this is not too much to ask – when Israel is forced to take military action against jihadis in defence of its citizens.

A law unto themselves

There can be no two ways about it: there are many important areas of society that only the authorities can fix. It goes without saying that exerting any influence over our borders lies beyond the power of ordinary citizens. Similarly, it is the responsibility of our leaders to protect our societies for future generations by banning the Muslim Brotherhood, Islamic Revolutionary Guards Corps and other such groups, and to place sanctions upon those universities which throw their Jewish students to the wolves, along with our common values, by indulging the young Stalins on their campuses. Authoritarianism must be avoided but far harsher penalties, such as expulsion, can be imposed upon students who cross the line between free expression and intolerable behaviour.

Especially since October 7, Jews have endured unacceptable levels of antisemitism on campus, including physical assaults, bomb threats, mockery and 'baby killer' slurs. One girl was taunted by her flatmate about her 'Jewish nose' and 'silly little Jewish brain'. A student at Swansea found bacon taped to the door of her room, while at a Cambridge college, a Jewish undergraduate was told over dinner to 'turn to the side so that he could gauge the size of my nose'.[18] This speaks of a culture of radicalism. Already, progressive fanatics have started turning violent. Two young Israeli diplomats were gunned down in Washington, DC, in May 2025, and a United Healthcare boss was murdered in Manhattan in what police called a 'symbolic takedown' of a figure of capitalist authority in December 2024.

The fact that this atmosphere is tolerated by the centrist fundamentalist authorities – or even enabled by their own radical sympathies – is nothing less than shameful. When Ronald Reagan, as governor of California, faced widespread civil disobedience in the sixties, he took flaccid university officials to task. 'All of it began the first time some of you who know better, and are old enough to know better, let young people think that they had the right to choose the laws they would obey so long as they were doing it in the name of social protest,' he declared, demanding that they take action.[19] Donald Trump picked up the baton in 2025, cutting federal funding to colleges that refused to comply. A similar approach must be taken across the West. As Douglas Murray told me on *The Brink*: 'I just really wish that people would realise that, like other places across the public square, universities must be de-politicised. It's not that there should be an endless litigation of foreign conflicts or domestic issues. They should be de-politicised.'

The same must apply to Islamist fanatics. If we are to restore order to our societies, the law must be applied equally: it is no good having policemen use horses and batons when the far-right takes to the streets, while employing a softly, softly attitude towards Gaza demonstrations. What message do these double standards send to the public? In Britain, it was clear from the start that leaders in several of the groups behind the Gaza marches had links to Hamas. Some had been pictured meeting terror chiefs in Gaza and had openly expressed support for the jihadis, in apparent defiance of British law.[20] Why were they allowed to proceed like that? Of course, the Palestine campaign groups call upon extensive legal firepower to steamroll the authorities, but this should have been confronted with determination and resolved.

Meanwhile, a London imam who called for Allah to 'destroy Jewish homes' in a sermon two weeks after October 7 was not even held responsible for a 'non-crime hate incident', a measure that has been applied liberally to those on the right. In one absurd example, a Jewish counterprotester was arrested by the Metropolitan police and accused of 'racially or religiously aggravated harassment' after he briefly held up a cartoon of the notorious terrorist Hassan Nasrallah, the late leader of Hezbollah.[21] He was held overnight and his house was searched by six police officers before the case was eventually dropped.

In one particularly notorious incident, Lucy Connolly, a nursery worker traumatised by the death of her baby, was locked up for thirty-one months for posting, 'mass deportation now, set fire to all the fucking hotels full of the bastards for all I care . . . if that makes me racist so be it', in the febrile aftermath of the stabbing of three little girls in Southport in October 2024. She was held without bail and later lost an appeal. These measures were harsher than those applied to a rapist, paedophile and terrorist fundraiser around the same time,[22] let alone that imam in London. Meanwhile, between 2021 and 2024, police failed to solve a single burglary in half of the country, and brought a charge in just 6 per cent of crimes.[23] To add insult to injury, when Connolly received news of her failed appeal in her cell, the government was busy releasing dangerous convicts early to free up space in overcrowded prisons.

What all this illustrates is that although legislation has its place, it is subservient to cultural norms and can be hijacked by unspoken priorities. The centrist fundamentalist belief system that cascades from government causes our police and courts to absorb double standards and implement them. Although it is never articulated, the true enemy is seen as the far-right – a category that has often been expanded to include anybody who does not share progressive views – while leftist radicals and Islamists are viewed as basically fine, or even supported. Indeed, when Sir William Shawcross's 2023 review of the government's 'Prevent' counterextremism programme found that jihadism was the greatest threat to Britain, it provoked fury from the left and allegations of 'Islamophobia'. Enforcement of the law, which is supposed to be blind to politics, is becoming an instrument of the culture wars.

Sometimes, as in the case of the Equality Act 2010 – which elevated 'protected' group identities above traditional individual rights, needlessly ushering in identity politics – laws can simply be bad. Sometimes, of course, they can be good and effective: legislation against sexual harassment, for example, helped create new social norms and taboos that helped repress it. Laws can also empower citizens who wish to do the right thing in an unhealthy cultural climate. Before the introduction of the 1964 Civil Rights Act, some restaurants that were imposing segregation lobbied the government to outlaw the practice. Why did they ask to be subjected to tighter laws? The answer was that they wanted to serve black people but lacked the courage to do so. Dropping segregation would widen their clientele and improve their business, but it was frowned upon under prevailing social norms. Once the legislation was passed, however, the restaurants could start serving black customers without incurring a social cost.[24]

Similarly, when Britain's Supreme Court delivered a landmark ruling that under the Equality Act 2010, a 'woman' was a biological female as recorded at birth, it released a wave of unabashed common sense across the country. People and institutions suddenly felt liberated to articulate their simple belief that a man was a man and a woman was a woman, without fear of social or legal censure, and without fear of cancellation.

Sometimes, however, laws may be undermined by the climate of norms in which they sit. A particularly egregious example was that of the child rape gangs in Britain, which took place while police and social workers looked the other way. The problem wasn't that we lacked the laws to prohibit such crimes. The problem was that these laws were not enforced. Rather than carrying out their duty to protect the public, figures of authority chose to obey the prevalent habits of centrist fundamentalism, which held greater weight in their minds.

Similarly, section 406 of the Education Act 1996 forbids 'political indoctrination' in schools. It says: 'The local education authority, governing body and head teacher shall forbid . . . the promotion of partisan political views in the teaching of any subject.' Moreover, section forty-three of the Education Act 1986, which covers colleges and universities, enshrines 'freedom of speech within the law'. Few people would stand against such principles. Yet this aspect of legislation is routinely flouted all over the country. Speaking on condition of anonymity, one teacher told me that a colleague had openly described her role as a teacher as 'advancing social justice'. Staff had been encouraged to gather to take 'anti-racism oaths' in the staffroom, 'equity, diversity and equality ambassadors' were found in every department, and external agencies pushing unabashed critical race theory had been brought in to give the school 'anti-racist' action plans.

A few years ago, at a parents' evening at our local secondary school, I noticed a display about the Holocaust on the wall. Surrounding it were posters supporting Black Lives Matter, a group viewed by many as stoking racial division. These included a quote from radical activist Ijeoma Oluo positing the controversial concept, deriving from critical race theory, that society is structurally racist and that all white people are inherently bigoted; it brought to mind the remark made by Whoopi Goldberg in 2022 that history's worst racist genocide was 'not about actual race' as it had taken place between 'two groups of white people', for which she was suspended as a television presenter.[25]

Beside it were posters promoting radical gender ideology, including the disputed theory that there are more than two types of gender, such as 'transgender', 'cisgender', 'non-binary', 'gender fluid' and 'genderqueer'. The display also featured material suggesting that the author J.K. Rowling was transphobic and lauding the actor Daniel Radcliffe's opposition to her without dignifying – or even portraying – her belief in the primacy of biological sex, with which the vast majority of people agree.

I wrote to the headmistress, explaining that promoting such radical views contravened the Education Act. 'This is, once again, a deeply political and partisan position that appears to be presented to children as fact,' I wrote. The material was removed and blamed on activist teachers who had created norms of their own in the education system. This demonstrated how easily the law may be pushed aside when dominant cultural trends lean in the opposite direction.

Chapter Nine

THE SCIENCE OF CHANGE

Unsilent majority

If we are to see a renewal of our society and the restoration of its values, it is vital to understand the science of group behaviour and cultural change. In 2016, three researchers – Leonardo Bursztyn from the University of Chicago, Georgy Egorov at Northwestern University and Stefano Fiorin from the University of California – conducted an experiment shortly before Trump was elected.[1] They gave participants control of a budget and told them that they would personally be paid a dollar for every donation they authorised to the Federation for American Immigration Reform, whose founder had written: 'For European-American society and culture to persist requires a European-American majority, and a clear one at that.' They found that those who were convinced that Trump would become president were happy to make the donation to the anti-immigration group publicly, whereas those who doubted his victory preferred to remain anonymous.

This study was cited by the American behavioural economist Cass Sunstein – who developed the influential 'nudge' theory –

in his excellent 2019 book *How Change Happens*. 'The central point is that information about Trump's expected victory altered social norms, making many people far more willing to give publicly,' the former Obama adviser wrote. 'Anonymity no longer matters, apparently because Trump's election has weakened the social norm against supporting anti-immigrant groups.'[2]

This research is an example of how powerful cultural changes can swim in the wake of political leadership. It is no surprise that under decades of downward pressure from centrist fundamentalist elites, often combined with progressive radicalism, society has naturally adapted to accommodate such self-undoing views, and people have come to propagate them even when they run contrary to their own deeply held beliefs.

In 1969, in a televised address to the American people amid widespread demonstrations against the war in Vietnam, President Richard Nixon famously said: 'And so tonight, to you, the great silent majority of my fellow Americans, I ask for your support . . . Let us be united for peace. Let us also be united against defeat.' Ever since, the notion of the 'silent majority' has been an essential part of political thinking, both during campaigns and when governing. It is all too easy – so the wisdom runs – to wrongly conclude that the views of the vocal minority represent those of the country. An astute politician will be able to read the centre of gravity of the people, without being distracted by the froth.

Since October 7, I have argued that the silent majority of Britons, and indeed of populations across the West, saw through the media bias and Hamas propaganda. These, I thought, were the people who felt in their bones that in a conflict between a democratic ally and jihadi butchers, there was no question where their support must lie. These were people, in other words, who remained in touch with the basic values of the democratic West. In a column for the *Sunday Telegraph* in December 2023, I wrote: 'Overseas, Jews are first slaughtered then scolded for defending themselves; meanwhile, their enemies hide behind babies, prepare the next atrocity and beckon the television cameras. At home, society seems divided between those who hate the Jews for fighting back and those who suspect they had it coming in the first place. The silent majority remains silent. What will it take to rouse them?'[3]

At first, there was some hope. Immediately after October 7, support for Israel among Britons rose to 21 per cent, and just 15 per cent backed the Palestinians. But then the Hamas propaganda strategy of human sacrifice kicked in and was embraced by the media, while Israel concentrated on winning the shooting war and fumbled the battle for hearts and minds. A rally in Manchester just days after the Hamas assault followed a large banner saying, 'Manchester supports Palestinian resistance'. Police officers walked alongside to ensure that those holding it could march freely. By 2 November, a week after Israeli forces had invaded Gaza, public sympathies were neck and neck at 19 per cent. Three weeks later, Israel was behind on 18 per cent, and the Palestinians hit 21 per cent. It was all downhill from there. These days, the gulf between those supporting our democratic ally and those backing their jihadi butchers is shamefully wide, with the majority skewed in favour of the latter. A similar story can be told across the West.

The media holds a great deal of the blame for this moral confusion. Although tens of thousands of jihadis have been killed in Gaza and many more wounded, the only footage that is broadcast to the world shows dead or injured civilians. This furnishes the public with 'evidence' that Israel is waging war on the innocent. People feel like they have seen it with their own eyes. As a result, anybody who tries to argue correctly that the Jewish state is harming proportionately fewer innocent people than any other army in history gets dismissed out of hand. As we have seen, Hamas supports this distortion by manipulating the casualty figures, telling the world that most of the dead are women and children, as if the IDF works some special voodoo that leaves the men unharmed. Once again, the media reports this with only the lightest dusting of context.

But the decline in support for Israel – and by implication the betrayal of the values of the West – may not have been as steep as the polls suggest. In a variety of ways, cultural pressure may cause individuals to internalise the prevailing social norms and repress their own dissenting instincts, sometimes burying them even from themselves. 'If a victim of sexual harassment genuinely believes that "it's not a big deal", it might be because it's most comfortable or easiest to believe that it's not a big deal', Sunstein writes.[4] So emerges the silent majority.

Kindred spirits

After October 7, the relentless propaganda and activism from all angles created a 'social cascade' in which supporting Israel rapidly became taboo in many parts of society. Although there are obvious differences, cascades of the past have involved shifts in attitude towards things like smoking and recycling, or towards black people during the civil rights movement or Jews in Nazi

Germany. Lacking firm convictions of their own, in the months following October 7, many people started to follow a pro-Gaza position simply because everybody around them appeared to do so, making it seem like the correct way of thinking. As this new norm became embedded, it was reinforced by four penalties identified by Jon Elster, the Norwegian philosopher and political theorist at Columbia University, in his 1994 paper *Rationality, Emotions, and Social Norms: Embarrassment, anxiety, guilt and shame.*[5] In many milieus, especially on the left, this uncomfortable quartet became the price of expressing support for the Jewish state. Many people lost friends and experienced an upheaval of their political alignments. Quite the deterrent.

In that potent climate, a kind of brainwashing may take place. Broadly, those affected can be split into three groups. In the most straightforward cases, people may remain aware that they hold unfashionable opinions but keep quiet to avoid reputational damage, loss of earnings or another social cost. They may even falsify their views, assuming a façade of hostility towards Israel that they do not feel deep inside, like actors on a stage.

In the second group, people disavow their own instincts and conform internally to the social norm, while failing to jettison their original views entirely. It often begins when they draw the conclusion that as nothing can be done to change things, they might as well keep their mouths shut. This then metastasises psychologically until they develop 'partially adaptive preferences', in which they grow convinced they have embraced hostility towards Israel but continue to be troubled by a quiet internal voice that tells them a different story.

Some may respond by attempting to silence the dissonant voice of their conscience, while others may grapple with it, trying to decide if it represents their true feelings. For example, in the Manchester Arena in 2017, when the security guard Kyle Lawler failed to stop the suicide bomber because he feared his own 'Islamophobia', he appeared to have internalised unhealthy social norms after years of browbeating by the elites. After an internal tussle, he became paralysed. The man didn't know what he thought any more.

If the culture changes, however, and the atmosphere becomes less repressive, people in this second group may feel liberated to give that voice full expression, again with great relief at the psychological wholeness it brings.

The third group is the one most deeply affected by social brainwashing. For those who are very concerned with the approval of their peers, it is frighteningly easy to become so dissociated from their own moral instincts that they lose touch with what they may have thought in the first place. Often, they do not know that this has happened, as they do not have the experience of being suppressed. They simply believe that they side against Israel, or have become pro-immigration, or believe that trans women are women, and even forget that they once held different views. When such people are taken out of their toxic environment, however, and placed among people who are not saturated with conformity, they may find their own hidden sentiments bubbling happily to the surface, making them feel liberated to articulate views that they did not even know they had. 'That is one reason that stunning surprises are inevitable,' Sunstein observes.

One of the effects of this silencing of unfashionable views is to create the false impression that everybody thinks the same way. On university campuses, or in the media or the arts, progressives may assume that everybody agrees with them, simply because conservatives have learned to hold their tongues. In this environment, dissenters move anonymously, like conspirators. This is not a sign of a healthy society.

On occasion, however, one of the silenced may catch a rebellious glint of a kindred spirit in the glance of a colleague, or after a few drinks, people will exclaim, 'I'd never have guessed that she was *gender critical*,' or 'did you know he was a *Christian*?' Sometimes, breaking cover may have disastrous consequences. But given the right circumstances, and if carried out with enough conviction, it may effect a change of social norms. This process of becoming 'unleashed', as Sunstein calls it, from the confines of social repression, is the starting point when it comes to restoring a voice to the silent majority and healing our society.

In psychological terms, the process may be quite deep. Once given the opportunity, people may find that they were harbouring feelings that they had not previously acknowledged, even to themselves. Or they may have been aware of those subterranean views but had written them off as incompatible with mainstream society; unearthing them may require courage amid an attendant risk of being socially snubbed.

The effects of these different ways in which the silent majority is kept silent may cause polling data to become unreliable. Consider a 2018 study of attitudes towards women working outside the home in Saudi Arabia,[6] where they customarily require permission from their husbands before doing so. The research, led by Bursztyn along with sociologist Dr Alessandra González and economist David Yanagizawa-

Drott, and cited by Sunstein, found that the overwhelming majority of Saudi men privately had no problem with their wives having jobs, but they kept these views to themselves in the mistaken belief that they were out of step with the social norm. They would probably have fallen into the first group listed above, the ones who resemble actors on a stage. When they learned from the researchers that most men shared their secret liberalism, however, they were emboldened to act upon their instincts and give their wives permission to look for a job. This was greatly liberating for both the men and, of course, the women.

Change entrepreneurs

On a drizzly London morning in November 2023, while we were still reeling from the pogroms in southern Israel, my family, friends and I joined a hundred thousand people marching through the centre of the city to raise our voices against the historic tsunami of antisemitism in which many of us had been engulfed since the Hamas atrocities. This was a quite remarkable event. Those trudging through the streets did not present a familiar coalition. There were many Jews, of course, from a spectrum of denominations, but there were also a great many Christians of different sorts, as well as Sikhs, Hindus, a small number of sympathetic Muslims and even a smattering of Buddhists, some of whom had travelled from the other end of the country. This was a most unusual rally, made up of unusual activists. Most people there were very unfamiliar with making a fuss in public, and some had never attended a demonstration before.

There were bobble hats. There were flasks of tea and children and paperbacks in pockets. There were attempts at chanting that were filled with awkwardness, and nobody wanted to be the last person left shouting a slogan when everybody else had stopped. There were mobile phones in wallet cases that flapped open when people took a video. There were gentle and self-effacing placards saying things like 'Dear Racists, Curb Your Enthusiasm' and many spontaneous yet vaguely apologetic renditions of 'God Save the King'. There were many expressions of a yearning for peace and much sympathy for the innocent victims of the war on both sides. The march had been preceded by a thoroughly Jewish argument between the various groups wishing to claim credit for the event. People ate sandwiches under brollies. There were jokes about the number of Jews and no catering. At the start of the march, police officers lining the route faced inwards, looking for troublemakers in the crowd, but by the end they were looking outwards into the streets, scanning for aggression towards us. When it was all over, one senior officer remarked that the demonstrators had only said two words to him: 'thank' and 'you'.

If there could ever be a scene showing the mobilisation of a silent majority, this was it. Here was the true beating heart of Britain and the West, and the beleaguered Jews were at the centre of it. For many I spoke to that day, the experience was a profoundly healing one. For weeks, people had been suffering in isolation, looking out at a world that seemed possessed by madness in which up was down and left was right. Now we realised that we were not alone. The depressing social norms in which we had been embedded – the result of an extraordinary propaganda effort on the part of centrist fundamentalists and

Islamist and progressive radicals – were lifted and we could finally raise our voices as friends.

This makes for a powerful metaphor for the change we need to see in society. Just as a cascade effect took place following October 7 in which the West slowly bent against itself and lent its support to Hamas, whether implicitly or explicitly (in May 2025, with their hostages chained in dungeons, the jihadis officially congratulated the leaders of Britain, France and Canada after they jointly condemned Israel) there is no reason why a social cascade couldn't turn in the opposite direction.

This isn't just about Israel. It is about the reawakening of the cherished values of the West that gave the world the greatest flourishing in history and now find themselves under grave threat. If a society can move against smoking, and racial segregation, and bigotry towards homosexuals, and if people can thumb their noses at the elites by voting for Brexit, and if the 'N-word' can become an almost superstitious taboo, and if postwar Japan can be demilitarised and democratised, then with enough determination and a bit of luck, we can regain those things that we have lost. We can revive a world of sanity in which Jews are not a target, humiliating a wartime leader in the Oval Office is viewed with disgust, Nazi fetishes are once again deplored, Islamist fanatics are no longer indulged, and we allow people to dress as they please while being permitted to laugh when told that a man literally is a woman. Over time, the previously unthinkable can become the accepted wisdom. For this to happen, we need one type of people above all. I like to think of them as 'change entrepreneurs'.

Sunstein, who christened them 'norm entrepreneurs' in his 1996 paper 'Social Norms and Social Roles', describes these brave souls as 'rebels, by nature of circumstance', for whom 'defiance of social norms, taken as such, might be a benefit rather than a cost'. In the right constellation of circumstances, they may spark 'norm bandwagons' and 'norm cascades', as they blaze a trail for more timid souls to follow, creating a whoosh effect.[7] Like the boy who pointed out that the emperor had no clothes, these people have the courage necessary to speak their minds, coupled with the conviction required to help others break free from the suffocating constraints of absurd or harmful social norms. The boldness to speak out alone isn't enough, however; it must be accompanied by a bloody-minded spirit that can change the mood, making those who still obey the old norms look like sheep. Wake up, says the change entrepreneur, shaking society by the shoulders. We all know right from wrong. Come alive.

Backward trousers

The social cascade, if it occurs, will certainly involve the unleashing of the silent majority, as during the civil rights uprising in the United States. But it might also involve the emergence of new norms so compelling that those who never held an affinity for such values become swept up in the cascade. Some people, in other words, may not be unleashed so much as influenced. 'Probably it is true enough that the great majority are rarely capable of thinking independently, that on most questions they accept views which they find ready-made, and that they will be equally content if born or coaxed into one set of beliefs or another,' wrote the philosopher Friedrich Hayek in *The Road to Serfdom*.

If this awakening results in political change, a new government may enact legal reforms that consolidate it. Society may start to take on new everyday beliefs, as happened with the successful normalisation of seatbelts between the late sixties and early eighties, or the criminalisation of drunk driving, both of which were enabled by new laws. Society may turn its back on the spread of Palestine cultishness and all it represents, as even those without firm convictions jump on a new and healthier bandwagon. It is certainly not impossible to imagine such a cascade. All across the West, people have had enough. Why should this anger continue to feed the various tribes of the new radicalism, rather than powering the restoration of our moral inheritance that the silent majority craves?

Given the numbers of citizens who do not acknowledge, or in some cases even know, what they believe, it is not easy to identify a moment when the touchpaper of a cascade may be lit. Many people suffer under social norms that they dislike, but it is not clear that jettisoning them in public will necessarily create the elusive bandwagon effect. Indeed, if the effort falls flat, the norm could become reinforced.

Think, for instance, of the American hip-hop duo Kris Kross, who shot to fame in the nineties, going quadruple platinum at the tender ages of twelve and thirteen. They tried to use this success to launch a new fashion trend: wearing their clothes backwards. The idea failed to catch on, however, leaving the two boys a laughing stock. Chris Smith, the older of the pair, ended up making a living selling clothing and home décor, while his younger partner, Chris Kelly, found himself running a daycare facility with his mother, while still wearing his trousers backwards; in 2013, he tragically died of a drug overdose.[8] It is fair to say that the efforts of Kris Kross made the public even more convinced that trousers were best worn the right way round.

This is why change entrepreneurs are so important. After October 7, a Mancunian journalist called Angela Epstein founded the Northern Advocacy Group (NAG), which coordinated email campaigns to 'NAG for Israel' and right particular wrongs, especially when it came to inaccurate reporting in the media. The NAGs just wouldn't shut up, and as a result they had a fair few successes. Along the way, they influenced others to challenge their assumptions, creating social momentum. (On the whole, Jewish mothers can make good change entrepreneurs. I think of the convoy that rolled out of north London during the Covid lockdowns, as they collectively defied meaningless government diktat to rescue their children from the universities in which they had been imprisoned. These women are an inspiration.)

On a larger scale, there may arise what Sunstein calls 'availability entrepreneurs', a kind of God-level change entrepreneur. These are people who campaign about a particular cause so vociferously that they render it 'available' to everybody, influencing large numbers. This can be especially effective when the cause in question taps into a body of resentment towards the status quo. One fine example was provided by the *Daily Telegraph* journalist Allison Pearson, who single-handedly took up the case of Lucy Connolly – the woman sentenced to a grossly disproportionate prison sentence after an offensive post on X – and shouted about it indefatigably. As a result, Connolly's plight as a 'political prisoner' became a matter of national debate, eventually even attracting the concern of the White House. It also made people more aware of the politicisation of the law, as well as the routine stifling of free speech, both of which have little to do with Britain's values.

In making this outrage 'available' to the public, facing down much scoffing and enmity from the centrist fundamentalist establishment, Pearson made the moment increasingly ripe for a social cascade. There are many other examples of such availability entrepreneurs. To begin with, they are prepared to be a lone voice in the wilderness, whatever the cost. As one of the change entrepreneurs in Ray Bradbury's dystopian novel *Farenheit 451* puts it: 'Don't ask for guarantees. And don't look to be saved in any one thing, person, machine, or library. Do your own bit of saving, and if you drown, at least die knowing you were heading for shore.' As momentum builds, others may be inspired to break their silence, encouraging even more people to do so. When the dam finally bursts, even those without firm convictions may be swept along in a new tide, causing a movement to which politicians will have to respond, if they have not done so already. There is no guarantee that this will happen, of course. Equally, it may be unleashed at the next election.

Embarrassment, anxiety, guilt and shame

One day, it could no longer be sexy to hate the Jews. Due to the unique position of antisemitism in our culture, the restoration of broad Western values, traditions and sensibilities would naturally stifle the radicalism that is oxygenating the oldest hatred. There will doubtless be great resistance, but it is hard to stand in the way of a social cascade. If fresh political leadership emerges that is in harmony with this movement, it could make the necessary legislative reforms and blaze a new path, providing powerful change entrepreneurialism. Then there will be no looking back.

Take the national flag, which has a profound significance in our sense of ourselves, both as individuals and as a nation. In the United States – whose citizens are aptly described by the American political scientist Samuel Huntington as 'a flag-oriented people' – great surges of flags accompany moments of national celebration, sorrow and solidarity. This is true to different extents across the world. 'Probably never in the past, however, was the flag as omnipresent as it was after September 11,' Huntington writes:

> It was everywhere: homes, businesses, automobiles, clothes, furniture, windows, storefronts, lampposts, telephone poles.
>
> In early October, 80 percent of Americans said they were displaying the flag, 63 percent at home, 29 percent on clothes, 28 percent on cars. Wal-Mart reportedly sold 116,000 flags on September 11 and 250,000 the next day, compared with 6,400 and 10,000 on the same days a year earlier. The demand for flags was ten times what it had been during the Gulf War; flag manufacturers went overtime and doubled, tripled, or quintupled production. The flags were physical evidence of the sudden and dramatic rise in the salience of national identity for Americans compared to their other identities.[9]

Given the power of the flag, when attempting to restore a national identity, normalising it is a good place to start. Not only will this cheer us up and revive our social bonds, it will also help to subdue antisemitism, since modern Jew-hatred is nothing if not a species of hatred of the West.

In 2012, David Cameron's government created a Behavioural Insights team to use the power of 'nudge' and other techniques to help shift popular norms. On one occasion, they drew upon the work of Robert Cialdini, a professor of psychology and marketing at Arizona State University and author of *Influence: The Psychology of Persuasion*, who found that people would be more likely to comply with a social norm if they knew that most other people were so doing. Seeing a collection of cyclists stopping at a red light, for instance, or observing that most people shun foul language, made individuals much more likely to do the same. Based on these principles, the Inland Revenue amended its letters to inform recipients that, for instance, 'nine out of ten people in your area pay their taxes on time'. It caused a 15 per cent drop in late payments, which would save the country £30 billion annually.[10]

The Covid years complicated our understanding of the use of 'nudges' in changing attitudes and behaviour, as well as damaging public confidence in it. But there's no reason why the careful use of such insights couldn't help future governments encourage and consolidate social restoration. In Britain, where the degeneration of national selfhood has caused an acute embarrassment in some quarters towards flying the national flag, the government might provide every school, university and place of worship with a Union Jack – as well as perhaps a George Cross, Saltire or Red Dragon – creating a social expectation of a celebration of our country. The campaign could be supported by availability entrepreneurs, programmes around national holidays and incentives.

If the cultural moment is not ripe for such an intervention, or it is rolled out in a cackhanded manner, such a policy could easily go the way of backward trousers. If deployed in the right way, however, and at the right moment, it could shine a spotlight on those radicals that may defy this trend, raising questions about why they are disinclined to conform. They may experience Jon Elster's four emotions of embarrassment, anxiety, guilt and shame, magnifying the pressure upon them and helping the new social norm to become embedded.

Take those Islamic communities that harbour hostility towards the '*kuffar*' countries where they live so freely. As things stand, given the hold exerted by the Muslim Brotherhood, embarrassment, anxiety, guilt and shame are more likely felt by those decent Muslims who would secretly like to fly our national flag above their mosque, perhaps in recognition of the millions of Muslims who fought for Britain during both World Wars. Reversing this sorry state of affairs would be a huge social boon. Extremists would be sidelined and mainstream Muslims could be more closely embraced by the national family. It is true, of course, that antisemitism is endemic to much of the Islamic world. But as we have seen, this was not always so; and if a social cascade may go in one direction, then with determination and a fair wind, it is not impossible to imagine it going in the other as well.

Such positive measures would need to be combined with a strict ban on the Muslim Brotherhood and other radicals, enforced relentlessly by the police and security services.

Together, this dual approach could evoke a cascade in society. Silent voices within the Islamic community may be unleashed. We may find more Muslim politicians representing a range of parties and views, not a rabble of sectarian independents exploiting a divisive conflict 3,000 miles away from their constituencies. In time, rather than hearing 29 per cent of British Muslims say that they support Hamas, a majority may find themselves free to back the West and even Israel.

It is worth bearing in mind that the 2024 Henry Jackson Society survey of the views of British Muslims,[11] which produced those disturbing results, would not have been able to record anyone keeping their true views hidden or repressed. Although the depth and scale of radicalism in Islamic communities is a very serious problem, and although it may indeed turn out to be indissoluble, it is not wrong to believe in the possibility of change. Bigger shifts have happened before, not least in the denazification of postwar Germany.

The baby and the bathwater

Consider the remarkable Bedouin Arabs, who, as Israeli Muslims, risked their lives to save their Jewish compatriots on October 7. Among them were four cousins, Dahesh, Ismail, Hamed and Rafi Alkrenawi, who together rescued some forty young people from the Supernova festival. 'Write this down,' Dahesh told reporters afterwards. 'This is very important for people to know. What happened there is not the Muslim religion. The Quran, our religion, our tradition, asks from us to help people, whether they are Jews or Arabs. This is not our religion that asks them to do this.'[12]

One of the things that allows such men to be patriotic Israelis in the face of widespread antisemitism in the Middle East is the strength of the national identity of which they are invited to partake. Not for Israel the habit of doing itself down, undermining its own history, culture and traditions and elevating those of others. Israel is nothing if not a society of strength, both in terms of its military and cultural might. It has a powerful national story. As it respects its own Jewish faith and tradition, Muslim citizens can be assured that theirs may be respected as well, as they become equals in a secular state. On Tel Aviv beach, women in bikinis stroll alongside those in hijabs, and mosques blare the Adhan from their minarets while Jews attend synagogues and Christians go to church. Muslims can assimilate, in other words, because there is something to assimilate into. Cultural renewal in the West, combined with the criminalisation and suppression of extremists, will allow more voices to emerge which denounce jihadism and express support for our values.

With radical groups banned, space would be created to help young people to move away from extremism they may have absorbed. Speaking on *The Brink*, Ayaan Hirsi Ali told me:

> I was brainwashed into hating Jews, growing up in a Muslim household in Somalia. We didn't have to be Islamists to hate Jews. We were just regular Muslims hating Jews. But because I studied in the Netherlands, I also went through the period of reckoning that the Dutch were going through about what they had done during the Holocaust. I was twenty-four years old when I first heard about the Holocaust, to my shame. But by 1998, when I went to Israel, I no longer hated the Jews.

Banning extremists may allow hardline interpretations of Islam to give way to a style of faith that is compatible with the West. In Hirsi Ali's view, a growing number of Muslims are 'ready' for such a change. 'I think there's a longing that most Muslims feel, just wanting to live in peace with one another, both as Muslims and with non-Muslims,' she said. 'They're basically saying, we live in a different time, we should modify our religion. But there's this struggle around who gets to have a last word about what to modify, and who has the authority to do that. These are the problems that twenty-first century Islam is struggling with.'

When I interviewed Ed Husain on *The Brink*, he emphasised that his deradicalisation as a teenager had occurred after an intervention from his father, who opposed jihadism from a conservative Muslim perspective. 'My father's heritage is originally from Yemen,' he told me. 'My family moved in the fourteenth century as traders and preachers into India and then my parents came to Britain. My mum's family to this day lives in Saudi Arabia, in Medina, and one of my cousins teaches in the prophet's mosque, so we have those credentials that over time forced me to rethink. Did I want to pursue their form of more mystical, rooted Islam? Or was I going to adopt this new Egyptian export called the Muslim Brotherhood?'

Vital to the subjugation of Islamist extremism, he said, were traditional Muslim figures who could command respect and create change from the inside. 'Banning the Muslim Brotherhood is absolutely right,' he said, 'but it's how we effect that ban, so that young Muslims realise that ideas of intolerance will not be tolerated here in the West. Muslims across the West have a home here but to maintain that home you've got to be friendly towards neighbours and those who have been on this land for millennia before us.' After the Egyptian leader Gamal Abdel Nasser executed Sayyid Qutb, whom Husain describes as 'the Lenin of the global Islamist movement', he was made into a martyr, Husain pointed out. 'This produced a more extreme form of Islamism that today we call jihadism, that led directly to the 9/11 terrorist attacks. So we ought to be careful as to how we deal with this problem. It's a very sensitive issue.' Of course, moderate Islamic voices are unlikely to emerge while the Muslim Brotherhood and other radical groups retain their iron grip on the community.

Globally, the reform of Islam may come not from the grassroots but from the leadership. 'For the last twenty-five years, we've been waiting for this silent majority of peace-loving Muslims to stand up, to organise, to get out there and say the Islamists don't speak for us,' Hirsi Ali told me. 'I haven't seen it.' In the Gulf, however, the seat of Sunni Islam, the United Arab Emirates has banned jihadi radicals, made peace with Israel and opened to the world without becoming Westernised. Its more powerful neighbour, Saudi Arabia, home of Mecca and Medina, is taking steps in the same direction, abandoning its former support for Wahabism, Salafism and jihadism and pursuing a programme of modernisation that may end up with an accord with the Jewish state. 'These are the changes that I find much more interesting than passively waiting for a large majority of Muslims to one day stand up to the Islamists and throw them out,' Hirsi Ali added.

Islamist fundamentalism, of course, is only one tribe of the new radicalism. Restoring our sense of self, coupled with firm but proportionate enforcement measures against radical disruptors, would help counter all of them. Seeing our flag taking its rightful place in the fabric of civic life, for instance, as it was for generations past and as it remains elsewhere, would act as a balm after decades of centrist fundamentalist repression; the rising military threat only lends this restoration a greater urgency. A similar buoyancy could follow the return of the national anthem. Until the sixties, it was even played at the end of films at the cinema. This isn't about nostalgia. We don't need the bathwater back, only the baby.

Society may not be able to retrieve all it has lost, but we can find new ways of articulating the old spirit. The school curriculum could be amended to include a greater focus on the positive aspects of our past, including our Christian heritage. These and similar measures would send the progressive radicals who are intent upon denigrating our history, culture and values a message that their views are roundly rejected by the mainstream, isolating rather than indulging them and sucking the wind out of their sails. One thing is certain: if society was healed to the extent that our flag and anthem were widely embraced once again, antisemitism would be squashed.

The intensity of resentment at the moral straitjacket of centrist fundamentalism, and the way this bitterness is already fuelling a radical backlash, suggest that the time for change may be coming. Of course, whether it will lead to a restoration of Western values is far from certain. It may spiral deeper into an age dominated by the new radicalism and the destruction of our democratic traditions. Avoiding this fate would likely rely upon the emergence of trailblazing and determined political leaders, activism by availability entrepreneurs, and any number of acts of historical serendipity, as well as an uprising of change entrepreneurs from different walks of life.

All those willing must embrace the spirit voiced by Percy Bysshe Shelley in 1819:

> *And rise like Lions after slumber*
> *In unvanquishable number*
> *Shake your chains to earth like dew*
> *Which in sleep had fallen on you –*
> *You are many – they are few.*

It may happen on a broad historical canvas, equivalent to the abolition of slavery, the collapse of communism or the triumph of the civil rights movement; or it may occur on a political scale, whether that resembles the votes for Margaret Thatcher or Brexit. It may happen gradually, or suddenly, or both. It may be triggered by an election, or conflict, or the assassination of a world leader, or a pandemic, or a natural or economic disaster. It will certainly rely on coincidences: the right conversations happening at the right time, the right story going viral, the right people posting the right messages on social media. Even if it occurs on a much smaller scale, heralding a shift simply in the culture of universities, or the media, or schools, it will come as a relief to many. Either way, the more enthusiastically the 'silent majority' embraces change entrepreneurialism, the more profoundly the West may heal.

Conclusion

UP WITH US!

Bacon sandwiches

If the centrist fundamentalist project can be summed up in Sir Roger Scruton's phrase 'down with us', then our response must be characterised by the opposite. Throughout human history, people have been inclined to exaggerate their positive qualities and whitewash their flaws. A dash of this is healthy, as it boosts feelings of solidarity and pride, while a surfeit of it, of course, may lead to jingoism. But the tendency to subject ourselves to the opposite, magnifying our evils and diminishing our achievements, is something new. It may have been born from a commendable instinct to undo the fascism of the twentieth century, but by disdaining the cultural inheritance that our forebears constructed and defended at such cost, we have betrayed the generations that preceded us, we have betrayed ourselves and we are betraying our children, who are in danger of never receiving it. Along the way, we have betrayed the Jews, who are more ourselves than ourselves.

From the Renaissance to the Industrial Revolution, from the advent of democracy to the spread of Christian values, the West, while hardly guiltless of all crimes, has been responsible for the greatest advances the world has ever seen. Yet we have become obsessed with picking our own scabs and inviting outsiders with their own resentments to join us in that endeavour. Is it any surprise that our national pride lies at an all-time low? In the United States, before the election of Donald Trump, fewer than half of adults described themselves as 'extremely' proud of their country, according to Gallup polling,[1] a measure that had been declining sharply over the previous ten years. The problem worsens among young people; in Britain, just 15 per cent of those between the ages of eighteen and twenty-four now describe themselves as 'very' patriotic,[2] according to a government survey, while more than half failed the 'Life in the UK' examination, designed to test a newcomer's knowledge of British values, traditions, culture, politics, history and laws before they immigrate to the country.

As the novelist Salman Rushdie pointed out in the aftermath of 9/11, it is sometimes easier to say what we are against. We are against flying commercial aeroplanes into buildings, blowing up parents and children at a pop concert, the rape, kidnap, murder and mutilation of Jews. But 'what are we for?' he asked in a 2001 essay entitled *Fighting the Forces of Invisibility*. 'What would we risk our lives to defend?' These are questions we have forgotten how to answer; and if we are to find a way to a better future, we must remember how to do so. Rushdie wrote:

> The fundamentalist believes that we believe in nothing. In his worldview, he has his absolute certainties, while we are sunk in sybaritic indulgences. To prove him wrong, we must first

> know that he is wrong. We must agree on what matters: kissing in public places, bacon sandwiches, disagreement, cutting-edge fashion, literature, generosity, water, a more equitable distribution of the world's resources, movies, music, freedom of thought, beauty, love. These will be our weapons. Not by making war but by the unafraid way we choose to live shall we defeat them.[3]

We may be able to improve on that. But first it is worth noting that in the decades since Rushdie wrote those words, it has become harder to state what we are against. Are we against child rape gangs? Yes, but not with sufficient conviction to stop them when the perpetrators are Pakistani. Are we against the disregard of our borders by boatloads of shysters from Albania, Afghanistan, Eritrea and Iran who were perfectly safe in France? Yes, but we keep putting them up in taxpayer-funded hotels and allowing them to work for Deliveroo. Are we against the bloody invasion of one's neighbours? Yes, but increasing numbers of our people are infatuated with Hamas and Putin. It is this 'yes, but' approach to our values that is the hallmark of centrist fundamentalism, which, in telling us how deplorable we are, has deprived us of the simple ability to know what we believe and to act upon it.

To return to Rushdie's challenge: what are we for? In recent years, we have seen the spread of a kind of plastic patriotism which dilutes itself into nothingness in a desperate attempt to avoid any sense of British exceptionalism. Our history, culture, achievements and spirit have been replaced by empty platitudes about how 'world leading' this or that industry is, an implausible faith in the substandard National Health Service,

Paddington Bear, a commitment to diversity and the trappings of British twee.

In this climate, people thirst for a meaningful sense of selfhood and belonging. Change entrepreneurs and their supporters must find the conviction to stand behind our culture, our language, our way of life and our armed forces, our great cities and our countryside, our traditions and customs, our cuisine and our history, but most of all our values and our freedoms, as well as our Jewish minority. This is not a pursuit of what Edmund Burke called the 'geometrical' politics of the French revolutionaries, which aimed to militate behind a rational and utopian goal. We seek not some planned society or reheated chauvinism, but simply a natural restoration of those things that we have lost in a way that feels native to the modern world.

It goes without saying that we must avoid the jingoism that stalks the other end of the spectrum. Ours must be an anti-chauvinist patriotism that is embedded in tolerance but allows our roots to feel their way back into the old soil, so that they can once again draw upon those nutrients that have always sustained our civilisation. Our great advantage is that deep down, our people have never really lost all this. We have just been persuaded to forget.

For the love of Christ

One aspect of our heritage that has groaned under the weight of 'down with us' is our national religion, which should in some ways hold as much value for non-Christian citizens as it does for the believers themselves. For the West, Christianity represents more than simply the sum of its particular beliefs. It represents a wealth of history, sacred art and architecture, a musical and literary tradition, a foundation stone of ethics, a sensibility, a common code of understanding and a way of living in the world. As Tom Holland has argued, all of us, to a greater or lesser extent, swim in these diluted waters, often without realising it. Yet the dilution cannot advance forever without that which it dilutes disappearing.

The fading of Christianity in civic life has slowly altered the spirit that animates the West. It seems undeniable that it has incubated moral relativism, disunity and what the political philosopher and German-Jewish émigré Leo Strauss called 'permissive egalitarianism'. In his critique of secular liberalism, Strauss argued that it dissolves the moral code that provides a vision of a just and good society, making ethics subservient to individual rights and universal freedom. The result, he believed, was either 'gentle nihilism', a meaningless drift in pursuit of pleasure, or 'brutal nihilism', the fascist and communist totalitarianism that disfigured the last century.

'The crisis of the West consists in the West having become uncertain of its purpose,' Strauss wrote:

> The West was once certain of its purpose, of a purpose in which all men could be united. Hence, it had a clear vision of its future as the future of mankind. We no longer have that certainty and that clarity. Some of us even despair of the future. This despair explains many forms of contemporary Western degradation. This is not meant to imply that no society can be healthy unless it is dedicated to a universal purpose, to a purpose in which all men can be united.

> A society may be tribal and yet healthy. But a society which was accustomed to understand itself in terms of a universal purpose cannot lose faith in that purpose without becoming completely bewildered.[4]

The eclipse of Christianity, in other words, has allowed radicalism to flourish in the dark. Those who rejected the supernatural claims of religion in the nineteenth century, like Matthew Arnold, John Stuart Mill and Henry Thoreau, can never have envisioned such loss. Their writings continued to dignify both the individual and mankind in a way that expressed a spiritual inheritance; the Christian traditions that had long governed their society, from marriage and morality to sacred art, had not been dismantled; and the standards of beauty previously applied to cathedrals found continued life in the designs of secular wonders like St Pancras Station and the classically inspired telephone box.[5] But this was a saint with a fatal wound staggering through his final steps. In today's world of TikTok, OnlyFans and fast fashion, the sacred has been almost entirely forgotten.

More than anything else, the degeneration of our spiritual tradition is the degeneration of ourselves, even for those of us who do not observe the national faith. Were Christianity to be rewilded, as it were, and find its way back to a respected and visible position in civic life, then much social goodness would naturally flow from it. This is not an argument for evangelism. It is simply a plea for cultural restoration. Whether they are Christians or not, why must so many children leave school with no knowledge of the Bible? Why must they be blighted with a lifelong ignorance of the most basic hymns? Why must

Christmas be only about indulgence and Easter, when it is not erased entirely, only about chocolate? Why have we done this to ourselves, or allowed our leaders to do it to us?

Knowledge of these things is not necessarily about being Christian. It is about being British. Occasionally, I accompany my wife to evensong and have observed the state of the Church of England from the perspective of an insider-outsider. My overall impression is of an institution that has so desperately adapted itself to the mores and sentiments of the day that it is in danger of losing the qualities that distinguished it in the first place. Our nearest cathedral, Winchester, recently staged a 'Whale Song Sound Bath', with tickets at £25 a pop.[6] What did this have to do with the Gospels? The event may have brought more visitors into the building, but I would wager that few of them took anything Christian away with them. As awesome as whales may be, the bump in footfall came at the expense of cheapening the sublimity of the church.

I once witnessed – it may have been at Norwich or at Salisbury – a glowing plastic orb, the size of ten beach balls, suspended in the apse. There has been a 55-foot helter-skelter in the nave at Norwich, fashion shows at St Paul's and silent discos at Canterbury.[7] Stunts such as these function to make formerly sacred spaces as ordinary as everywhere else, depriving them of the very thing that set them aside in the first place. This creates a depressing flattening effect in which even the domains of the sublime have thrown off their inheritance in favour of uniformity with shallow secular modernity. Ironically, this coincides with what Huntington saw as the dawning of a 'century of religion' around the globe. 'Virtually everywhere, apart from Western Europe, people are turning to religion for comfort, guidance, solace, and identity,' he wrote:

> In many countries powerful movements have appeared attempting to re-define the identity of their country in religious terms. In a very different way, movements in the United States are recalling America's religious origins and the extraordinary commitment to religion of the American people. Evangelical Christianity has become an important force, and Americans generally may be returning to the self-image prevalent for three centuries that they are a Christian people.[8]

Something similar may be seeking to move in Britain and Western Europe, albeit on a smaller scale. A recent study has found that Gen Z Britons – people in their teens and twenties – are much more likely to describe themselves as 'spiritual' than their middle-aged parents of Gen X or their Baby Boomer grandparents. Whereas a quarter of the middle-aged are atheists, that figure declines to just 13 per cent of those under twenty-five, 62 per cent of whom say they are 'very' or 'fairly' spiritual.[9] The established Church seems embarrassingly out of touch with this pulse. From the point of view of the religious seeker, or even the non-believer seeking inspiration, what is the purpose of a church that has stopped offering a spiritual sanctuary? Balm for the soul must be sought elsewhere.

Predictably, it isn't long before the Jews are hit by this stuff. All too often, priests use their pulpits to deliver liberal political hectoring rather than spiritual sustenance. The journalist Quentin Letts recalled a sermon in which congregants were informed that 'they would not progress to Heaven unless they denounced the Balfour declaration'.[10] These views always take on a particular irony when juxtaposed – as, given the nature of the Bible, they often are – with scripture in which God protects the people of Israel and ruins their enemies. What is the purpose of dragging a spiritual tradition into the grubby and divisive realms of identity politics, let alone modish Israelophobia? In many ways, the church has always been political. But when combined with the dilution of the faith, it feels like it has been exchanged for centrist fundamentalism in frocks.

As if this was not bad enough, the Church of England has even imposed the indignity of the new radicalism upon its congregations. In a bovine response to the death of George Floyd, four thousand miles away, it commissioned an investigation that three years later, when the Black Lives Matter moment had long faded, discovered that the Church had had an eighteenth-century fund which invested in the South Sea Company, which transported slaves. While parishes all over the country struggled with leaking roofs, elderly congregations and sparse attendance, the commission recommended absurd reparation payments of a billion pounds. After swallowing hard, the Church committed to handing over a staggering £100 million to 'black-led businesses', whatever those may be. Yet even this vast sum was immediately condemned as 'not enough'.[11]

Nobody questioned the absurd implication that every injustice in the last three centuries must attract a monetary claim, nor addressed the impossibility of identifying worthy recipients of this wealth after so long. Given demographic and geographical movements over the generations, it is quite possible that the descendants of slaves living in Britain would end up contributing through their taxes to reparations that went to the descendants of the slavers. Indeed, nobody even mentioned the fact that driven by Christian principles, Britain had already spent 1.8 per cent of GDP each year between 1808 and 1867 on hunting down the traders, making abolition the most expensive moral foreign policy in human history. Like many other societies all over the world, we had profited from slavery. Unlike them, however, we put a stop to it, losing two thousand sailors of the Royal Navy in the process.

The late American historian David Brion Davis, a leading authority on slavery and abolition at Yale University, noted in an essay for the *New York Review of Books*: 'The participants in the Atlantic slave system included Arabs, Berbers, scores of African ethnic groups, Italians, Portuguese, Spaniards, Dutch, Jews, Germans, Swedes, French, English, Danes, white Americans, Native Americans, and even thousands of New World blacks who had been emancipated or were descended from freed slaves but who then became slaveholding farmers or planters themselves.'[12] Yet Britain, driven by the moral voices of William Wilberforce, Thomas Clarkson and the others, saw the moral error and took the lead in correcting it.

At great cost in blood and treasure, the West Africa Squadron stopped slave ships crossing the Atlantic and Indian oceans and suppressed the Arab slave trade across the continent. African kings of the nineteenth century resisted George III's efforts to abolish the practice, viewing enslavement as an economically advantageous aspect of the natural order. Thanks to the heroism of the Royal Navy, however, 1,600 slave ships were captured and more than 150,000 Africans were freed in the first part of the nineteenth century. (Ironically, the British Empire supported action against Arab slavers in Nyasaland in the 1880s and 1890s through the British South Africa Company, which was led by a certain Cecil Rhodes.)

This moral victory, which was driven by a deep Christian faith, can only evoke a great patriotic cry of 'up with us!' which may inspire us with the courage to pursue similarly worthy goals in the future. Yet it has been all but erased from our island story, while we are placed beyond forgiveness for our ancestors' part in the original sin. Other countries are entitled to celebrate their achievemants and leave their evils behind, even with scant atonement; indeed, a great many have more than enough evils of the present with which to contend. Yet our participation in slavery is weaponised to undermine our national selfhood. 'Down with us,' the centrist fundamentalists and radicals chorus. 'Down with us!'

This affects our morale – which may need to be urgently called upon as the dogs of war bark louder – in the here and now. 'There is, therefore, a more historically accurate, fairer, more positive story to be told about the British Empire than the anti-colonialists want us to hear,' Nigel Biggar writes. 'And the importance of that story is not just past but present, not just historical but political. What is at stake is not merely the pedantic truth about yesterday, but the self-perception and self-confidence of the British today, and the way they conduct themselves in the world tomorrow. What is also at stake, therefore, is the very integrity of the United Kingdom and the security of the West.'[13]

Show me hostility towards Western culture and I'll show you mendacity towards the Jews. All three tribes of the new radicalism are at it; Louis Farrakhan, leader of the Nation of

Islam, David Duke, the former Ku Klux Klan Grand Wizard, and the progressive activist Jackie Walker[14] have all claimed that the Jews were in some way a dominant power behind the slave trade. YouTube hosts more than 50,000 videos on the topic, mostly posted by the Nation of Islam and Duke and their supporters.[15] Once again, it is a question not of particular facts but the warping of the overall narrative to suit an agenda. It is true that Jews could be found among those individuals who traded and owned slaves. But it is equally true that they did not dominate the industry, with one study concluding that their role was 'exceedingly limited'.[16] As David Brion Davis concluded: 'The small number of Jews who lived in the Atlantic community took black slavery as much for granted as did the Catholics, Muslims, Lutherans, Huguenots, Calvinists, and Anglicans.'[17]

Dig a little deeper and it becomes apparent that the smear originated in the first volume of a 1991 trilogy called *The Secret Relationship Between Blacks and Jews*, which carried the name of no author and was published by the Nation of Islam, the radical black nationalist movement. It accused the Jews of 'carv[ing] out for themselves a monumental culpability in slavery – and the black holocaust'. Black holocaust? Needless to say, the book's scholarship was flawed and it has been roundly rejected by mainstream experts, including David Brion Davis, the late Ralph Austen, professor emeritus of African history at the University of Chicago, and the late Winthrop D Jordan, professor of history and Afro-American studies at the University of Mississippi. In an essay entitled 'Black Demagogues and Pseudo-Scholars', Henry Louis Gates Jr, director of the Hutchins Centre for African and

African American Research at Harvard, described *The Secret Relationship* as 'one of the most sophisticated instances of hate literature yet compiled', which 'massively misrepresents the historical record, largely through a process of cunningly selective quotation of often reputable sources'.[18] In other words, like so much of the enmity facing Jews and the West today, it was clever propaganda.

The Church of England may not blame the Jews for slavery, but it has fallen for this benighted social contagion. And as it has chased secular trends in a bid for popularity, it has been punished by demographics. Christian identity has been on the wane in Britain for years. To see the old pillars of the Church – the numinous choral music, the sacred architecture – remaining standing while the religion is diluted and toxified is especially poignant. The foothills through which people may find their way to the mountains have been desecrated, yet the mountains themselves still tower in the distance.

Those denominations that have remained in touch with their heritage, however, and do not shy away from 'up with us', are able to tell a different story. Amid the overall decline there has been a surprising surge in church attendance recently, rising from four million people worshipping at least once a month in 2018 to six million in 2024. The largest increase came among those under twenty-five, which quadrupled from 4 to 16 per cent, especially among young men. Significantly, however, that growth occurred not in Anglicanism but in the Catholic and Pentecostal churches, both of which have seen dramatic increases in popularity.[19] 'When you meet [converts] and hear their stories, they say they are looking for clarity and stability,' Catholic Archbishop Mark O'Toole told the *Daily*

Telegraph. 'They are attracted to the Catholic Church's strong sense of identity and clarity around the teaching of Jesus.'[20]

Immigration is driving some of this change and the allure of faith schools plays a part. But conversions are also in the ascendency. Remarkably, if these trends continue, Catholicism will soon become the country's largest churchgoing denomination for the first time since the Reformation. If this blazes a direction for the revival of faith in civic life, it also suggests how deeply many people in our deracinated society thirst for old values. If the Church of England were to rediscover its soul and believers were to cast off the awkwardness that so often lingers around people of faith, then Christianity may become part of 'up with us'. As it should rightfully be.

Family matters

If faith and flag must play their roles in the restoration of the West, family also deserves our attention. Here we find ourselves returning to Israel, that most unjustly derided of nations, and what it may have preserved that we have lost. In 2024, the number of live births in the European Union fell below four million for the first time in modern history, producing one of the lowest fertility rates on earth. As a measure of decline, in 1960 that figure topped six million and it sank below five million in 1990. As an OECD report pointed out: 'The Total Fertility Rate has halved from 3.3 children per woman in 1960, on average across the OECD, to 1.5 in 2022, below the "replacement level" of 2.1 children per woman. This decline will change the face of societies, communities and families and will potentially have a significant impact on economic growth and prosperity.'[21] The United States has a fertility rate of 1.64. By contrast, Western and Central Africa has a fertility rate of 4.98, followed by Eastern and Southern Africa at 4.35 and the Arab world at 3.14. If these demographic trends continue, huge upheaval will be upon the West within the coming generations.

The economic vortex this creates provides a force of its own. Take Britain: research by the Centre for Policy Studies showed that when the state pension was introduced in 1909, only 5 per cent of the population were over sixty-five.[22] By 2072, however, that number will have risen to 27 per cent, more than doubling public spending on health and pensions over the coming fifty years. The shifting ratio between younger taxpayers and the older people they fund tells its own story: in 2022, there were 3.3 productive workers per pensioner, but by 2072 there will be just 1.9. If the state is to avoid digging even deeper into other people's pockets – the tax burden is already at record highs – it will require an average annual economic growth of 2.9 per cent for the next five decades, something that has not been achieved in recent memory.

Add to this growing worklessness among the native population, which both hammers productivity and increases the burden on the public finances, and the easy solution is the one to which governments have been turning ever since the Blair years. Maintaining a balance of 3.5 workers per pensioner would draw 666,000 productive immigrants into the country each year. Of course, as many will come with dependants and many will be unproductive, the true number will be far higher. By the 2070s, more than a third of the population would be first-generation newcomers. The addition of enough foreigners to fill Leeds plus the surrounding villages every year would place its own strain on the system, draining the public purse and further accelerating the doom loop. The collapse in our culture and exploitation of ordinary people, who must compete for jobs, housing and services while seeing their country slip away from them, will require increasingly authoritarian management by the state, making a furious backlash increasingly likely. A similar picture may be applied across much of the West.

There could be no deeper expression of pessimism and deracination than having fewer babies. Practical worries like economic insecurity, the expense of raising children, increased housing costs and inhospitable job markets all place downward pressure on birth rates, but social norms and culture are a more powerful part of the story. Speaking to me on *The Brink*, Douglas Murray saw this pessimism reflected in other ways. Kamala Harris, for instance, campaigned for president on a platform principally consisting of the right to kill your unborn child. 'You would have thought people would talk about abortion with an air of sadness,' Murray said. 'But it is talked about with a sense of glee. This is just anti-human.' He also lambasted Britain's preoccupation with euthanasia. 'Last Christmas, the main issue of parliamentary debate – and it was a very shallow debate – was how to kill the elderly,' he said. 'How about having a society which cherishes the elderly?'

Israel, which tops the OECD table with a fertility rate of 2.9, is the only democracy to sit above replacement level. It's not that it has somehow resolved the list of economic deterrents. Far from it. In fact, certainly since October 7, it may add existential insecurity and, of course, dangerous military service to the list. Rather, its people have retained pride in their national story, tight family bonds, devotion to their fellow citizens, vibrant traditions rooted in faith and their collective selfhood. Moreover, if having children is an expression of joy, Israel, which also scores exceptionally highly for happiness, certainly has that. In the face of heartbreak, trauma and political strife, in generational terms, all these good things point in only one direction. It is remarkable how many of them flow from a people's simple ability to say with their whole chest: 'Up with us.'

Of course, 'up with us' does not have to mean 'down with everybody else' (though it must certainly mean 'down with our enemies', a sentiment that the comfort democracies have allowed themselves to forget, with increasingly disastrous results). Nor does 'up with us' need to translate into jingoism. Like all other countries, the Jewish state is a place of heroes and villains, light and darkness, but none of this means that it is not worth defending. A person who makes loyalty to his country conditional upon its politics holds no loyalty to his country at all. In the final analysis, human flourishing is about love. If we in the West can reach into the recesses of our souls and remember how to love our history, our traditions, our culture, our achievements, our values, our people and ourselves, we may find a way to once again say 'up with us' like the Israelis do. In fact, we can join their chorus. All good things, from higher birth rates to greater happiness, will no longer be out of our grasp. The restoration will be underway.

Orphans of the time

Of course, fortune may be against us. A critical mass of stars may fail to align or the enemy may go unstoppably berserk. Centrist fundamentalists are fundamentalists for a reason, and their radical allies can be very radical, and as the Remainer project, the anti-Trump campaigns, the Covid authoritarianism and the collective hectoring of Israel as it fights for its life reminded us, the grownups do not take kindly to challenge.

The Islamists have spent decades threading their networks through our body politic, at great expense and driven by fanaticism; expect to see relentless allegations of 'Islamophobia', widespread legal action, street movements and a political alliance with the socialists and Greens. Moreover, every political earthquake will be met with such resistance from the civil service that any new leader will have to face down a mutiny before he or she can govern the country. Depressingly, the Jews will find themselves in the eye of the storm.

An even more impossible set of dynamics apply stateside, of course, with Trumpistan providing an opposition of its own. How can 'up with us' be reclaimed when it has been so crudely hijacked? While the president flogs 'Trump 2028' merchandise with a call to 'rewrite the rules' – meaning the Constitution, which forbids a third term – and hones his ability to destroy political opponents of all stripes with his trademark bile, the white supremacists and other radicals that form part of his coalition are as fanatical as they are heavily armed. A certain Rubicon was crossed when they stormed Capitol Hill on 6 January 2021. What will come next? Will Trump resist the temptation to harness a greater portion of that force? Like everything else in America, even Christianity is becoming radicalised. How can the country begin to plot a course between the extremes of chauvinism and progressivism that represents the silent majority?

Underpinning all this is another question: how far can our culture stretch before it snaps? Huntington wrote:

> Historically, the substance of American identity has involved four key components: race, ethnicity, culture (most notably language and religion), and ideology. The racial and ethnic Americas are no more. Cultural America is under siege. And as the Soviet experience illustrates, ideology is a weak glue to hold together people otherwise lacking racial, ethnic, and cultural sources of community.
>
> Reasons could exist, as Robert Kaplan observed, why 'America, more than any other nation, may have been born to die'. Yet some societies, confronted with serious challenges to their existence, are also able to postpone their demise and halt disintegration, by renewing their sense of national identity, their national purpose, and the cultural values they have in common. Americans did this after September 11. The challenge they face in the first years of the third millennium is whether they can continue to do this if they are not under attack.[23]

As artificial intelligence develops apace and social media continues to drain trust in institutions, the disruptive effects of the digital revolution also constitutes another great and unprecedented obstacle. In 1997, *The Sovereign Individual*, written by William Rees-Mogg and James Dale Davidson, foretold much of the disorder and confusion that would follow in the coming decades. Everything from the rise of the gig economy to digital currencies and fake news made an appearance, within an overarching argument that both the nation state and democracy were doomed. In their place, they predicted, would emerge the age of powerful and self-ruling figures who compete in a Hobbesian battle for supremacy.

The book concludes with a warning that is as relevant today as it was nearly thirty years ago. 'The shift from an Industrial to an Information society is bound to be breathtaking,' they wrote. 'The transition from one stage of economic life to another has always involved revolution. We think that the Information Revolution is likely to be the most far-reaching of all. It will reorganise life more thoroughly than either the Agricultural Revolution or the Industrial Revolution. And its impact will be felt in a fraction of the time. Fasten your seat belts.'[24]

It is easy to fall prey to despondency. But when the culture shifts, it shifts. Any restoration that does emerge will likely take the form of a Hegelian zeitgeist as much as the leadership of some Great Man; like the tides, the very movement of time and human society that brought us away from ourselves may wash us back towards those things we have lost.

In his masterpiece *Life and Fate*, the twentieth-century Russian Jewish novelist Vasily Grossman gave us one of the most astute observations of this phenomenon in all of literature. 'Time flows into a man or State, makes its home there and then flows away,' he wrote. 'The man and the State remain, but their time has passed. Where has their time gone? The man still thinks, breathes and cries, but his time, the time that belonged to him and to him alone, has disappeared . . . Such is time: everything passes, it alone remains; everything remains, it alone passes. And how swiftly and noiselessly it passes. Only yesterday you were sure of yourself, strong and cheerful, a son of the time. But now another time has come – and you don't even know it.'[25] There can be no doubt that for both the diaspora Jews and the silent majority, these last decades have made us orphans of the time. One day, however, it may be the turn of those who led the betrayal to be orphaned in their turn, as the time that was taken by them is returned to us.

What is good for the Jews is good for the West and what is good for the West is good for the Jews. The Jewish story will always lie at the heart of the Christian one, just as the Christian story lies at the heart of the secular revolution, and over the millennia the entwining of our peoples has been so elaborate that it has become impossible to separate one of our fates from the other. Why should we want to? If this is a question of family, then we rise or fall together. Those who have turned with petulant vengeance against the Jewish state may have dark centuries of tradition upon which to draw, but they have failed to learn the lesson of where such history inevitably leads. Blood, as they say, is thicker than water, and a betrayal of the Jews is a betrayal of themselves. If the West in its lethargy has forgotten what it means to feel the prick of danger, perhaps that is something else that it may take from the Jews.

In 1938, while German generals planned the invasion of Poland, the charismatic Jewish leader Ze'ev Jabotinsky made a speech at a synagogue in Warsaw in which he warned of the coming cataclysm. 'For three years I keep addressing you, Jews of Poland, the crown of world Jewry,' he said:

> I keep warning you time and again that the catastrophe is approaching. My hair has turned white, and I grew old during all those years, because my heart is bleeding for you, dear brothers and sisters, for not seeing that the volcano is about to erupt and spit the fire of destruction. I foresee a terrible vision; there is not much time left to save your life. I know, you are too preoccupied and busy with your daily concerns to see it.

> Listen to my words at the very last moment. For heaven's sake, save your lives, every one of you, so long as there is time. And time is short![26]

We are not yet staring down a second Holocaust. For one thing, we have the mighty state of Israel. Almost ninety years on from Jabotinsky's speech, however, as Jews around the world face the triangulated threat of the new radicalism, too many remain locked in timidity, equivocation, obsequiousness or despair. While these same dangers close in upon the West, great swathes of the population remain somnambulant, softened by addiction to screens and to comfort. We cannot run on the fumes of previous generations forever. As Grossman observed: 'Time is a transparent medium. People and cities arise out of it, move through it and disappear back into it. It is time that brings them and time that takes them away.'[27] Whether in defence of a Jew on Holocaust Memorial Day or at any other moment, if we are to take back the time and make it our own, both political leaders and the ordinary men and women of civil society must respond to this great emergency by jumping to their feet.

ACKNOWLEDGEMENTS

Firstly, of course, I must thank my fabulous publisher, Andreas Campomar, and his team at Constable, particularly Holly Blood and James Nightingale, as well as my superb agents, Neil Blair and Rory Scarfe, and their colleagues. It goes without saying that this book would not exist without them. I hope it does them proud.

For their generous advice while my manuscript was in incubation, I am greatly indebted to Ed Husain, Colin Brazier, Paul Davies, Tomiwa Owolade, Nick Timothy, Emily Critchley, Bob Low and David Del Monté. Thanks also to Douglas Murray, Bari Weiss, Sir Niall Ferguson, Aayan Hirsi Ali, Tom Holland and Bernard-Henri Lévy for their invaluable contributions, and to my dear comrade Simon Sebag Montefiore along with all those who so kindly endorsed this book: Andrew Neil, Nigel Farage, Kemi Badenoch, Andrew Roberts, Daniel Hannan, Michael Gove, Boris Johnson and Allison Pearson. I am very moved by your support.

But I owe the most gratitude to my lovely wife, Roxanna. Not only did her conversations help a great deal in the formation of my ideas, but she kept every practical detail of our lives ticking over beautifully while I was locked in my study, emerging only to take delivery of obscure tomes or to make tea.

For three and a half months, I jettisoned everything other than writing. I suffered eyestrain and backache, and took on the drained and wild look of a man possessed. On one occasion, I was hospitalised. They thought I'd had a stoke but embarrassingly, it turned out to be a migraine. Apologies to everybody I neglected and especially to my wonderful wife; I cannot emphasise enough just how tolerant, supportive and uncomplaining she has been.

My thanks also to the children, who have had to get used to the madman in the study and the shed.

Up with us!

Notes

INTRODUCTION

1 https://www.telegraph.co.uk/world-news/2025/01/27/irish-president-holocaust-speech-reference-gaza-plight/
2 https://www.thetimes.com/uk/article/antisemitism-uk-anti-jewish-incidents-britain-james-cleverly-k5lcgjbx7
3 https://www.bbc.co.uk/news/articles/cx285v8djejo
4 https://www.france24.com/en/france/20240619-french-teens-charged-with-anti-semitic-rape-in-attack-condemned-by-political-leaders
5 https://www.bbc.co.uk/news/articles/cx2y33ee1klo
6 https://www.bbc.co.uk/news/articles/c5ydr228jyko
7 https://apnews.com/article/poland-synagogue-attacked-warsaw-jewish-firebomb-antisemitism-d51fa5305907bf10bbb7a1ecd02f126e
8 https://www.theguardian.com/news/article/2024/may/14/antisemitism-in-europe-leading-some-to-hide-jewish-identity-says-leading-rabbi
9 https://www.telegraph.co.uk/world-news/2024/11/18/jews-gay-people-hide-identity-arab-areas-germany/
10 https://www.adl.org/resources/press-release/us-antisemitic-incidents-skyrocketed-360-aftermath-attack-israel-according
11 https://edition.cnn.com/2024/05/16/us/loay-alnaji-paul-kessler-death-will-stand-trial/index.html
12 https://www.jns.org/18000-terrorist-attacks-in-israel-in-2024/
13 Jabotinsky, Ze'ev, 'Instead of Excessive Apology', 1911: https://web.archive.org/web/20080102223444/http://www.csuohio.edu/tagar/boris.htm
14 Sacks, Jonathan, *Future Tense* (London: Hodder & Stoughton, 2010), p. 262.
15 https://www.visionofhumanity.org/wp-content/uploads/2024/02/GTI-2024-web-290224.pdf

16 https://slate.com/news-and-politics/2005/09/the-legacy-of-darkness-at-noon.html
17 A wonderful history of my paternal family can be found in a biographical cookbook written by two of my relatives: Anderson, Bridget, and Anderson, Stephen, *Burma: Food, Family and Conflict* (London: Ma Khin Markets SL, 2018).
18 Murray, Douglas, 'The Crime of Noticing', *The New Criterion*, vol. 43, no. 9, May 2025.
19 Huntington, Samuel P., *Who Are We?* (New York: Simon & Schuster, 2004), p. 10.
20 https://www.timesofisrael.com/israels-former-pm-golda-meir-has-become-a-symbol-of-hope-for-ukrainians/
21 Anderson and Anderson *Burma: Food, Family and Conflict.*

1. CENTRIST FUNDAMENTALISM

1 Montefiore, Simon Sebag, *The World: A Family History* (London: Hachette, 2022), p. 1256.
2 https://www.telegraph.co.uk/news/2025/05/31/vikings-were-not-all-white-pupils-to-be-told/
3 https://www.gov.uk/government/history/king-charles-street
4 https://www.thetimes.com/uk/politics/article/the-great-british-dividesomewheres-v-anywheres-s8qm908f0
5 https://www.telegraph.co.uk/news/2025/05/30/benefits-foreigners-near-cost-1bn-month/
6 https://www.jstor.org/stable/42897520
7 https://www.euronews.com/business/2014/01/22/the-globe-s-biggest-business-meeting-in-davos-aims-to-reshape-the-world
8 https://www.thetimes.com/article/putting-the-world-to-rights-is-thirsty-work-for-party-people-3m53cj3ztfl
9 Strauss, Leo, *Natural Right and History* (Chicago: Chicago University Press, 1965), p. 14.
10 https://www.telegraph.co.uk/news/2025/05/19/poll-shows-support-for-starmers-island-of-strangers-warning/
11 https://www.telegraph.co.uk/news/2025/01/23/the-far-centre-thats-where-the-real-extremist-threat-lies/
12 Kolakowski, Leszek, *Modernity on Endless Trial* (Chicago: University of Chicago Press, 1990), p. 162.
13 Popper, Karl, *The Open Society and Its Enemies* (London: Routledge, 2011), p.107.
14 Lewis, Bernard, *Semites and Anti-Semites* (New York: Norton, 1999), p. 194.
15 Strauss, *Natural Right and History*, p. 6.

16 Dawkins, Richard, *The Selfish Gene* (Oxford: OUP, 2016).
17 Scruton, Roger, *How to Be a Conservative* (London: Bloomsbury, 2015), p. 83.
18 https://www.democracywithoutborders.org/36317/autocracies-outnumber-democracies-for-the-first-time-in-20-years-v-dem/
19 Bellow, Saul, *To Jerusalem and Back* (London: Penguin, 1998), p. 27.
20 https://www.spectator.co.uk/article/are-you-ramadan-ready/
21 https://www.telegraph.co.uk/news/2025/03/17/islamophobia-law-censorship-muslims-already-have-protection/
22 https://www.telegraph.co.uk/news/2025/03/22/primary-school-scraps-easter-service-respect-religions/
23 https://yougov.co.uk/politics/articles/17971-only-55-brits-associate-jesus-christ-easter
24 https://www.dailyecho.co.uk/news/25062576.supporters-defend-norwood-school-headteacher-protest/
25 https://www.facebook.com/TPointUK/videos/activists-from-the-disciples-of-christ-crashed-a-bbc-staff-party-due-to-their-pr/2142951212828602/
26 https://www.dailymail.co.uk/news/article-14459289/Council-BANS-Christian-prayers.html
27 https://www.telegraph.co.uk/news/2025/03/20/young-men-drawn-toxic-masculinity-schools-not-boy-positive/
28 https://www.adl.org/resources/article/andrew-tate-five-things-know
29 https://www.bbc.co.uk/news/uk-politics-30142579
30 https://www.tiktok.com/@footballworld2756/video/7287965157274242336?lang=en
31 Murray, Douglas, 'The Crime of Noticing', *The New Criterion*, vol. 43, no. 9, May 2025.
32 Holland, Tom, *Dominion* (London: Abacus, 2019), p. 500.
33 Quoted in Murray, 'The Crime of Noticing'.
34 https://www.theguardian.com/world/2019/may/02/persecution-driving-christians-out-of-middle-east-report#:~:text=In%20the%20Middle%20East%20the%20population%20of,to%20be%20about%2020%;%20now%20it's%205%.%E2%80%9D&text=The%20report%20shows%20that%20a%20century%20ago,than%204%%2C%20or%20roughly%2015%20million%20people.
35 https://www.thejc.com/news/over-90-per-cent-of-uk-jews-give-to-charity-with-orthodox-and-over-60s-most-generous-report-finds-uur1or4a
36 https://www.martingilbert.com/blog/winston-churchill-and-the-foundation-of-israel/
37 Makovsky, Michael, *Churchill's Promised Land: Zionism and Statecraft* (New Haven: Yale University Press, 2007), p. 61.
38 https://www.theguardian.com/world/2002/jun/27/globalisation.russia

39 https://www.telegraph.co.uk/news/uknews/1494182/Soldiers-forced-to-shout-bang-as-the-Army-runs-out-of-ammunition.html

40 https://www.ceicdata.com/en/indicator/united-states/government-debt--of-nominal-gdp#:~:text=United%20States%20Government%20Debt%3A%20%25%20of%20GDP,-1969%20%2D%202024%20%7C%20Quarterly&text=United%20States%20Government%20debt%20accounted,Mar%201969%20to%20Dec%202024.

41 https://www.ons.gov.uk/employmentandlabourmarket/peopleinwork/employmentandemployeetypes/bulletins/employmentintheuk/february2025#:~:text=In%20the%20year%20to%20October,inactivity%20rate%20decreased%20to%2021.5%25.

42 https://www.telegraph.co.uk/business/2025/02/26/more-than-half-million-sick-benefit-claimants-never-worked/#:~:text=Analysis%20of%202021%20census%20data,not%20just%20those%20claiming%20benefits.

43 https://www.ons.gov.uk/census/maps/choropleth/work/economic-activity-status/economic-activity-status-3a/economically-active

44 https://www.telegraph.co.uk/business/2025/03/05/one-in-10-children-workless-households-welfare-spending/

45 https://www.telegraph.co.uk/news/2025/03/06/labour-punishing-middle-england-to-fund-the-underclass/

46 https://www.telegraph.co.uk/money/benefits-bill-surges-25pc-working-age-britons-disabled/

47 https://www.bbc.co.uk/news/articles/crewng29zgno

48 https://commonslibrary.parliament.uk/research-briefings/cbp-8175/

49 https://www.ft.com/content/8cc0f584-45fa-11e2-b7ba-00144feabdc0

2. WAR AND PEACE

1 https://yougov.co.uk/politics/articles/48473-more-than-a-third-of-under-40s-would-refuse-conscription-in-the-event-of-a-world-war

2 https://www.gallup-international.com/survey-results-and-news/survey-result/fewer-people-are-willing-to-fight-for-their-country-compared-to-ten-years-ago

3 Lewis, Bernard, *Semites and Anti-Semites* (New York: Norton, 1999), p. 123.

4 https://www.timesofisrael.com/israel-ranked-4th-best-performing-economy-among-oecd-countries-in-2022/

5 https://www.theguardian.com/technology/2025/mar/18/google-parent-alphabet-buy-cybersecurity-wiz-israeli-startup#:~:text=Google's%20owner%2C%20Alphabet%2C%20has%20agreed,the%20competitive%20cloud%20services%20market.

6 https://www.timesofisrael.com/israels-birth-rate-remains-highest-in-oecd-by-far-at-2-9-children-per-woman/

7 https://www.haaretz.com/israel-news/culture/health/2025-01-10/ty-article/.premium/israel-sees-wartime-baby-boom-with-10-percent-rise-in-births-in-final-months-of-2024/00000194-4caf-da5e-abbd-5eff33d70000

8 https://podcasts.apple.com/gb/podcast/a-new-u-s-president-and-the-middle-east-with-tal-becker/id1539292794?i=1000685255127

9 https://podcasts.apple.com/gb/podcast/call-me-back-with-dan-senor/id1539292794?i=1000698530577&r=4079

10 Senor, Dan, and Singer, Saul, *The Genius of Israel* (London: Constable, 2023).

11 https://www.thetimes.com/uk/society/article/gen-z-survey-police-racism-crime-nhs-hlghh0pxw

12 https://yougov.co.uk/politics/articles/46034-do-britons-want-bring-back-national-service

13 https://data.worldhappiness.report/table?_gl=1*8knx25*_gcl_au*MTQyMjE0MzEwMi4xNzQxMzQ3NTgz

14 https://www.jstor.org/stable/44613021

15 https://www.jstor.org/stable/24721536

16 https://www.ons.gov.uk/peoplepopulationandcommunity/wellbeing/bulletins/unityanddivisioningreatbritain/24aprilto28june2020

17 https://www.thetimes.com/uk/society/article/gen-z-survey-police-racism-crime-nhs-hlghh0pxw

18 https://www.britainschoice.uk/media/wqin4k4x/britain-s-choice-full-report-2020.pdf

19 https://www.newsweek.com/israel-has-created-new-standard-urban-warfare-why-will-no-one-admit-it-opinion-1883286

20 https://press.un.org/en/2022/sc14904.doc.htm

21 https://www.timesofisrael.com/gaza-tunnels-stretch-at-least-350-miles-far-longer-than-past-estimate-report/

22 Arendt, Hannah, *The Origins of Totalitarianism* (New York: Harcourt Brace & Co, 1979), p. 459.

23 https://www.thejc.com/news/israel/terror-groups-use-all-hospitals-in-gaza-for-operations-pij-spokesperson-admits-whrgcjrr

24 https://www.telegraph.co.uk/news/2025/04/20/israel-bbc-incapable-getting-simplest-thing-right/

25 https://henryjacksonsociety.org/wp-content/uploads/2024/12/HJS-Questionable-Counting-%E2%80%93-Hamas-Report-web.pdf

26 https://www.ipsos.com/en-uk/uk-attitudes-toward-conflict-israel-and-gaza

27 https://www.researchgate.net/publication/390889419_Citizens_in_democratic_countries_have_more_benevolent_traits_fewer_malevolent_traits_and_greater_well-being

28 https://www.thejc.com/opinion/how-terrorists-acquire-deploy-and-weaponise-western-empathy-against-israel-kiubfl6b
29 Elon, Amos, *The Pity of It All* (London: Penguin, 2002), p. 386.
30 Turner, Henry Ashby, *Hitler's Thirty Days to Power* (New York: Basic Books, 1996), p. 159.
31 Ibid., p. 394.
32 https://www.spectator.co.uk/article/blm-should-look-to-martin-luther-king-not-malcolm-x-for-inspiration/
33 https://www.jewishnews.co.uk/young-jews-defend-saying-kaddish-for-gaza-dead-despite-knowing-many-were-in-hamas/
34 Romerstein, Herbert and Levchenko, Stanislav, *The KGB Against the 'Main Enemy'* (Massachusetts: Lexington Books, 1989), p. 307.
35 Marcus, Jacob Rader, *The Jew in the Medieval World* (New York: Praeger Publishers Inc., 1975), p. 19.
36 https://www.thejc.com/news/community/hmdt-apologises-unreservedly-for-referring-to-israel-gaza-war-in-holocaust-memorial-ceremony-invitation-dhvsxtqf
37 https://morningstaronline.co.uk/article/f/jeremy-corbyn-open-letter-fighting-antisemitism-and-islamophobia
38 Burke, Edmund, *Reflections on the Revolution in France* (London: Yale University Press, 2004), p. 82.
39 https://www.jewishnews.co.uk/board-have-significant-concerns-over-rishi-sunaks-illegal-migration-bill/
40 https://www.thejc.com/news/board-of-deputies-accused-of-political-grandstanding-bmga6mn2
41 https://www.thejc.com/news/politics/ex-board-of-deputies-president-marie-van-der-zyl-joins-labour-mxsgeqlz
42 https://www.thejc.com/opinion/its-wrong-to-say-holocaust-memorial-day-has-been-diluted-we-must-back-it-kamrldcw

3. DADS AND MUMS

1 https://www.telegraph.co.uk/opinion/2024/09/28/kemi-badenoch-migrants-britain-tradition/
2 https://www.thetimes.com/article/e4fce705-2a56-4e4a-aa04-0b55effb5bc0?shareToken=e8ccfb91a43625e44a12b7f106042012
3 https://www.dailymail.co.uk/news/article-14424959/Knock-knock-Thought-Police-thousands-criminals-uninvestigated-detectives-call-grandmother-crime-went-Facebook-criticise-Labour-councillors-centre-Hope-Die-WhatsApp-scandal-exposed-MoS.html

4 https://www.telegraph.co.uk/news/2025/03/31/toddler-kicked-out-of-nursery-for-being-transphobic/
5 https://www.thetimes.com/uk/education/article/school-whatsapp-group-maxie-allen-dmr2bhltg
6 https://www.telegraph.co.uk/news/2025/03/27/kathleen-stock-criticises-sussex-university-free-speech/
7 https://www.telegraph.co.uk/news/2025/05/10/retired-police-officer-arrested-over-thought-crime-tweet/
8 https://www.telegraph.co.uk/news/2024/11/28/housewife-police-interview-calling-man-pikey/
9 https://www.thejc.com/opinion/this-was-the-year-the-jews-were-told-the-holocaust-is-not-about-you-fjtnb1q0
10 https://www.telegraph.co.uk/news/2025/02/08/how-unprecedented-immigration-of-10m-will-reshape-britain/
11 https://www.bbc.co.uk/news/uk-england-manchester-54695580
12 https://static1.squarespace.com/static/599c3d2febbd1a90cffdd8a9/t/5bfd1ea3352f531a6170ceee/1543315109493/Islamophobia+Defined.pdf
13 https://www.theguardian.com/politics/2025/jan/10/wes-streeting-new-zealand-mosque-massacre-warning-grooming-gang-rhetoric
14 https://www.theguardian.com/commentisfree/2024/jan/30/age-of-dadcast-podcast-george-osborne-alastair-campbell-rory-stewart
15 https://x.com/intothefuture45/status/1886818649593278493
16 https://www.samharris.org/podcasts/making-sense-episodes/352-hubris-chaos
17 https://pressgazette.co.uk/podcasts/first-political-podcast-election-youtube-rest-is-politics-goalhanger/
18 https://www.samharris.org/podcasts/making-sense-episodes/356-islam-freedom
19 Holland, Tom, *Dominion* (London: Abacus, 2019), p. 505.
20 https://www.wsj.com/world/europe/antisemitism-among-muslim-migrants-unsettles-a-germany-haunted-by-the-holocaust-ff359e73
21 https://www.politico.eu/article/henry-kissinger-germany-let-in-way-too-many-foreigners/
22 https://www.statista.com/statistics/894223/immigrant-numbers-germany/
23 https://www.ajc.org/news/what-is-the-alternative-for-germany-or-afd-party
24 https://www.telegraph.co.uk/news/2025/03/13/germany-has-been-betrayed-again-on-migration/
25 https://www.thetimes.com/world/europe/article/what-is-afd-germany-party-pnkrmx5p0
26 https://www.facebook.com/hanspeter.friedrich/posts/1243584958990041?pnref=story

27 https://www.focus.de/politik/deutschland/uebergriffe-an-silvester-koelner-polizeichef-sex-uebergriffe-waren-keine-organisierte-kriminalitaet_id_5277005.html

28 https://www.welt.de/politik/deutschland/article156038699/Polizeiversagen-bestaerkte-die-Koelner-Sex-Taeter.html

4. NAZIS OF ISLAM

1 https://www.thejc.com/news/politics/tory-candidate-rabbi-hit-with-blood-libel-abuse-and-called-snake-during-visit-to-mosque-epw8wzya

2 https://www.cage.ngo/articles/british-muslim-organisations-scholars-and-activists-defend-palestinian-rights-to-resistance-and-self-defence

3 https://www.telegraph.co.uk/news/2024/04/06/one-in-four-british-muslims-believe-hamas-israel/

4 https://www.telegraph.co.uk/news/2025/03/17/islamophobia-law-censorship-muslims-already-have-protection/

5 https://www.algemeiner.com/2023/12/18/new-poll-registers-strong-support-hamas-among-french-muslims/

6 https://www.nationalgeographic.com/history/article/french-jews-fleeing-country#:~:text=Facing%20record%20levels%20of%20anti%2DSemitism%2C%20many%20French%20Jews%20are,a%20free%20flight%20to%20Israel.

7 https://www.jura.uni-hamburg.de/die-fakultaet/professuren/kriminologie/media/san-francisco-asc-2024-wetzels-et-al-final1.pdf

8 https://www.gu.se/sites/default/files/w-12/si-rapport-13-en.pdf

9 https://fra.europa.eu/sites/default/files/fra_uploads/fra-2019-2nd-survey-on-discrimination-and-hate-crime-against-jews-in-eu-ms-country-sheet-netherlands_en.pdf

10 https://www.annefrank.org/en/anne-frank/go-in-depth/netherlands-greatest-number-jewish-victims-western-europe/

11 https://encyclopedia.ushmm.org/content/en/article/france

12 https://www.jns.org/cygnal-poll-57-5-of-muslim-americans-say-hamas-at-least-somewhat-justified-in-attack-on-israel/

13 https://mcb.org.uk/2021-census-as-uk-population-grows-so-do-british-muslim-communities/

14 https://www.pewresearch.org/religion/2012/12/18/global-religious-landscape-muslim/

15 https://www.theguardian.com/world/2020/oct/25/europes-jewish-population-has-dropped-60-in-last-50-years

16 https://assets.publishing.service.gov.uk/media/5a80c4fded915d74e6230579/The_Casey_Review_Report.pdf

17 https://www.thetimes.com/uk/politics/article/my-sons-living-hell-j72t7fppc
18 Rushdie, Salman, 'Yes, This Is About Islam', New York Times, November 2, 2001.
19 https://www.amdigital.co.uk/insights/blog/ajex-british-jewry#:~:text=British%20Jews%20have%20served%20in,including%204%2C000%20refugees%20from%20Nazism.
20 https://www.thejc.com/news/israel/arab-israeli-family-risked-their-lives-to-save-dozens-of-jews-on-october-7-cr9z0vre
21 https://www.timesofisrael.com/taibe-bike-shop-torched-after-arab-israeli-owner-donates-bikes-to-jewish-kids/
22 https://www.i24news.tv/en/news/israel-at-war/1697432316-arab-israeli-news-anchor-lucy-aharish-saves-families-from-hamas-massacre
23 https://x.com/EylonALevy/status/1711988611502281183?ref_src=twsrc%5Etfw%7Ctwcamp%5Etweetembed%7Ctwterm%5E1711988611502281183%7Ctwgr%5E18efa3d9144667cc2eb93c78141f42045815dc86%7Ctwcon%5Es1_&ref_url=https%3A%2F%2Fwww.i24news.tv%2Fen%2Fnews%2Fisrael-at-war%2F1697432316-arab-israeli-news-anchor-lucy-aharish-saves-families-from-hamas-massacre
24 https://www.timesofisrael.com/liveblog_entry/raam-party-demands-resignation-of-mk-for-casting-doubt-on-october-7-massacres/
25 https://www.jpost.com/israel-hamas-war/article-809892
26 Husain, Ed, *The Islamist* (London: Penguin, 2007), p. 279.
27 Montefiore, Simon Sebag, *The World: A Family History* (London: Weidenfeld & Nicolson, 2023), p. 270–1.
28 Holland, Tom, *In the Shadow of the Sword* (London: Abacus, 2013), p. 388.
29 Stillman, Norman A., *The Jews of Arab Lands: History and Source Book* (London: The Jewish Publication Society, 1998), p. 241.
30 Gilbert, Martin, *In Ishmail's House* (New Haven: Yale, 2011), p. xxiii.
31 Lewis, Bernard, *Semites and Anti-Semites* (New York: Norton, 1999), p. 124.
32 Ibid., p. 130.
33 Ibid., pp. 121–2.
34 Ibid., p. 137.
35 https://referenceworks.brill.com/display/entries/EMHO/COM-021720.xml?language=en
36 Haim, Sylvia G., 'The Palestine Problem in al-Manar', in Cohen, Amnon and Baer, Gabrial (eds.), *Egypt and Palestine: A Millennium of Association* (New York: St Martin's Press, 1984), p. 300.
37 Altoma, Salih J., *The Image of the Jew in Modern Arabic Literature 1900–1947* (Colombus: Al-Arabiyya, 1978), pp. 51–3, 62.

38 Lewis, Bernard and Braude, Benjamin, (eds.), *Christians and Jews in the Ottoman Empire: The Functioning of a Plural Society*, vol. I (New York: Holmes & Meier, 1982), p. 30.

39 https://www.youtube.com/watch?v=TxX_THjtXOw

40 Hirszowicz, Lukasz, *The Third Reich and the Arab East* (London: Routledge, 2016), p. 30.

41 Carpi, Daniel, 'The Mufti of Jerusalem, Amin el-Husseini, and His Diplomatic Activity During World War II (October 1941–July 1943),' *Studies in Zionism*, 7, 1983, pp. 104–5.

42 al-Jundi, Sami, *Al Ba'th* (Beirut, 1969), p. 27.

43 Hitler, Adolf, *Mein Kampf* (New York: Hutchinson Publications Ltd, 1969), p. 294.

44 Hirszowicz, *The Third Reich*, p. 30.

45 http://memri.org/bin/latestnews.cgi?ID=SD227809

46 Lewis, *Semites and Anti-Semites*, p. 155.

47 Aglion, Raoul, *The Fighting French* (New York: Holt, 1943), p. 217.

48 Satloff, Robert, *Among the Righteous* (New York: Public Affairs, 2007), pp. 85–6.

49 https://www.aljazeera.com/news/2024/4/10/israeli-forces-kill-three-children-of-hamas-leader-ismail-haniyeh-in-gaza

50 Aaron, David, *In Their Own Words: Voices of Jihad* (Santa Monica: Rand Corporation, 2008), p. 103.

51 Beevor, Antony, *Berlin: The Downfall 1945* (London: Penguin, 2002), p. 238.

52 https://www.samharris.org/podcasts/making-sense-episodes/410-the-whole-catastrophe

5. THE ART OF DEATH

1 Patterson, David, *A Genealogy of Evil* (Cambridge: Cambridge University Press, 2011), p. 69.

2 Mitchell, Richard P., *The Society of the Muslim Brothers* (Oxford: Oxford University Press, 1993), p. 207.

3 Montefiore, Simon Sebag, *The World: A Family History* (London: Weidenfeld & Nicolson, 2023), p. 1093.

4 Ibid., p. 1092.

5 Musallam, Adnan, *Sayyid Qutb: The Emergence of the Islamist 1939–1950* (Jerusalem: Passia Publication, 1997), p. 34.

6 Tibi, Bassam, *Islamischer Fundamentalismus, moderne Wissenschaft und Technologie* (Frankfurt am Main: Suhrkamp, 1992), p. 124.

7 Lawrence, Bruce (ed.), *Messages to the World: The Statements of Osama Bin Laden* (London: Verso, 2005), p. 229.

8 Küntzel, Matthias, *Jihad and Jew-hatred* (New York: Telos Press, 2007), p. 82.

9 Murawiec, Laurent, *The Mind of Jihad* (Cambridge: Cambridge University Press, 2008), p. 98.

10 https://www.iium.edu.my/deed/articles/muslim_nation.html#:~:text=There%20is%20only%20one%20place,the%20state%20with%20mutual%20consultation.

11 Aaron, David, *In Their Own Words: Voices of Jihad* (Santa Monica, CA: RAND Corporation, 2008), p. 62.

12 Herf, Jeffrey, *Nazi Propaganda for the Arab World* (New Haven: Yale University Press, 2009), p. 259.

13 Ibid., p. 259.

14 https://www.amnesty.org.uk/press-releases/egypt-sentencing-death-more-500-people-grotesque-ruling

15 Trifkovic, Serge, *The Sword of the Prophet* (Boston: Regina Orthodox Press, 2002), p. 188.

16

17 Wickham, Carrie Rosefsky, *The Muslim Brotherhood* (Oxford: Princeton University Press, 2013), p. 302.

18 https://www.counterextremism.com/blog/muslim-brotherhood-britain-analysis-recent-sanctions

19 https://www.counterextremism.com/blog/muslim-brotherhood-britain-analysis-recent-sanctions

20 https://www.elysee.fr/en/emmanuel-macron/2020/11/04/letter-france-is-against-islamist-separatism-never-islam

21 https://assets.publishing.service.gov.uk/media/5a8076bfe5274a2e8ab504ab/53163_Muslim_Brotherhood_Review_-_PRINT.pdf

22 https://www.spectator.co.uk/article/france-is-waking-up-to-the-threat-of-the-muslim-brotherhood-is-britain/

23 https://www.telegraph.co.uk/opinion/2025/04/30/michael-gove-ipso-decision-chilling-free-speech/

24 https://x.com/amjadt25/status/1912452766410371232

25 https://www.dailymail.co.uk/news/article-14402727/Counter-extremism-advisor-warns-UK-powerbase-radical-Islam.html

26 https://www.thejc.com/news/islam-channel-fined-40-000-over-antisemitic-conspiracy-theory-documentary-xpo3xkd4

27 https://www.telegraph.co.uk/news/2025/03/15/islam-channel-watched-millions-facing-ofcom-investigation/

28 https://www.dailymail.co.uk/news/article-14463533/speak-english-neighbourhood-interactive-map-language.html

29 https://www.ampereanalysis.com/press/release/dl/frequent-viewing-of-foreign-language-content-up-24-in-english-speaking-markets-in-four-ye
30 https://www.telegraph.co.uk/news/2025/03/17/more-than-one-million-foreigners-claim-benefits/#:~:text=Benefits%20are%20being%20claimed%20by,and%20Pensions%20(DWP)%20show.
31 https://www.telegraph.co.uk/politics/2024/07/11/jonathan-ashworth-hid-from-palestine-protesters-vicarage/
32 https://www.telegraph.co.uk/politics/2024/07/04/labour-general-election-2024-latest-starmer-rayner-reeves/

6. WHITE RUSSIANS

1 https://www.gu.se/sites/default/files/2024-12/si-rapport-13-en.pdf
2 https://www.thelocal.se/20180830/two-sweden-democrats-kicked-out-of-party-for-nazi-purchases-hitler-support
3 https://www.etc.se/inrikes/sd-topp-medlem-i-nazistgrupp-god-sak
4 https://www.timesofisrael.com/german-far-right-party-to-drop-fascist-spokesman-proud-of-aryan-grandfather/
5 https://www.france24.com/en/france/20240704-black-sheep-embarrass-the-national-rally-ahead-of-decisive-parliamentary-vote
6 Strauss, Leo, *Natural Right and History* (Chicago: Chicago University Press, 1965), p. 2.
7 https://www.adl.org/resources/report/right-wing-extremist-terrorism-united-states
8 https://www.visionofhumanity.org/wp-content/uploads/2024/02/GTI-2024-web-290224.pdf
9 Schumer, Chuck, *Antisemitism in America* (New York: Hachette, 2025), p. 108.
10 https://www.nytimes.com/2022/12/07/opinion/trump-2024-republican-party.html
11 https://www.prri.org/spotlight/replacement-theory-is-not-a-fringe-theory/
12 https://www.splcenter.org/resources/guides/year-hate-extremism-2023/
13 Kendi, Ibram X, *How to Be an Antiracist* (London: Vintage, 2023), p.18.
14 https://cbsaustin.com/news/nation-world/squad-members-oppose-house-resolution-condemning-global-rise-of-antisemitism-progressive-congress-cori-bush-rashida-tlaib-ilhan-omar-jewish-israel-palestine
15 https://www.pbs.org/newshour/politics/trump-begins-openly-embracing-and-amplifying-false-fringe-qanon-conspiracy-theory
16 https://www.prri.org/spotlight/replacement-theory-is-not-a-fringe-theory/
17 https://www.adl.org/resources/article/fuentes-delivers-antisemitic-christian-nationalist-rant-fellow-white-supremacists
18 https://www.adl.org/resources/backgrounder/candace-owens

19 https://rumble.com/v5p0e2e-champion-poker-player-businessman-dan-bilzerian-questions-holocaust-during-.html
20 https://www.telegraph.co.uk/business/2025/05/11/kanye-west-heil-hitler-song-blocked-streaming-platforms/
21 Schumer, *Antisemitism in America*, p. 106.
22 https://www.youtube.com/watch?v=4fqHriOpQo4
23 https://www.theatlantic.com/magazine/archive/2017/12/the-making-of-an-american-nazi/544119/
24 https://www.adl.org/resources/news/andrew-anglin-five-things-know
25 https://www.theatlantic.com/magazine/archive/2017/12/the-making-of-an-american-nazi/544119/
26 https://talkingpointsmemo.com/livewire/trump-julia-ioffe-anti-semitic-threats
27 Dugin, Alexandr, *Putin vs Putin: The View from the Right* (New York: Arktos Media, 2014), p. 201.
28 Kalugin, Oleg, *Spymaster* (New York: Basic Books, 2009), p. 445.
29 Dugin, Alexandr, *The Fourth Political Theory* (New York: Arktos Media, 2012), p. 72.
30 https://monitoring.bbc.co.uk/product/b0003cev
31 https://www.theatlantic.com/magazine/archive/2017/12/the-making-of-an-american-nazi/544119/
32 https://www.adl.org/resources/article/white-supremacists-applaud-tucker-carlsons-promotion-replacement-theory
33 https://www.pewresearch.org/religion/2025/02/26/decline-of-christianity-in-the-us-has-slowed-may-have-leveled-off/#:~:text=The%20first%20RLS%2C%20fielded%20in,about%203%25%20of%20U.S.%20adults.
34 https://www.ons.gov.uk/peoplepopulationandcommunity/culturalidentity/religion/bulletins/religionenglandandwales/census2021
35 https://faithsurvey.co.uk/uk-christianity.html
36 https://faithsurvey.co.uk/uk-christianity.html
37 https://www.pewresearch.org/religion/2023/12/07/spiritual-beliefs/
38 https://religionnews.com/2024/05/06/how-trumpism-has-pushed-a-fringe-charismatic-theology-into-the-mainstream/
39 https://markoppenheimer.substack.com/p/the-atlantics-fear-mongering-about
40 https://www.nytimes.com/2011/04/30/us/30beliefs.html
41 https://www.motherjones.com/politics/2024/09/jd-vance-just-decried-political-violence-but-he-endorsed-a-book-celebrating-it/
42 Strauss, Leo, *On Tyranny* (Illinois: The Free Press, 2015), p. 1.
43 https://en.kremlin.ru/events/president/transcripts/24034
44 https://www.academia.edu/2082958/The_Eurasian_Idea
45 https://www.ynetnews.com/article/hynwgvglr

7. YOUNG STALINS

1 https://president.ie/en/media-library/news-releases/statement-by-president-michael-d.-higgins-on-the-death-of-fidel-castro
2 https://www.irishtimes.com/news/higgins-pays-tribute-to-chavez-1.1318927
3 https://www.businesspost.ie/analysis-opinion/lucinda-creighton-higgins-has-no-legitimacy-lecturing-the-government-about-foreign-policy-peace-or/
4 https://www.independent.co.uk/news/uk/michael-d-higgins-jeremy-corbyn-micheal-martin-bloody-sunday-londonderry-b2001865.html
5 https://www.irishnews.com/news/northernirelandnews/2023/08/04/news/jeremy_corbyn_urges_republic_not_to_forsake_neutrality-3503096/
6 https://www.spectator.co.uk/article/jeremy-corbyn-sides-with-russia-again-/
7 https://www.independent.co.uk/news/uk/politics/jeremy-corbyn-brexit-eu-lisbon-treaty-europe-empire-military-video-a8766421.html
8 https://www.theguardian.com/politics/2022/aug/02/jeremy-corbyn-urges-west-to-stop-arming-ukraine
9 https://www.theguardian.com/politics/2022/apr/20/jeremy-corbyn-would-like-to-see-nato-ultimately-disband
10 https://www.jewishvirtuallibrary.org/yasser-arafat-s-kgb-connections?utm_content=cmp-true
11 https://www.nytimes.com/1974/11/14/archives/dramatic-session-plo-head-says-he-bears-olive-branch-and-guerrilla.html
12 Fanon, Frantz, *The Wretched of the Earth*, (New York: Grove Press, 1963), p. 37.
13 Saïd, Edward, *The Question of palestine*, (London: Fitzcarraldo Editions, 2024), p. 5.
14 Saïd, Edward, *Between Worlds: Reflections on Exile and Other Essays* (Massachusetts: Harvard University Press, 2001), p. 563.
15 https://www.amherst.edu/media/view/307584/original/The+Question+of+Orientalism+by+Bernard+Lewis+%7C+The+New+%20York+Revue+de+Livres.pdf
16 Biggar, Nigel, *Colonialism: A Moral Reckoning* (London: William Collins, 2023), pp. 6–7.
17 John Rees, *The ABC of Socialism* (London: Bookmarks, 1994), p. 55.
18 https://www.politico.eu/article/labour-hamas-london-ira/
19 Montefiore, Simon Sebag, *Young Stalin* (London: Weidenfeld & Nicolson, 2007), p. xxix.
20 https://www.timesofisrael.com/rape-is-not-resistance-london-rally-calls-for-release-of-women-held-by-hamas/

21 https://web.archive.org/web/20070627183623/http://www3.cnn.com/SPECIALS/cold.war/episodes/21/interviews/kalugin/
22 https://www.youtube.com/watch?v=yErKTVdETpw
23 Kalugin, Oleg, *Spymaster* (New York: Basic Books, 2009), p. 297.
24 https://www.youtube.com/watch?v=yErKTVdETpw
25 https://www.jstor.org/stable/j.ctt9qg47z
26 https://www.commentary.org/john-podhoretz/derrick-bell-jewish-neoconservative-racists/
27 https://www.adl.org/resources/backgrounder/farrakhan-his-own-words
28 https://www.commentary.org/john-podhoretz/derrick-bell-jewish-neoconservative-racists/
29 https://www.aljazeera.com/news/2022/2/21/malcolm-x-quotes
30 https://extramuralactivity.com/2020/09/14/you-cant-have-capitalism-without-racism/
31 https://x.com/JakeWSimons/status/1913917952073642173
32 https://www.euronews.com/green/2023/11/13/no-climate-justice-on-occupied-land-man-grabs-greta-thunbergs-mic-over-pro-palentinian-cha#:~:text=Thunberg%20wrestled%20the%20mic%20back,climate%20justice%20on%20occupied%20land%22.
33 https://www.france24.com/en/live-news/20231108-black-lives-4-palestine-us-activists-find-common-cause
34 Pascal, Blaise, *Pensées* (New York: Penguin, 1966), p. 75.
35 https://www.dailymail.co.uk/news/article-13342245/nyu-pro-palestine-protest-washington-square-park-israel.html
36 https://chinadigitaltimes.net/chinese/321001.html
37 https://www.telegraph.co.uk/news/2023/07/20/ofcom-tiktok-biggest-news-source-young-teenagers/
38 https://focus.cbbc.org/how-is-chinas-version-of-tiktok-different/
39 https://www.thejc.com/news/world/exclusive-irans-shadowy-uk-network-revealed-fwseyhtt
40 Haidt, Jonathan, *The Anxious Generation* (London: Penguin, 2024), p. 315.

8. WHO ARE WE ANYWAY?

1 Montefiore, Simon Sebag, *The World: A Family History* (London: Weidenfeld & Nicolson, 2023), p. 1261.
2 https://www.economist.com/united-states/2023/12/07/one-in-five-young-americans-thinks-the-holocaust-is-a-myth
3 https://www.theguardian.com/world/2025/jan/26/uk-young-adults-unable-to-name-auschwitz-holocaust-education-disinformation

4 Montefiore, *The World*, p. 1261.
5 https://www.telegraph.co.uk/news/2025/04/19/anti-woke-backlash-right-wake-of-supreme-court-trans/
6 https://www.telegraph.co.uk/news/2025/05/14/i-was-wrong-only-net-zero-immigration-can-save-britain/
7 https://www.telegraph.co.uk/news/2025/05/19/poll-shows-support-for-starmers-island-of-strangers-warning/
8 Scruton, Roger, *How to be a Conservative* (London: Bloomsbury, 2015), p. 21.
9 Ibid., p. 91.
10 https://www.telegraph.co.uk/news/2025/05/14/i-was-wrong-only-net-zero-immigration-can-save-britain/
11 https://www.telegraph.co.uk/news/2025/05/20/migrant-who-pleaded-time-make-up-excuse-to-stay/
12 https://www.telegraph.co.uk/news/2025/05/16/iranian-criminal-spared-deportation-to-cut-sons-hair/
13 https://www.telegraph.co.uk/news/2025/05/28/pakistani-drug-dealer-stay-in-uk-to-teach-son-about-islam/
14 https://www.telegraph.co.uk/news/2025/03/17/albanian-criminal-cannot-be-deported-video-calls-harsh/
15 https://x.com/NJ_Timothy/status/1925465441561907611
16 https://www.telegraph.co.uk/news/2025/05/21/taxpayers-funding-dog-crossed-channel-migrant/#:~:text=Taxpayers%20are%20funding%20a%20dog,last%20week%2C%20The%20Sun%20reported.
17 https://www.telegraph.co.uk/news/2025/05/24/denmark-act-against-migration-and-preserve-its-culture/
18 https://www.thejc.com/news/uk/jewish-students-reveal-scale-of-hostility-on-uk-campuses-ce3muwze
19 https://www.youtube.com/watch?v=05xJk9CnoRI
20 https://www.thejc.com/news/leaders-of-groups-behind-london-pro-palestinian-march-have-links-to-hamas-ng34ql4i
21 https://www.telegraph.co.uk/news/2025/05/23/jewish-protester-arrested-mocking-terrorist-leader/
22 https://www.telegraph.co.uk/politics/2025/06/01/lord-hermer-declined-review-unduly-lenient-sentences/
23 https://www.telegraph.co.uk/news/2024/03/03/police-fail-to-solve-single-burglary-in-half-of-country/
24 Sunstein, Cass R., *How Change Happens* (Cambridge, MA: MIT Press, 2019), p. 14.
25 https://www.nytimes.com/2022/02/01/us/whoopi-goldberg-holocaust.html

9. THE SCIENCE OF CHANGE

1 https://www.wallis.rochester.edu/assets/pdf/conference24/Egorov.pdf
2 Sunstein, Cass, R., *How Change Happens* (Cambridge, MA: MIT Press, 2019), p. 16.
3 https://www.telegraph.co.uk/news/2023/12/02/weak-britain-failed-to-crush-anti-semitism-succumbed-hamas/
4 Sunstein, *How Change Happens*, p. 12.
5 https://www.jstor.org/stable/20117856
6 https://www.aeaweb.org/articles?id=10.1257/aer.20180975
7 https://chicagounbound.uchicago.edu/cgi/viewcontent.cgi?article=12456&context=journal_articles
8 https://www.nytimes.com/2013/05/03/arts/music/chris-kelly-of-the-duo-kris-kross-dies-at-34.html?searchResultPosition=1
9 Huntington, Samuel P., *Who Are We?* (New York: Simon & Schuster, 2004), pp. 3–4.
10 https://www.nytimes.com/2012/07/08/business/behavioral-science-can-help-guide-policy-economic-view.html?pagewanted=all
11 https://henryjacksonsociety.org/wp-content/uploads/2024/04/HJS-Deck-200324-Final.pdf
12 https://www.jpost.com/israel-news/article-789981

CONCLUSION

1 https://news.gallup.com/poll/259841/american-pride-hits-new-low-few-proud-political-system.aspx
2 https://yougov.co.uk/politics/articles/12796-decline-british-patriotism?redirect_from=%2Ftopics%2Fpolitics%2Farticles-reports%2F2015%2F07%2F14%2Fdecline-british-patriotism
3 Rushdie, Salman, *Step Across This Line: Collected Nonfiction 1992–2020* (New York: Random House Inc, 2002).
4 https://archive.org/details/leo-strauss-the-crisis-of-our-time-1963/mode/2up?view=theater
5 See Scruton, Roger, *How to be a Conservative* (London: Bloomsbury, 2015), p. 176–7.
6 https://www.winchester-cathedral.org.uk/event/how-to-be-a-whale/
7 https://www.spectator.co.uk/article/the-c-of-es-tragic-misuse-of-its-sacred-spaces/
8 Huntington, Samuel P., *Who Are We?*, p. 15.
9 https://www.thetimes.com/uk/religion/article/gen-z-half-as-likely-as-their-parents-to-identify-as-atheists-wp2vl0l29

10 https://www.spectator.co.uk/article/my-manifesto-for-the-next-archbishop-of-canterbury/
11 https://www.bbc.co.uk/news/articles/cjrjv9r1jyko#:~:text=The%20%C2%A3100m%20earmarked%20by,tens%20of%20thousands%20of%20slaves.
12 https://www.nybooks.com/articles/1994/12/22/the-slave-trade-and-the-jews/
13 Biggar, Nigel, *Colonialism: A Moral Reckoning* (London: William Collins, 2023), p. 7.
14 https://www.bbc.co.uk/news/uk-england-kent-36203911
15 https://www.myjewishlearning.com/article/jews-and-the-african-slave-trade
16 https://www.kirkusreviews.com/book-reviews/eli-faber/jews-slaves-and-the-slave-trade/
17 https://www.kirkusreviews.com/book-reviews/eli-faber/jews-slaves-and-the-slave-trade/
18 https://www.nytimes.com/1992/07/20/opinion/black-demagogues-and-pseudo-scholars.html
19 https://www.biblesociety.org.uk/research/quiet-revival
20 https://www.telegraph.co.uk/news/2025/04/13/extraordinary-comeback-catholicism/
21 https://www.oecd.org/en/publications/society-at-a-glance-2024_918d8db3-en.html
22 https://cps.org.uk/wp-content/uploads/2023/11/CPS_JUSTICE_FOR_THE_YOUNG.pdf
23 Huntington, Samuel, *Who Are We?* (New York: Simon & Schuster, 2004), p. 12.
24 Rees-Mogg, William, and Davidson, James Dale, *The Sovereign Individual* (New York: Simon & Schuster, 1997), p. 394.
25 Grossman, Vasily, *Life and Fate* (London: Vintage, 2006), p. 21.
26 https://en.jabotinsky.org/media/59013/ninth-of-ab-speech.pdf
27 Grossman, *Life and Fate*, p. 21